P9-CQP-725

Emily Brontë, portrait by Branwell Brontë, c. 1833.
(By courtesy of The National Portrait Gallery)

Emily Brontë

HER LIFE AND WORK

Emily Brontë

HER LIFE AND WORK

By MURIEL SPARK
and
DEREK STANFORD

Coward-McCann, Inc. New York

First American Edition 1966

Library of Congress Catalog Card Number: 66-20161

PRINTED IN THE UNITED STATES OF AMERICA

To

HUGO MANNING

ACKNOWLEDGMENTS

Acknowledgments are due to the following for inclusion in the text of this study of material under their copyright. Above all, to Columbia University Press, whose edition of *The Complete Poems of Emily Jane Brontë* by C. W. Hatfield is indispensable for scholarly purposes, and for quotations from *The Brontë's Web of Childhood* by Fannie E. Ratchford; and, next, to Longmans, Green & Co. Ltd. for quotations from Phyllis Bentley's *The Brontë Sisters,* published for the British Council; Constable & Co. Ltd. for quotations from Arthur Symons; Hutchinson & Co. (Publishers) Ltd. for quotations from May Sinclair; The University of Chicago Press for quotations from Lord David Cecil's *Early Victorian Novelists,* copyright 1958 by The University of Chicago; Sir Herbert Read for quotations from his various works; Hastings House, Publishers, Inc. for quotations from Laura L. Hinkley's *Charlotte and Emily: The Brontës,* copyright 1945.

Contents

Part I—BIOGRAPHICAL

Part II—CRITICAL

LIST OF ILLUSTRATIONS

Part One

BIOGRAPHICAL

by

MURIEL SPARK

1

FACT AND LEGEND

Emily Brontë was born in 1818, on 30th July, and she died on 19th December, 1848. From first to last, there is no evidence that she laid any plans for the course of her life. She seems, above all, to have wished to avoid "doing something about" her life, and when, from time to time, the obligation was put to her, to make some sort of career for herself, and so prepare for her future, she tried to meet these demands, and failed.

Indeed, Emily Brontë seems to have been determined that her life should come under the category of "uneventful"; not because she was apathetic about life, but on the contrary, because she was intensely taken up with her own particular calling in life. Life, as she experienced it in her home was meaningful. She bent all her efforts towards defining this meaning, by the direct methods of her literary work, and by indirect means, which included her household and family duties. Any time apart from this which she was persuaded to spend towards improving her lot, went against the grain. To the end, she caused very little to happen to herself by her own agency.

The result of this compressed, instinctive discipline, was the singular achievement for which we remember her name: her poems and her novel, *Wuthering Heights*. These are the principal facts in the life of Emily Brontë; so important as to place her character in the realm of legend.

All great genius attracts legend to itself. Legend is the common means of expressing the manifestation of genius in certain people, who cannot be described in ordinary terms. For this reason the legendary data which adhere to people of genius, should be respected. A recent Brontë biographer claims to "clear away the heaped rubbish of legend." This is not the present writer's aim. Such legend is the repository of a vital aspect of truth; and ought not to be swept aside simply because it is not ascertainable; neither, of course, should it be taken as literal truth.

The literal facts about Emily Brontë, we get from family correspondence and from the industry of subsequent researchers; there is little from Emily Brontë herself. The way in which these facts are presented—references to her, in letters and diaries—shows that, up to the time when she began to reveal her genius in her work, she was regarded by those most familiar with her, with the sympathy and understanding which near-relatives are wont to bestow on "nervous" members of the family. Emily was not thought of as a genius until her work attracted attention; this is natural enough, for without her work she was merely a daughter in a clergyman's home; one whose special nature called for special consideration: Emily was shy, often to the point of rudeness, with strangers. ("How did Emily behave?" was her sister Charlotte's anxious question to a visitor who had returned from a walk with Emily.) Her relatives feared for her on the few occasions when Emily forced herself to leave her home for a few months. So far, she was loved and understood. During this first phase, Emily (who in the later, legendary light appears as a monolith of self-generated strength) is referred to simply with protective loyalty. Only strangers were patronising; as late as Emily's twenty-fourth year, her master at the finishing school in Brussels, where she had spent a few uneasy months, wrote to her father that "Miss Emily was learning the piano, receiving lessons from the best professor in Belgium, and she herself already had little pupils. She was losing whatever remained of ignorance, and also of what was worse—timidity."

The facts to be gained from references to Emily Brontë in documents dating from her birth to the year 1846, are in significant contrast to the statements made about her as her worth became known, during the remaining three years of her life and after her death. More remarkable, is the contrast between what was said at the time about Emily up to her twenty-eighth year, and what was put forward, later, concerning the same period, by people who remembered, now they came to think of it, that the author of *Wuthering Heights* had been remarkable for this or that quality.

So, after 1846, a new note appears, very gradually at first, in family references to Emily. This is apparent in her sister Charlotte's letters. Charlotte had always respected Emily; the new note is not simply a deepening of respect, although it contains an element of awe. Charlotte began, now, to see her sister as a *dramatic* being, and as Emily proceeded to her dramatic death, Charlotte was ever more taken up with this new image of her younger sister as a creature of concealed and terrible powers hacking her relentless way through a fatal consumption for which she would accept no alleviation. Emily took on the aspect of a legendary being.

All this was, of course, justified. Charlotte, in her anguished letters relating to Emily's last illness, invented nothing. Had this larger-looming Emily, in fact, existed all along?

In 1841, the youngest sister, Anne, who, like Charlotte, was then working as a governess away from home, had written "Emily . . . is as busy as any of us, and in reality earns her food and raiment as much as we do." In 1844, one of Charlotte's chance remarks about Emily when the sisters contemplated starting a school, was that "Emily does not care much for teaching, but she would look after the housekeeping, and, although something of a recluse, she is too good-hearted not to do all she could for the well-being of children." Such casual comments reveal nothing of the passionate lonely genius who, it seems, was revealed to her family in the last three years of her life.

It may be that Emily did not herself realise her own nature until she had produced *Wuthering Heights*. Perhaps she then became conscious of a new self-image, whose role she grimly pursued. This is speculative; but it is clear that, from contemporary sources we have two pictures of Emily Brontë. One, of a shy, quiet country girl, a girl who was useful in the house, and who had not shown any of her writings to her family since her childhood, when all the children had been prolific in writing. The later picture is more richly adorned. Everyone who had met the now-famous woman, however briefly, contributed to the portrait of Emily Brontë the poet and novelist. M. Héger, the Brussels master who had once written to tell her father that she was losing her "ignorance and what was worse, timidity," now pronounced on Emily, in retrospect. "She should have been a man—a great navigator" runs the celebrated passage. "Her powerful reason would have deduced new spheres of discovery from the knowledge of the old; and her strong, imperious will would never have been daunted by opposition or difficulty; never have given way but with life."

M. Héger had not seen Emily since the time when, nearly fifteen years before, he had assured her father of his hopes for her ignorance and timidity. It is difficult to reconcile his first opinion, which he no doubt modified to accommodate a father's pride, with the "strong imperious will" and the "powerful reason" he ascribed to Emily after her posthumous fame had caused him to think again. Still, these discrepant statements, like those made by her family before and after Emily had revealed herself, can be reconciled—they must be reconciled, because they represent impressions which we have every reason to believe were recorded in good faith.

It happens from time to time that we meet someone; we don't catch his name; we note he is shy, or hearty, or dull; perhaps he has some mannerisms which irritate us; or he may leave the vaguest impression on us; or we may put him down as "unusual". Some weeks later, we learn "who he is"; someone we have heard about; whose books we have read; or whose piano recitals, which we have never attended, are famous. Returning to our impression of the man, we change it, though we may never see him again. The irritating mannerisms are quite understandable, they are charming. If he was too jovial, he now seems to have been surprisingly friendly. Shy, he is now modest. The vagueness of his features in our memory is illuminated by our new knowledge. We remember some strong quality, as befits genius. The first impression is obscured, unless we happen to have described him in a diary or a letter, on our meeting with him. Anyone comparing this impression with the later reconstruction of it, would scarcely recognise the same man in each. Which is the more accurate portrayal, that of the real man whom we chanced to meet, or that of our reconstruction—the legendary figure, in other words? The second impression is the more real. The first merely prefigured the legend. But the legend alone is not enough; we need concrete as well as legendary impressions to bring us somewhere near a true picture of the man.

Emily Brontë's biographer faces a similar situation; but this is intensified by the fact that her earliest interpreters, those on whom we rely for most information, had known her in varying degrees of intimacy before they gained this new insight into her character. Her sister Charlotte was of course the best informed. Charlotte's friend, Ellen Nussey, was frequently in her company. M. Héger, a man of intelligence, had observed her daily throughout most of her ten-months' residence at his school. Was he insincere in his first assessment of Emily—concerning her timidity for instance? It is most unlikely; this was the accepted opinion of Emily at that time. Nor was the good man insincere in his oracular utterance, fifteen years later, as to her "strong imperious will" among other heroic attributes—this legendary aspect of Emily had been current at least seven years by this time, initiated by Charlotte's introduction to *Wuthering Heights*.

It would be nothing new in Brontë biography to have opened this question merely to close it again by assuming that everything recorded of Emily Brontë by her contemporaries before they became aware of her talent, can be worked in with what was said afterwards, forming a composite picture. The two aspects, it is true, are to be reconciled.

But the distinction between them exists to a remarkable degree. To assume simply that Emily Brontë's contemporaries were not aware of her deeper nature until they discovered it in her work, does not adequately reconcile the reserved, "problem" girl with the impassioned superwoman subsequently described by Charlotte. This would not explain the nature and extent of the change in Emily's reputation, it would merely explain that there was a change.

A comparison with the case of her sister Charlotte may make this clear. Charlotte's success with *Jane Eyre,* her first-published novel, was immediate; as it gradually became known, amongst their friends and neighbours that she was the author, there was a certain stir; a new aspect of Charlotte was observed, but the records do not suggest that anyone's previous impressions of Charlotte's character were suddenly put out of gear by this discovery. Causing some surprised comment at first, Charlotte Brontë nevertheless continued to be recognisable as her old self in the eyes of her acquaintances and intimates; her personal reputation never reached fever-heat. Whereas Charlotte's success called forth some respect, some disapproval, and some back-biting, Emily's book made no immediate impact, at first, outside her family circle. But gradually, as the author of *Wuthering Heights* was discovered in Emily, her reputation underwent a spectacular change; she became a mysterious force, a woman larger than life, increasing in stature after her death three years later.

Moreover the rhetoric of Charlotte in her biographical notes on Emily, and the rhetoric of M. Héger in his panegyric, can be cited as instinctive acknowledgements of their belief that Emily Brontë was no normal being. This was by no means due to literary discernment. Charlotte probably considered herself a better novelist than Emily; and justifiably so. M. Héger was traditional in taste; he would have been impressed but not satisfied with *Wuthering Heights*. It is clear, however, that some powerful element in the work moved them to employ a highly impassioned style to illuminate the character of the author. They used the language of legend as though this were Emily's natural due. Many modern biographical writings on Emily show a similar tendency (and though this is an implicit definition of her nature, it is not perhaps the most lucid method of approach).

From Charlotte's letters describing Emily's last illness and death, there is "internal evidence" of a more than usually elevated prose style: an implicit sign, possibly, of Charlotte's revised conception of her sister some years before the public became curious about the person of Emily Brontë. The more direct evidence of this, however, lies in the substance of Charlotte's statements. Emily's incapacity to cope with the world had always evoked her sister's sympathy. In the last phase of Emily's life, Charlotte, who had hitherto expressed her fears for Emily, now expresses something very close to a fear *of* Emily. Accompanying the agony of mind which Charlotte experienced in watching her sister's brutal self-neglect, an objective and terrified fascination can be detected.

Emily Brontë was established as a legendary woman, first by those who had read her work, and next by people who had heard the legend. Villagers who remembered her, though seldom having spoken with her, obliged her first biographers by recounting this or that eccentricity. Legend-making is infectious. The Brontës' old servants added their reminiscences. Their stories are remarkably in keeping with the highly-charged aura surrounding Emily's posthumous name. The making of legend is of course unconscious, and though the singularities attributed to Emily may not be accurate in detail, they are probably highly typical of her.

The purpose of this essay is not to discredit the accepted view of Emily Brontë, but to claim, first, that this conception is legendary in nature and so lending itself to diverse interpretations; (theories about Emily Brontë are, perhaps, only exceeded in number by theories about Shakespeare.) Next, it is intended to consider what was the essence of this legend; the essence which apparently lay concealed from

Emily's closest intimates until the last years of her life. The method employed in the following pages is of analysis rather than synthesis, through which it is hoped to promote some fresh thoughts on the subject. The following essay is planned to reconstruct Emily Brontë's life-story exclusively from documents concurrent with the events. The posthumous records will be found to add little in the way of information, although, of course, they enrich any Brontë narrative.

Where Emily Brontë is concerned, the commonest fallacies held are those which attribute the qualities she acquired in the last three or four years of her life, to previous stages in her development. The result of this is that she seems to show no development. She is puzzle enough as it is, but invested with the right attributes at the wrong time it is no wonder that Mr. Clement Shorter called her "the sphinx of our modern literature".

The tone of these 'afterthoughts' seems to follow Charlotte, whose special attitude after Emily's death prevents her from being a reliable witness to a progressive life-study of Emily. Charlotte, and Mrs. Gaskell after her, and Miss Mary Robinson in turn, adopt some of Charlotte's fallacies, the principal being that which takes the last years of Emily's life to represent the whole. Emily was, as we will see, a more forceful proposition at the age of thirty than she was at nineteen. Yet they will have her a silent morose orgulous genius at a time when Emily was patently the most buoyant and accommodating member of the family.

For this reason, the following experiment has been undertaken, and for the same reason, of course, makes no claim to be a full or broad account of Emily's career. The narrow way is taken for the purpose of tracing Emily's development. This is supplemented by a general chapter considering some of the special qualities which distinguish Emily Brontë.

The method of interpretation should perhaps be mentioned. Attention is given to the impressions Emily Brontë made on the people she met, particularly during her stay in Brussels, so that by comparing the reactions of her acquaintance, it is possible to deduce something of Emily's state of mind, even though we have no direct references to her feelings. This oblique method of interpretation is not, of course, always called for.

THE BASIC STORY

The Brontë Parents

Emily Brontë was the fifth of six children—five girls and one boy. Patrick Brontë, her father, was Irish, a clergyman of the Church of England; her mother, Maria Branwell, was Cornish, of modest merchant stock.

Both were evangelically-minded, touched by Methodist teaching. At the time of their marriage in 1812, however, the Methodists had been separated from the Established Church for some seventeen years, and while Maria Branwell's relatives appear to have become professing Methodists, her uncle, a Methodist minister at whose home she had met Patrick Brontë, later returned to the Church of England, to which she herself adhered after her marriage.

Patrick Brontë was the son of a poor Protestant farmer and a Catholic mother of County Down. He had earned the friendship of local patrons, through whose influence he was able to enter St. John's College, Cambridge. The expenses were variously contributed to by his own savings of seven pounds, an annual grant from benefactors who included William Wilberforce, and the leniency of the College itself. Patrick Brontë fulfilled their hopes, took his degree and was ordained. While at Cambridge it is known that he joined a Home Guard corps, formed to resist a possible French invasion.

Six years later, while holding his fourth curacy at Hartshead, near Dewsbury, he married Maria Branwell. In the previous year he had published his first book *Cottage Poems,* "chiefly designed for the lower classes of society"; of which a sample:

> Once she was gentle, fair and kind,
> To no seducing schemes inclined,
> Would blush to hear a smutty tale.

There was a second volume the next year. His children loyally carried with them to the grave their private opinion of their father's verse. He next published two prose tales, of similar merit, after which his literary activities are spasmodic.

The mother had no pretensions to authorship, and she did not see the publication of the one essay by her hand which remains to us. It is entitled *The Advantages of Poverty in Religious Concerns,* in which the author reasserts the traditional blessings of poverty, adding that she is in a position to speak impartially, never having been impoverished herself; she maintains, however, that no respectable person need partake of the blessings of poverty, there being plenty of charitable institutions in England.

Emily Brontë's parents were in no way extraordinary people. The few surviving letters written by her mother to her father during their courtship, reveal an independent woman with a respect for the current proprieties. She considered Patrick Brontë sufficiently expansive to address him on one occasion as her "Saucy Pat". In his own letters, written after her death at Haworth Parsonage nine years later, we find a rhetorical style—he was consistently attracted to metaphors of tempest and thunder—combined with ingenuous optimism.

Early Environment
1820—1825

By the time the family moved finally to Haworth, where Patrick Brontë had obtained a perpetual incumbency, Emily was in her second year. Haworth, a village situated on a moorland steep in the West Riding of Yorkshire, was to be the Brontë's home until the last survivor, the father, died there some forty years later. In this gaunt house with a graveyard at the bottom of the garden, all but one of the Brontës died. Facing the broad unchanged moorland prospect, the parsonage and graveyard still stand isolated. Their characteristics seem inseparably blended; the gravestones leaning awry like so many disused out-houses; and the house itself, a slab-like oblong memorial.

This, then, was the immediate physical environment in which Emily Brontë grew to awareness, with the other Brontë children—Maria, Elizabeth, Charlotte, and Branwell, her seniors; and her younger sister Anne. To these children, death was no hushed-up affair: its outward tokens resided next door, and could be visited through a gate in their own garden wall. The younger children especially — Emily and Anne who were still in babyhood when the family settled at Haworth—were therefore in the enviable position of growing up as conscious of death as they were of life. Whatever Emily Brontë's later preoccupations with the subject of death, the phenomenon itself caused her no bewilderment or wonder; she had never needed to exercise a conscious effort to accept the idea of death and so was free to consider its complex implications with an advanced simplicity which distinguished her attitude from that of contemporary writers.

Emily was cared for by young servant-women from the village during her mother's illness which began shortly after their removal to Haworth, ending with Mrs. Brontë's death in September 1821.

In a letter written soon after her death, Patrick Brontë recorded the painful course of his wife's illness, during which time all the children contracted scarlet fever. After their recovery, Miss Branwell, a sister of Mrs. Brontë, arrived from Penzance to take charge; and thereafter the young Brontës were in her care. Emily was now aged three.

There is little recorded of Aunt Branwell during her lifetime. So far as we are interested in her influence in the home, it can here be deduced rather from what this admirable woman refrained from doing, than from anything she did or said. We know that she was always referred to by the Brontës with restraint and respect, never with warmth, and on the other hand, never with fear or resentment. In fact, from the earliest references to Aunt Branwell in the childrens' writings and letters, it seems she was looked upon as 'part of the fittings.'

Miss Branwell was a Methodist, and with the method of Methodism, she organised the household, allotted duties and tasks to the children, and gave them elementary lessons, without any apparent pressure of her will. If there had been any suggestion of tyranny in Aunt Branwell's administration, we may be sure she would have put in a recognisable appearance in the Brontë sisters' novels. She was a woman of small independent means, accustomed to a mild Cornish climate and the sociable interchanges common to Methodists. Her residence, during the next twenty-odd years, in this harsh isolated northern parish, with the responsibility of six children, was undertaken from a sense of duty. But her sense of duty must have been of an exceptional order. The highest testimony to Miss Branwell's conception of her duty lies in the prolific juvenile writings of Charlotte and her brother Branwell. This juvenilia shows evidence of the abundant freedom of spirit and the leisure to occupy themselves without hindrance, which all the children enjoyed under their Aunt's dominion. It is clear that Miss Branwell's sense of duty included a voluntary self-effacement. She neither imposed herself on the family as a monument of self-sacrifice, nor did she pose as a second mother. To highly advanced children like the Brontës, this was an enormous advantage. Their aunt's restrictions extended no farther than that required for a moderate domestic education. Beyond that they were at liberty to develop along their own lines. Miss Branwell made no emotional demands upon them, the artificiality of which they would easily have detected. Nor does it seem that she made any attempts to pry into their leisure activities. She must have known about the piles of notebooks filled with page after page of close script, of which a hundred-odd have survived. These bear no trace of censorship, nor of having been composed with a weather-eye open in the adult direction. The Brontë Aunt, who has received little credit from commentators, gave the Brontës what they most needed, failing the presence of their mother: she represented the principle of practical order. Many years later, Charlotte, when touching her aunt for a loan, reminded her of her practical virtues: "You always like to use your money to the best advantage; you are not fond of making shabby purchases; when you do confer a favour, it is often done in style . . ."

As Miss Branwell was a Methodist, her religious influence in the household would certainly introduce a lyrical and fervent note into the Brontës daily family worship. Differences in practice between Methodism and the Evangelical Anglicanism of their father were not great; the theological issues involved would hardly be apparent where the outward manifestations of these two forms of Christianity were so similar. We learn of no dichotomy between the religious teachings of the father and the aunt, neither of whom were contemplatives, neither of whom were doctrinaire, both of whom had been reared in a Wesley-minded tradition.

Towards the beginning of Miss Branwell's stay at Haworth, Mr. Brontë proposed marriage to a Miss Burder, a former love, whom he invited to share with him his "*small* but *sweet* little family" on whose "endearing little ways" he expatiated. Miss Burder bethought her of the fact that she had been spurned by this same Mr. Brontë. She did not accept. Her refusal was pronounced in letters vibrating with so much pent-up venom that it seems a mercy for the "sweet little family" that they were spared her presence at Haworth. There were no further attempts to replace Miss Branwell, whose company Patrick Brontë does not seem to have relished greatly. He took to living in his study, for the most part, but we have the impression that they observed a companionable reserve, making an agreeable and placid household background for the children.

The family were not much involved in the social life of the district, but the spirit of Haworth was borne in to them by many agencies, and must be reckoned as part of the early Brontë environment. The household now included 'Tabby', a Haworth woman who served them up to the last weeks of Charlotte's life. With Tabby, the children enjoyed a warm kitchen-fireside communion, which is implied in their frequent references to her from childhood days onward. It was she, principally, who brought the lore of the countryside to life for them. From their father they heard something of local affairs, although he was most communicative on issues of national politics, a grasp of which the children quickly acquired; imaginatively, they transformed the famous military and parliamentary figures of the newspaper reports into Haworth - inhabiting heroes. Parliamentary debates, expounded by Papa, combined with the peculiar spirit of the population of local hills and wolds, to form new embodiments of fancy. Presently the Brontës were to "establish" as they called it, their well-known day-dream epics, documented with intense industry. And from these sprang the Gondal dispensation, of which Emily and Anne were the exclusive proprietors. The Gondal invention served Emily as a motivating force for her poems, up to her last years. Gondal has its roots in the locality of Haworth; its nature and traditions were daily insinuated into Emily's infant understanding. She, alone of the Brontë's, made use of the most primitive elements thus conveyed to her; the others were more social, political and civil-minded.

The village and neighbourhood were then recovering from the disruption in local conditions of life caused by the Industrial Revolution. As recently as 1812, unemployment and starvation had been followed by riots and the wrecking of machines in the neighbourhood. By now, the wool-trade had passed from the cottages to the factories, but amongst the older people these memories persisted in a general anti-machine feeling. The new generation of mechanics were however, rising in hopeful numbers to seize all opportunities for the new adult-educational movements, embodied in the Mechanics Institute. It was from the Mechanics' Institute Library at Keighley that the Brontë family borrowed books for their home reading, years later.

Haworth had, in the mid-eighteenth century, enjoyed some fame as a sort of showpiece for the Evangelical Revival, spurred by the energy of its pastor, the Rev. William Grimshaw. He transformed the parish and its agricultural neighbourhood by means of thunderings and threats, and claimed to have raised the number of communicants at Haworth Church from twelve to twelve hundred. This militant worthy has been cited as having introduced Methodism to Haworth, Mechanics' Institutes. It was from the Mechanics' Institute This may well be; he welcomed the Wesleys as preachers in his church. He established a chapel for Methodists in the village, and in fact it was his practice to set up chapels throughout the countryside, so that country-people had no excuse for defection. But it should be noted that his support of Methodism preceded the Methodist break with the Established Church. Thereafter, Grimshaw wrote to Charles Wesley, "The Methodists are no longer members of the Church of England. They are as real a body of Dissenters from her as the Presbyterians, Baptists, Quakers, or any body of Independents. I hereby assure you that I disdain all further and future connection with them."

Thus, his influence made Haworth a heated centre of a controversy between the Church and the Chapels, which was continued during Mr. Brontë's career. The combined religious note of Haworth, stemming from this Mr. Grimshaw of fervent memory, was strongly evangelical with a puritan tendency. Independence and hard work seem to have been Haworth's prime virtues.

This was the world Emily had come to know by the time she was six years old. The house next door to the graveyard—an orderly, unnoticeable Aunt—a Papa secluded in his study or absent on parish work, intruding with occasional information about parliamentary feuds—Tabby in the kitchen representing the Haworth Idea, in her dialect, her manners, her opinions and her gossipy narratives — a brother and three sisters, active in imaginative speculations on all the above items—and one infant sister who was compliant with all suggestions, as yet. At the age of six, Emily went to school.

Emily's stay at the Clergy Daughters' School at Cowan Bridge was brief. Her two elder sisters, Maria and Elizabeth, contracted illnesses there of which they were brought home to die. Charlotte and Emily were withdrawn. The school was run on the bleak lines associated with 19th century concepts of 'Charity' establishments. The experience left a burning resentment with Charlotte, but Emily has left no token of her impressions. The school record describes her thus: "Emily Brontë. Entered Nov. 25, 1824. Aged 5¾. Reads very prettily and works a little. Left June 1, 1825. Subsequent career, governess."

1826—1832

"Our plays were established; *Young Men,* June, 1826; *Our Fellows,* July 1827; *Islanders,* December, 1827. These are our three great plays, that are not kept secret. Emily's and my best plays were established the 1st of December, 1827; The others March, 1828. Best plays mean secret plays; they are very nice ones. All our plays are very strange ones." Thus Charlotte, in 1829; from henceforth she was to be the main family recorder. It is to Charlotte that we have to turn for most of our facts.

Of the "great plays" established by the Brontë children about a year after the deaths of Maria and Elizabeth, we know a considerable amount. These were, as Charlotte stated, "not kept secret." The "secret" plays were the best plays—those exclusive to herself and Emily, and concealed under so firm a pledge that no trace of them survives, other than this reference. We only know that they were "very nice ones" and that they share with the not-secret plays, the quality of being "strange ones." In these latter, Emily too participated. In her newly assumed role of Brontë biographer, fourteen-year-old Charlotte recalled how, three years past, in 1827, their *Young Men's Play,* "took its rise".

"The *Young Men's* play took its rise from some wooden soldiers Branwell had; *Our Fellows* from Aesop's Fables; and the *Islanders* from several events which happened. I will sketch out the origin of our plays more explicitly if I can. First, *Young Men*. Papa bought Branwell some wooden soldiers at Leeds; when Papa came home it was night, and we were in bed, so next morning Branwell came to our door with a box of soldiers. Emily and I jumped out of bed, and I snatched up one and exclaimed, 'This is the Duke of Wellington! This shall be the Duke!' When I had said this Emily likewise took one up and said it should be hers; when Anne came down, she said one should be hers. Mine was the prettiest of the whole, and the tallest, and the most perfect in every part. Emily's was a grave-looking fellow, and we called him 'Gravey.' Anne's was a queer little thing, much like herself, and we called him 'Waiting-boy'. Branwell chose his, and called him 'Buonaparte' "

It seems clear that the children did not only record these legendary sagas of their invention, they first enacted them. The stories were conceived and worked out in their play-time; the Brontës' childhood games were really drama in the making. Charlotte, as if perceiving instinctively that the physical scene which accompanied the inception of each Play was itself meaningful, elaborates upon the domestic picture, once more, when she writes her introduction to their *Tales of the Islanders,* which appeared in miniature 'magazine' form.

June the 31st, 1829.

"The play of the *Islanders* was formed in December, 1827, in the following manner. One night, about the time when the cold sleet and stormy fogs of November are succeeded by the snow-storms, and high piercing night-winds of confirmed winter, we were all sitting round the warm blazing kitchen fire, having just concluded a quarrel with Tabby concerning the propriety of lighting a candle, from which she came off victorious, no candle having been produced. A long pause succeeded, which was at last broken by Branwell saying, in a lazy manner, 'I don't know what to do.' This was echoed by Emily and Anne.

"*Tabby*. 'Wha ya may go t'bed.'

"*Branwell*. 'I'd rather do anything than that.'

"*Charlotte*. 'Why are you so glum to-night, Tabby? Oh! Suppose we had each an island of our own.'

"*Branwell*. 'If we had I would choose the Island of Man.'

"*Charlotte*. 'And I would choose the Isle of Wight.'

"*Emily*. 'The Isle of Arran for me.'

"*Anne*. 'And mine should be Guernsey.' "

"We then chose who should be chief men in our islands. Branwell chose John Bull, Astley Cooper, and Leigh Hunt; Emily, Walter Scott, Mr. Lockhart, Johnny Lockhart; Anne, Michael Sadler, Lord Bentinck, Sir Henry Halford. I chose the Duke of Wellington and two sons . . ."

And from Charlotte again, we have a third picture of Haworth Parsonage and its inmates, accompanied by many casual curiosities of information which build up, as if by design for posterity, the real background to their fantastic activities. She tells us, in the *History of the Year 1829,*

"While I write this I am in the kitchen of the Parsonage, Haworth; Tabby, the servant, is washing up the breakfast things, and Anne, my youngest sister (Maria was my eldest), is kneeling on a chair, looking at some cakes which Tabby has been baking for us. Emily is in the parlour, brushing the carpet. Papa and Branwell are gone to Keighley. Aunt is upstairs in her room, and I am sitting by the table writing this in the kitchen. Keighley is a small town four miles from here. Papa and Branwell are gone for the newspaper, the *Leeds Intelligencer,* a most excellent Tory newspaper, edited by Mr. Wood, and the proprietor, Mr. Henneman. We take two and see three newspapers a week. We take the *Leeds Intelligencer,* Tory, and the *Leeds Mercury,* Whig, edited by Mr. Baines, and his brother, son-in-law, and his two sons, Edward and Talbot. We see the *John Bull;* it is a high Tory, very violent. Mr. Driver lends us it, as likewise

Blackwood's Magazine, the most able periodical there is. The Editor is Mr. Christopher North, an old man seventy-four years of age; the 1st of April is his birthday; his company are Timothy Tickler, Morgan O'Doherty, Macrabin Mordecai, Mullion, Warnell, and James Hogg, a man of most extraordinary genius, a Scottish shepherd . . ."

We see Emily, in the first picture, aged eight years, following the initiative of Branwell and Charlotte. Emily and six-year-old Anne were subordinates. Allowing for the fact that this account was written by Charlotte who would understandably portray herself in a leading light, it seems reasonable to conclude that Emily had not yet begun to make much impression on the family. Charlotte, besides being the eldest, was evidently the most precocious and leader-like of the Brontës; she had more power of endurance than Branwell, who was, at this time, equally with Charlotte respected as an elder by the two younger girls. When eventually Emily does begin slightly to assert her presence, it is never as a leader; she is seen in varying stages of separation from the rest of her family. From the episode of th etoy soldiers, we can deduce no more than that she preferred a "grave-looking fellow" to any other among these wooden heroes.

By the next year, 1827, Emily has become co-equal with Charlotte in one respect: in the secret, or best plays. That they were kept secret was possibly Emily's own provision, since at this time, Charlotte appears eager to make known all her inventions to the other children. In December of the same year, in the scene which led to the inauguration of their play, *Islanders,* Emily is depicted still as following the lead of Charlotte and Branwell.

Their Tory heroes were derived from their father's enthusiasms. We learn from Charlotte's girlhood narrative how the children would gather round him while he read out the reports on occasions of important parliamentary debates. Branwells choice of Leigh Hunt as one of his literary heroes was more récherché than Emily's Sir Walter Scott. Scott was, in fact, a constant favourite with the Brontës; next year they received a copy of his *Tales of a Grandfather*, inscribed "to her dear little nephew and nieces" from Miss Branwell. *The Lay of the Last Minstrel* was amongst their father's books, to which the children had access. It was from these plays that the 'Angrian' sequence later took shaps; as also the independent 'Gondal' narrative of Emily and Anne.

The last-quoted account by Charlotte offers a different picture of their home; this is an active morning scene, everyone is doing something. Of eleven-year-old Emily, we know only that she was brushing the carpet in the parlour. We see Emily during her childhood, through an elder sister's eyes, where she is naturally given a secondary position. But it is clear from Charlotte's accounts, that no-one at this time considered Emily remarkable, and we may take it that her qualities were as yet not too distinct from those of this whole remarkable family.

Charlotte's absence at school—a Miss Wooler's establishment at Roe Head near Dewsbury—left Emily and Anne to develop a closer intimacy. Branwell, whose status as the only son, and whose obvious cleverness, had earned him some deference from the girls, was not inclined to co-operate with the two younger sisters. Gondal was founded about this time; Emily and Anne were regarded, at first, as a rebel faction of the official body which was centred at "Glass Town", a scene of fabulous high-society activity. Gradually Gondal became accepted as an independent unit. And on Charlotte's return in the summer, Angria was initiated under the joint management of herself and Branwell, continuing on the more orthodox lines already set forth in the Glass Town narrative.

Gondal (of which no early narratives survive) seems to have differed from Angria in its more legendary characteristics even at this early stage of its development. Angria is nearer to social fantasy, with direct or implicit reference, always to the world of contemporary politics. Angria was much more civilised. Gondal was a northern island territority in the North Pacific; there, the characters enacted their near-archetypal feuds, loyalties, loves, treacheries, slaughters, and what was worse, imprisonments. From the Gondal poems of Emily and Anne—those written when they were grown women—this mythological scene appears peopled with medieval characters nourishing primitive passions: a compound as of Scott and Homer. It may be that Gondal was an offshoot of those "best" and "secret" plays which, Charlotte tells us, she was sharing with Emily in 1827.

A list of Gondal place names is given by Anne; she jotted them down at the back of a geography book which the girls had presumably consulted for the purpose, if not of accuracy, of stirring up the imagination. The names recur in the surviving adult poems of Emily and Anne:

Alexandia, a kingdom in Gaaldine.

Almedore, a kingdom in Gaaldine.

Elseraden, a kingdom in Gaaldine.

Gaaldine, a large Island newly discovered in the South Pacific.

Gondal, a large Island in the North Pacific.

Regina, the capitol of Gondal.

Ula, a kingdom in Gaaldine, governed by 4 Sovereigns.

Zelona, a kingdom in Gaaldine.

Zedora, a large Provence in Gaaldine, governed by a Viceroy.

Apart from the few months she spent at school as an infant, Emily's education had comprised her aunt's instruction in general and domestic rudiments, religious instruction from both her aunt and her father, self-instruction from her father's library, information gathered from her brothers and sisters, and her personal observations. It was not a formal or in any way organised education, but it was not considered inadequate by current standards, nor can we possibly presume to judge otherwise. Charlotte, an avid thirster for knowledge, seems to have hankered after formal schooling; but from Emily, we get the opposite impression. We cannot

Haworth Church and Parsonage
(By courtesy of Walter Scott, Bradford)

Original water-colour of her dog, Keeper, by Emily Brontë.
(By courtesy of Walter Scott, Bradford. Copyright The Brontë Society)

say that her instinct in this matter was wrong. When Charlotte left Roe Head, she undertook the further instruction of Emily and Anne, aged 14 and 12 respectively. "In the mornings from 9 o'clock to half-past 12, I instruct my sisters and draw, then we walk till dinner," writes Charlotte to her schoolfellow Ellen Nussey. At about the same time, this sober routine was enlivened by the visits of a drawing master from Leeds, who encouraged the family's high hopes of Branwell as an artist; and of a music master from Keighley.

1833—1840

At Roe Head School Charlotte had formed her lifelong friendship with Ellen Nussey; Charlotte's letters to Ellen form the bulk source for biographical information. From these letters we obtain an enormous amount of useful facts; and also some sidelights on the characters of her brothers and sisters, in employing which, we must try to judge from the context which of her statements represent an opinion or bias of Charlotte's own, and which stand for the view accepted by the whole family. The fact that she mentions Emily very infrequently amongst some hundreds of letters written during her sister's lifetime, does not necessarily mean that Emily appeared insignificant to those who knew her; but it does show that Emily had no *particular* significance within the family circle; otherwise, it would have been in keeping with Charlotte's dramatic nature to emphasise the fact.

With these reservations in mind, and remembering that Charlotte was always, to some extent, the spokesman of the family, we may find her references to Emily useful for the factual data they supply, or for the suggestions they supply towards a reconstruction of Emily Brontë in her earlier years. These considerations have been mentioned, because it has often been the case with writers on Emily Brontë, that, faced with a lack of biographical documents by her own hand, and with a paucity of day-to-day comment upon her, they have seized upon every chance reference to make of it an event of luminous significance.

Ellen Nussey paid a visit to Haworth in the summer of 1833, the first of a series of visits of which she has left some interesting accounts, and which, since they were written long after Emily's death, are excluded from this narrative. If her opinion of Emily was expressed at the time, it is not recorded, but shortly after Ellen's departure Charlotte quotes Emily and Anne as saying "they never saw anyone they liked so well as Miss Nussey". This compliment seems quite sincere; indeed Emily and Anne hardly saw any new faces at all, and Ellen Nussey reveals herself always as an "amiable" person, as her friends said of her. It is customary to describe Emily, even at this stage of her career, as a reserved, silent, scornful genius. An ordinary sociable girl like Ellen Nussey, it is assumed, would secretly appal Emily. There is no hint of such a situation in any of the correspondence between Charlotte and Ellen. Emily, at fifteen, is no morose misanthropist; she is normally capable of liking people, and she much liked Ellen; Charlotte was not given to expressing excessive flattery.

Anne and Emily continued to study under Charlotte's tutelage for the next two years. Meanwhile we have one autobiographical statement written in November 1834. It is set down in Emily's script, on behalf of herself and Anne.

> "I fed Rainbow, Diamond, Snowflake, Jasper Pheasant (alias).
>
> This morning Branwell went down to Mr. Driver's and brought news that Sir Robert Peel was going to be invited to stand for Leeds. Anne and I have been peeling apples for Charlotte to make a pudding and for Aunt's . . . Charlotte said she made puddings perfectly and she . . . of quick but limited intellect. Tabby said just now Come Anne pillo-putate (i.e., pill a potate). Aunt has come into the kitchen just now and said Where are your feet Ann Anne answered On the floor Aunt. Papa opened the parlour door and gave Branwell a letter saying Here Branwell read this and show

it to your Aunt and Charlotte. The Gondals are discovering the interior of Gaaldine. Sally Mosely is washing in the back kitchin.

"It is past twelve o'clock Anne and I have not tided ourselves done our bed work, or done our lessons and we want to go out to play. We are going to have for dinner Boiled Beef, Turnips, potatoes and apple pudding. The kitchin is in a very untidy state. Anne and I have not our music lesson which consists of a *b major* Taby said on my putting a pen in her face Ya pitter pottering there instead of pilling a potate. I answered O dear, O dear, O dear I will derectly With that I get up, take a knife and begin pilling. Finished pilling the potatoes Papa going to walk Mr. Sunderland expected.

"Anne and I say I wonder what we shall be like and what we shall be and where we shall be if all goes well, in the year 1874—in which year I shall be in my 57th year. Anne will be in her 55th year Branwell will be going on in his 58th year and Charlotte in her 59th year. Hoping we shall all be well at that time. We close our paper.

Emily and Anne."

Anne's contribution to this production is a drawing of a lock of hair, described: "A bit of Lady Juliet's hair done by Anne."

What does this interesting document reveal?—It has been much adapted for the purpose of revelation. We learn something about Emily's daily activities; we can infer something of her personal disposition towards the household; we can gather what some of her habits were, and also the degree of general tolerance which prevailed at Haworth. We also get an insight into Emily's power of expressing herself, in her seventeenth year: her mental equipment, her intelligence.

Taking the composition, first, as a means of assessing Emily's intellectual ability, it surely is not a remarkable composition for a girl of sixteen; and those who say it is, may possibly have in mind the "great navigator" of M. Héger's posthumous description. In fact, it strikes the present writer as being rather backward in expression; and this, in view of the undoubted genius which Emily displayed at a later date, is an interesting discovery.

It is not only a matter of punctuation and spelling; there is a note of childishness running through the whole piece. It is in no way organised: not anything like so accomplished as are Charlotte's compositions (previously quoted) written at the age of thirteen. Emily's commentary on what is going on before her eyes is, of course, charming to all who enjoy close-up portrayals of the Brontë scene. Had it been set down purposely for the benefit of readers of Brontë biography, the thing would be almost too clever to be true; it has all the requisite "atmosphere". The narrative gives the same ingenuous illogical string of incidents, all in one breath, without any suggestion of a discriminative sense, that a lively child of ten might deliver. "The Gondals are discovering the interior of Gaaldine. Sally Mosely is washing in the back kitchin." Were these two items of equal value to Emily? Perhaps they were. Maybe it was as vital, to her mind, that Sally Mosely's wash-day should be celebrated, as the latest Gondal developments. On the other hand, we have heard of Gondal before, and will hear of it again, in Emily's scheme of things; Sally Mosely enjoys no further fame.

It is true that an advanced sense of mimicry emerges from her description of Tabby's dialect speech: this was a trick, also, of Charlotte, and the speculations concerning the far-future date 1874 present signs of sophistication. On the whole, however, the piece is enjoyably juvenile; few schoolgirls of sixteen could ever have written anything so enjoyable or so childish. If this is so, it might have some bearing on the nature of genius; so far as Emily is concerned, we must observe, as no doubt had her family, that she was in many ways young for her years. But we must not forget that the very fact that she felt compelled to make even this voluntary record—one which, possessed no function, like for instance a letter; one which, for practical purposes was quite useless—in this she was old for her age, in common with the rest of the Brontës.

The information contained in this paper tells us much about the conditions in which the Brontës came to maturity. We get the impression of a warm slapdash harmony; a close intimacy between Emily and Anne. Tabby's invitations to lend a hand with the potatoes are repeatedly ignored. Aunt Branwell urges Anne to get up and do something; Anne cheeks back, but Aunt doesn't bother, she is already occupied elsewhere. Papa presents a letter to Branwell which is to be shared with Charlotte and Aunt, the Elders. The kitchen is untidy, and so are Emily and Anne, whose daily duties are disclosed by the list of those not yet done. Nothing seems to have been "done" in fact, except the feeding of their pet pheasant of four-fold "alias". Emily's attitude to everyone and everything concerned shows a genial satisfaction with life. It represents one day in an ocean of years; she may have been in uncommonly good spirits on this one day; on the other hand, this random piece might be taken, as is more likely, for an account of an average day in Emily Brontë's girlhood.

Charlotte, in a satirical Branwell-baiting story, gives his alleged opinions of his sisters at this time—"miserable silly creatures not worth talking about. Charlotte's eighteen years old, a broad dumpy thing, whose head does not come higher than my elbow. Emily's sixteen, lean and scant, with a face about the size of a penny, and Anne is nothing, absolutely nothing": Exaggerated, of course, for Charlotte's purpose. Emily's leanness is in keeping with all accounts; it is Anne's being "nothing" which deserves attention. This sentiment was a more or less lifelong conviction, not only of Branwell, but of Charlotte, who always tended to demote Anne's personality and talent. However, there is abundant evidence to show that Anne had a tenacious will and a good mind. She was far from being "nothing" to Emily; in fact, she came closer to Emily than any other person ever did.

In July, 1835, Charlotte announced, "We are all about to

divide, break up, separate. Emily is going to school, Branwell is going to London, and I am going to be a governess." Charlotte was to return to Roe Head as a teacher, and there, too, Emily was entering as a pupil.

Neither cared for the idea, for Charlotte adds, "Emily and I leave home on the 29th of this month; the idea of being together consoles us both somewhat." Now that Branwell, off to London to enrol in the Royal Academy, seemed to be about to make his way in the world, the time had come for the girls to consider their future livelihood. The only suitable occupation open to them was teaching. Charlotte had had her schooling, she was equipped for the job. As for Emily, she would have to go to school first, in order to become a governess later. So it was planned. They left in July, and by November Emily was back at Haworth. Anne took her place at Roe Head. Branwell's hopes failed.

It was said after Emily's death, notably by Charlotte, and reaffirmed by Mrs. Gaskell, that the trouble with Emily was homesickness. It is curious that no mention was made of Emily's distress at the time; it may be that Charlotte entertained some fears concerning her sister's future, which she would not reveal. How would Emily support herself when their father should die, and Haworth Parsonage be no longer their home? Some sort of systematic learning seemed necessary. But there was no further attempt to send Emily to school,

Her first extant poems date from the following year. She may possibly have destroyed her earlier pieces before she died; this is more likely than that they were destroyed by Charlotte or any other member of the household, as some suggest; both because Emily showed a strong proprietory interest in the disposition of her work, and because there is no evident reason why, had they destroyed anything at all, her executors should have chosen to destroy everything up to this particular year, and to preserve so much subsequent unfinished work. (Many of her poems are simply fragments put down as a poet's working notes.)

From 1836 forward, we have, in her poems, the material for some insight into Emily Brontë's mind, and yet we have not. In the first place, some of the poems are composed for the specific requirements of the Gondal epic which was in constant process of elaboration by herself and Anne. It has been usual to assume that, from the first, Emily dominated Anne in the Gondal transactions. There is no evidence to support this. The only direct evidence of the attitude of Emily to Anne, and of Anne to Emily, comes in the secret papers they addressed to each other. These papers, as we shall see, do not suggest that Emily was the dominant party. That she was the superior poet is true. But in matters of collaboration, it is not always the superior partner who leads, organises and directs the proceeding.

There seems to have been a mutual interchange between the two sisters, on sufficiently loose a basis to allow each some freedom of individual expression. All the same, neither was entirely free; the demands of Gondal's development and action imposed on their Gondal work certain limits from which, as individual writers, they were free. So far as action was concerned, we do not know exactly what was Emily's contribution, and what Anne's, to the Gondal story. We only know which of the Gondal poems was produced individually by the sisters. The attitude and substance of these poems might have been pre-arranged by both partners.

Therefore it is impossible to assume, in Emily's Gondal pieces, any disposition of mind which would have a reliable bearing on her general outlook; it is true we may, from the point of view of literary criticism, declare that this or that poem is pantheistic in its philosophy, or mystical in tone. But we cannot, so far as the Gondal work is concerned, deduce that Emily was a pantheist or a mystic at the date of composition. If she had been the sole creator of Gondal, we would be able to reconstruct Emily's personal frame of mind much better. For even her 'personal' poems, from which she herself separated her Gondal pieces, are touched with Gondal heroics. The personal poems have, on the whole, nothing like the fullness of poetic *intention* which the Gondal productions convey. In fact, Emily appears at her most vital in the Gondal poems; we can truly judge these as her poems, but not as pure manifestations of her thought. The action of Gondal was the dominating factor, and this was devised only in part by herself, so far as we know. We cannot, either, assume that each partner's contribution was made without previous consultation—that, in other words, the poems themselves dictated the pattern of Gondal events. It is unlikely that such a haphazard arrangement could have produced the organic results, which even the fragmentary evidence of the extant poems discloses.

There are the particular dangers in adducing evidence from Emily Brontë's poems towards reconstructing her state of mind at any given time. Still less could one safely trace outward events of her life in them. For, apart from present considerations, few poets can be said to have experienced the physical or psychological events portrayed, during the precise month or year in which a particular poem was composed. Years may go by before actual events emerge in a poem. No poem by Emily Brontë can possibly tell us whether in 1836 she was unhappy; in 1838, bitter; in 1840, transported with mystic joy. We cannot tell the date on which these emotions stirred within her; we only know the month and year on which her poems were completed (for she has recorded the dates); from this we can tell only that on those particular dates she was neither overwhelmed with despair nor in the transports of mystical rapture; she was absorbed in writing a poem about despair or rapture, as it may be. Such complete absorption in work is what most poets would describe as happiness, whether it lasts a whole afternoon, several days, or half-an-hour. Only in the retrospect of her completed life's-work, can we make deductions as to the philosophical bias of Emily Brontë's mind. We can then see the bent of her thought as it mastered the Gondal epic. For the present, we see her poems, month by month, in the contrary position of being in subjection to Gondal.

It is not proposed, therefore, to use Emily's poems as a biographical source. It is legitimate, however, to consider the implications of the fact of her poems' existence. This fact means that there were few periods in her life, especially from 1836 onwards, when she was not deeply engaged in her work. If her poems cause us to speculate that she had suffered greatly, had been frustrated in the most ardent longings of her spirit, had been many times melancholy, we do also know quite definitely that there were many and frequent intervals of happiness, on the occasions when she was practising her art. And since we can see the influence of other poets in her work, we must also recognise the fact that she had been happily reading these poets on many occasions. That she was seldom hilarious does not mean that she was often mournful.

Of course, some of her working hours yielded unsatisfactory results, as we know from the results themselves, and from an early hint contained in her comment, written underneath a poem: "I am more terrifically and idiotically STUPID—than ever I was in the whole course of my incarnate existence. The above precious lines are the fruits of one hour's most agonizing labour between ½ past 6 and ½ past 7 in the evening of July — 1836."

We may assume from this that she took her work seriously, as a vocation, something worth labouring at. She appears to have learned later, not to force poems which showed signs of fruitlessness; not to try always to salvage something for her labours; instead, she simply left the poem unfinished.

Emily made no effort to gain public recognition. Branwell had been submitting his work, with more and more forcefulness, to Blackwood's magazine. Charlotte sent a specimen of her prose to Southey, from whom she got a kind answer, advising her to forgo the career of letters. Emily's anxieties were not towards the publication, but the perfecting of her work.

Charlotte was still teaching at Miss Wooler's school, now

moved to Dewsbury Moor, when, in the October of 1837, she wrote, "My sister Emily is gone into a situation as teacher in a large school of near forty pupils, near Halifax. I have had one letter from her since her departure; it gives an appalling account of her duties—hard labour from six in the morning until near eleven at night, with only one half-hour of exercise between."

In later years it was said that Emily endured her teaching enterprise at Law Hill School for six months, and returned once more, homesick. As with her departure from Roe Head, there is complete silence in Charlotte's letters about Emily's further experiences at Law Hill, and her return. As nothing more is spoken of Emily until mid-1839, it has been suggested that she was at Law Hill for as long as eighteen months. The earliest authorities, however, agree on the period of six months, for the harrowing experience described by Emily, as Charlotte transmits it. Emily's first letter to Charlotte was probably her way of giving notice of her impending return. It may be that her duties were described with complete accuracy; or perhaps some excess of loathing of the work forced Emily to a poetic excess in order to hint her desire to be advised to leave. Either way, she deserves equal sympathy. "Hard labour from six in the morning until near eleven at night" may be decoded into "I am altogether unfit for this sort of work. I don't take to routine. I wish to get out of it."—(especially remembering Emily's exaggerated phrase, "agonizing labour" to describe an hour's difficulty with a poem). If it is true that Emily only had half-an-hour's exercise between rising and retiring, she must have written her poems in her daily half-hours; for during her first three months stay there, she wrote fourteen poems, some of them her longest pieces; whereas, during the previous nine months of that year, at Haworth, she had written only twenty poems. Law Hill, therefore, increased Emily's incentive to write. This may imply that she was so miserable that she took her only escape in the practice of poetry. But it cannot be said to imply that she had less leisure there than she enjoyed at home. Poems so complete as those which Emily wrote at this period, are unlikely to have been composed in a half-hour's break in a seventeen-hour working day. And unless we prefer to enchant ourselves with a picture of Emily working at her poems far into the night, by the dim light of an ever-sinking tallow, at the top of a sleeping school-house, we might, perhaps, take Emily's "appalling account" with moderation.

She returned home, as she desired. The family perhaps understood that Emily was queer about going from home. It is unlikely that she herself felt any sense of personal failure; she applied herself to painting some of her pets. Her poems continued to absorb her, and began to develop into maturity during 1838. There is a possibility that Emily was content to play the queer sister, so long as she was left in peace. On the other hand any assumption of her eccentricity at this time, is purely speculative, if we are to suspend full reliance on Charlotte's memory. At present, Charlotte's ambitions for the family do not seem to have troubled Emily, who did not share them.

In the spring of 1839 Charlotte and Anne took their first situations as private governesses, Charlotte having had some temporary frictions with her old employer, Miss Wooler. Anne expressed herself "very well satisfied" with her employer in spite of difficulties in managing the children. Charlotte, however, discovered that working for a friendly headmistress of a girl's school, and being employed by a stranger in a private house, were very different propositions. She complained bitterly to Emily, in a letter addressing her as "Dearest Lavinia" about the trials of her new life. "I see now more clearly than I have ever done before that a private governess has no existence, is not considered as a living and rational being except as connected with the wearisome duties she has to fulfil" wrote Charlotte. Perhaps this was the very point Emily had made, when she decided Law Hill was not for her; Charlotte was only now realizing the truth of the matter.

1840—1842

The arrival of a gay and charming curate, William Weightman, at Haworth, caused a flutter of high spirits amongst the girls. He was attentive to all, including Ellen Nussey on her visits to Haworth. Charlotte, with the authority of one who had already refused two clergymen in marriage, made much game of him. Amongst themselves, the girls referred to this young gallant as "Miss Celia Amelia", sometimes merely "Miss Weightman". He despatched Valentines to all of them, and made himself pleasant to other female hearts in the countryside as well. While on holiday, he would send large consignments of game to the parsonage. Only Anne seems to have taken him seriously; he was observed by Charlotte to be glancing and sighing in Anne's direction, one day in Church. Emily's nickname 'The Major', was subsequently explained as having originated in a walk she took with Weightman and Ellen Nussey, when Emily walked protectively between the two. There is no question of Emily having needed protection from William Weightman, nor he from her. Although her work is constantly concerned with the subject of love, she had no realistic conception of it. We get no clue from her work that she ever experienced a love affair, far less that she ever entertained amorous feelings for a living person; love is a conceptual though passionate emotion in Emily Brontë's work. In contemporary reports, there is no indication of her falling in love with anyone; moreover, there is no sign that, merely lacking the opportunity of meeting men, she did not fall in love. She does not appear to have needed any object of amorous or sexual attention. That is not to say she was without passion, but to say that passion in her, was not focussed towards attachments to her fellow men. In other words, she appears to have been a born celibate, about which condition, as it applies to Emily, fuller comment will be made in the latter part of this essay.

For Emily, alone with her aunt and father, housework and leisure to think and write were the daily fulfilments. Charlotte and Anne were rarely at Haworth during the next two years. Branwell had taken and lost a job as a tutor. While at Haworth he was not much in the house; he met his friends at the local inn. Presently, he left home again, having obtained a job as a clerk on the Railroad. Charlotte and Anne changed their jobs but were little happier. "We are all separated now" Charlotte informs one of her former suitors, Henry Nussey, "and winning our bread amongst strangers as we can — my sister Anne is near York, my brother in a situation near Halifax, I am here (Rawdon, in the Leeds vicinity). Emily is the only one left at home, where her usefulness and willingness make her indispensible."

If Emily made herself indispensible at home, this reveals not only her wisdom, but a true enjoyment of manual work in the familiar ease of her home. She was wise, because she safeguarded herself in this way from being uprooted. Both Charlotte and later, Anne, make a point of expressing Emily's household usefulness, as if to silence criticism, and to reassure themselves, that Emily was not shirking at home while her sisters slaved for strangers.

Charlotte, Branwell and Anne all possessed, in some measure, a desire to get on in the world. Their literary work was, to them, but half-fulfilled if it remained unheard-of outside the family. In 1840 Charlotte had submitted work to Wordsworth who had replied in a tone which provoked a saucy retort from her. Branwell had got so far in his endeavours as to have spent a day at Ambleside on the invitation of Hartley Coleridge. But these two Brontës were dissatisfied with any advice or response, however sanguine, however courteous, so long as it led nowhere in terms of publication. In reality, they submitted their work, not for critical consideration, but for approval. Charlotte especially, took no notice of any man of letters who advised her to stop writing; and she proved right.

Emily was not without ambition; if this had been so, her acquiesence in the common lot of clergymen's spinster daughters, would have been more noticeable. She would have resigned herself to the necessity of taking a job as a governess. But her apparent listlessnesss, her willingness to be the useful stay-at-home, concealed a determined resistance to any attempt to make her useful elsewhere. This fact seems to have been tacitly assumed by her family. The cause of this strong preference for home life in Emily seems at first sight explicable in terms of Charlotte's posthumous statement to the effect that Emily was passionately attached to the moors around her home, and spent a great deal of her solitude in their familiar embrace; away from the moors, Emily pined; Haworth drew back the ailing homesick girl like a magnet. Whether this was wholly the case, is a question which now becomes prominent. So far we have observed from the current data, that Emily had been evidently dissatisfied with her life at Miss Wooler's school and at Law Hill school; and was now fairly satisfied with her life at Haworth.

It should be noted that Emily had been from home during her childhood on two previous occasions: once at Cowan Bridge where the school records suggest only that the authorities were pleased with her; there is no word from Charlotte, in all her later commentary on the Cowan Bridge episode, that her infant sister Emily was pining for home. Again, Emily had, at the age of ten, spent a holiday with Charlotte, Branwell and Anne, at the home of their great-uncle John Fennell. From there, Charlotte wrote home to tell of the drawings executed by all four children; there is no suggestion that Emily was pining.

It may be, then, that the irresistible call of the Haworth moorland did not affect Emily until she was past childhood. If this is so, we should expect to find stubborn resistance from Emily to a proposition put forward in July 1841, while Charlotte was home on vacation, which would entail leaving Haworth. "There is a project hatching in this house" writes Charlotte to Ellen Nussey, "which both Emily and I anxiously wish to discuss with you . . . Papa and aunt talk, by fits and starts, of our—*id est,* Emily, Anne, and myself—commencing a school." Their aunt had offered to lend them the capital, to Charlotte's surprise. She goes on to discuss the many details of their plan. "Aunt Branwell might go as far as £150; would it be possible to establish a respectable (not by any means a *showy*) school and to commence housekeeping with a capital of only that amount?" Then, the question of where the school should be. Charlotte had thought of the neighbourhood of Burlington as offering some scope for their project. "This is, of course" she added "a perfectly crude and random idea . . . We have no connections, no acquaintances there; it is far from here, etc . . ."

We learn, then, that Emily was far from troubled about the prospect of leaving Haworth to start a school with her sisters. Charlotte says that, like herself, Emily was "anxious to discuss" the plan with Ellen. And from the arguments propounded in Charlotte's letter, we may assume that the project had been the subject of much discussion at the Parsonage, without any personal objections from Emily. But we also have Emily's own testimony of her reactions to this proposal. This comes in one of her 'birthday papers'. There was an arrangement between Emily and Anne that each should write a personal reminiscence every few years on Emily's birthday; these papers were opened in a later year. Of these interesting compositions, only four remain—two by Emily and two by Anne. These were intentionally private communications; it is unlikely that anyone but the two sisters concerned was aware of this pleasant habit. Here is Emily's contribution for the year 1841.

A PAPER to be opened
when Anne is
25 years old,
or my next birthday after
if
all be well.
Emily Jane Brontë. July the 30th, 1841.

It is Friday evening, near 9 o'clock—wild rainy weather. I am seated in the dining-room, having just concluded tidying our desk boxes, writing this document. Papa is in the parlour—aunt upstairs in her room. She has been reading *Blackwood's Magazine* to papa. Victoria and Adelaide are ensconced in the peat-house. Keeper is in the kitchen—Hero in his cage. We are all stout and hearty, as I hope is the case with Charlotte, Branwell, and Anne, of whom the first is at John White, Esq., Upperwood House, Rawdon; the second is at Luddenden Foot; and the third is, I believe, at Scarborough, inditing perhaps a paper corresponding to this.

A scheme is at present in agitation for setting us up in a school of our own; as yet nothing is determined, but I hope and trust it may go on and prosper and answer our highest expectations. This day four years I wonder whether we shall still be dragging on in our present condition or established to our hearts' content. Time will show.

I guess that at the time appointed for the opening of this paper we i.e. Charlotte, Anne, and I, shall be all merrily seated in our own sitting-room in some pleasant flourishing seminary, having just gathered in for the midsummer ladyday. Our debts will be paid off, and we shall have cash in hand to a considerable amount. Papa, aunt, and Branwell will either have been or be coming to visit us. It will be a fine warm summer evening, very different from this bleak look-out, and Anne and I will perchance slip out into the garden for a few minutes to peruse our papers. I hope either this or something better will be the case.

The *Gondaland* are at present in a threatening state, but there is no open rupture as yet. All the princes and princesses of the Royalty are at the Palace of Instruction. I have a good many books on hands, but I am sorry to say that as usual I make small progress with any. However, I have just made a new regularity paper! and I must *verb sap* to do great things. And now I close, sending from far an exhortation of courage, boys! courage, to exiled and harassed Anne, wishing she was here.

Emily was now twenty-three.She has had practice in prose as well as verse. Her 'paper', though not impressive in its style, is adequately framed. Had we no more than this to go by, Emily appears to be all at rights with the world. She is perfectly normal in tone, as she mentions each member of the family, their plans and prospects. It has not, indeed, so far been hinted in the current Brontë correspondence that Emily was anything but a normal contented young woman. In addition, we know from the poems that she was highly gifted. Charlotte had no access to the poems as yet.

Emily had every reason for satisfaction — even for the buoyancy of spirit which her birthday note suggests. Her literary work has been making progress. Her verse prospers, as we know from her verse; the Gondal narrative continues, and although there is some congestion at present—("I have a good many books on hand . . ." is a reference to the Gondal "volumes", also referred to, below, by Anne)—the epic of Gondal is generally flourishing. The relationship of Emily Brontë to her work at this stage is not one of interwoven identity. There seems little similarity between the tragic mood of her recent poems—with their stress on themes of death, remorse, revenge, imprisonment—and the mood of personal well being which Emily conveys in her birthday note. The poems which took their place in the prose narrative of Gondal, would be seen by Anne, as well as the birthday paper; and so it is not a question of Emily concealing the true state of her mind in her personal memorandum, whilst revealing it in the poems. The most simple and obvious explanation of the striking contrast which exists between the tone of Emily's creative work, and that of her personal statement, is that her writings were, at this time, more objectively conceived than they appear to be. The Augusta, the Julius, the Douglas, and all the rest of Gondal's characters are not subjective variants on Emily Brontë herself because the biographical evidence shows otherwise; and also, for the reason already mentioned that the Gondal characters were not Emily's sole creation. And those poems which do not come into the Gondal category also apparently partake of poetic, not personal and actual, experience at this date. Poetic experience is, however, such that it may be prophetic; it may express a real tendency present in the poet's mind as one of many potentialities. Thus, Emily's lines, written a few days before her birthday note,

> I see around me tombstones grey
> Stretching their shadows far away.
> Beneath the turf my footsteps tread
> Lie low and lone the silent dead;
> Beneath the turf, beneath the mould—
> Forever dark, forever cold,
> And my eyes cannot hold the tears
> That memory hoards from vanished years;
> For Time and Death and Mortal pain
> Gives wounds that will not heal again.
> Let me remember half the woe
> I've seen and heard and felt below,
> And Heaven itself, so pure and blest,
> Could never give my spirit rest. . . .

—these lines may be said to prefigure a possible development in Emily Brontë's thought, but they do not furnish a picture of her mind to supplement that of her autobiographical birthday note. Both were written in July 1841; but the poem belongs to the realm of potential experience: it tells us only that in July 1841, Emily Brontë *had it in her* to suffer greatly from memories of horror; it does not tell us that she already bore those memories. The autobiographical fragment, on the other hand, expresses what we are concerned with at this point: Emily's state of mind in July 1841.

She was satisfied because she was fulfilling her innate will to write. Had the school project threatened her literary activity, we may suppose she would have resisted it. As she would be working together with her own accustomed kin, this fear did not present itself: they knew each others' ways. If she had suffered from a serious dread of being away from

Haworth, she would not have embraced the scheme with the words "I hope and trust it may go on and prosper and answer our highest expectations". She acknowledged the fact that the present arrangement was unsatisfactory, with Charlotte and Anne miserably situated in private employment, herself with no provision for earning her living after their father's death. "This day four years" she writes, anticipating the time when the paper should be opened "I wonder whether we shall still be dragging on in our present condition or established to our hearts' content." She allows herself to speculate on the delightful possibilities, should the scheme come to fruition. She allows herself a guess: "all merrily seated in our own sitting-room in some pleasant and flourishing seminary, having just gathered in for the mid-summer lady-day".

As for the moors from which, it has been told, she could never tear herself away, Emily does not here repine them. Instead, she is concerned with something quite as important to a practitioner of the art of letters: cash. They would have paid off their debts and possess also, a considerable sum in hand. Money meant leisure; freedom from the pressure of uncongenial work, freedom to pursue a vocation. It meant freedom for the sisters to sit merrily together in a pleasant room. She does not seem to realise that she is supposed to be passionately devoted to the Haworth scene; she is busy anticipating the luxuries in store, this day four years. Will she not be homesick for the moors? We are not told that the thought occurred to her. "It will be a fine warm summer evening" she declares "very different from this bleak look-out." Emily adds her hope that "this or something better will be the case."

The spirit of the document is one of sensitive optimism. Everyone at home is "stout and hearty" including herself; she has drawn up a new work-sheet to get herself out of the difficulty of having too many fragments in hand; she has high hopes for getting work done; and she wishes only for the company of Anne.

This was true. Anne's paper is pitched on a more sober key. She writes from her employers' holiday residence in Scarborough, "I dislike the situation and wish to change it for another." Her hopes for the future were not therefore nourished by a present sense of well being, as with Emily. Anne records the school plan without enthusiasm:

"We are thinking of setting up a school of our own, but nothing definite is settled about it yet, and we do not know whether we shall be able to or not. I hope we shall. And I wonder what will be our condition and how or where we shall all be on this day four years hence; at which time, if all be well, I shall be 25 years and 6 months old, Emily will be 27 years old, Branwell 28 years and 1 month, and Charlotte 29 years and a quarter. We are now all separate and not likely to meet again for many a weary week, but we are none of us ill that I know of, and all are doing something for our own livelihood except Emily, who, however, is as busy as any of us, and in reality earns her food and raiment as much as we do.

How little know we what we are
How less what we may be!

Four years ago I was at school. Since then I have been a governess at Blake Hill, left it, come to Thorp Green, and seen the sea and York Minster. Emily has been a teacher at Miss Patchet's school, and left it. Charlotte has left Miss Wooler's, been a governess at Mrs. Sidgwick's, left her, and gone to Mrs. White's. Branwell has given up painting, been a tutor in Cumberland, left it, and become a clerk on the railroad. Tabby has left us, Martha Brown has come in her place. We have got Keeper, got a sweet little cat and lost it, and also got a hawk. Got a wild goose which has flown away, and three tame ones, one of which has been killed. All these diversities, with many others, are things we did not expect or foresee in the July of 1837. What will the next four years bring forth? Providence only knows. But we ourselves have sustained very little alteration since that time. I have the same faults that I had then, only I have more wisdom and experience, and a little more self-possession than I then enjoyed. How will it be when we open this paper and the one Emily has written? I wonder whether the *Gondaland* will still be flourishing, and what will be their condition. I am now engaged in writing the fourth volume of *Solala Vernon's Life . . .*"

Anne's quotation,

> How little know we what we are
> How less what we may be!

had perhaps more relevance than she knew. Charlotte and Branwell both possessed a conscious conviction that they had great possibilities within them. Charlotte directed herself as best she could, to doing something to bring these possibilities to light. Branwell's talent was dissipated by eloquence; he entertained his friends with his wit, while Charlotte kept quiet, planned, and acted. Anne herself was Emily's closest friend, and in the general belief that she was overpowered by Emily, the possibility that Anne might have exerted some personal influence on her sister, has been overlooked. Anne, who was the most realistic of the Brontës, did not seem to think of her own potential talent so long as there was little opportunity to exercise it. As we see, she continues with her Gondal volumes, but she wonders whether Gondaland will still be flourishing four years hence. She will not commit herself, like Emily, to guessing the future; nor like Charlotte, to putting plans in motion. But Anne was observant and reflective. She knew that many unforseen things had occurred, and would occur. When at last she did get her independence, Anne was assiduous to act upon it; meantime she kept her aims within the limits of her present duty. Anne was a persuaded Christian: it was deliberate practise of her principles which prevented Anne from launching forth before her due time; she submitted to Charlotte's suggestions, and continued to do work she disliked while Charlotte experimented with life. These signs of Anne's strength of character have somehow earned her a reputation for weakness of purpose. It is, however, necessary to consider the obvious tenacity of will which kept Anne Brontë at the same tedious job for four years, during which time she started her first novel. She was not afraid to face the likelihood of the school plan coming to nothing, and indeed, of all their circumstances being altered. Anne, like Emily, had her reputation fixed for all time by the commentaries of her friends. "Sweet gentle Anne" they said. Indeed she was gentle and sweet. But it does not follow that she was easily influenced in her opinions or actions; quite the opposite: she was the more released from obligations to concede matters of principle. Where her family was concerned, she acquiesced in Charlotte's plans; as youngest, she waited her turn; Emily she looked upon, for the present, as her fellow-fantastic, her playmate, and it may be that she detected possibilities of Emily's genius before Emily did herself. "How little know we what we are . . ."

Judging from Anne's work and the conduct of her life, it seems likely that she had, by now, tired of the Gondal legend. She was the least romantic of the Brontës. Anne had been in love, it is supposed with William Weightman, and possibly had by now given up hopes of him. She made the best of life as it was, nor would she relinquish her participation in the Gondal epic, since its continuance meant so much to Emily. From later indications, however, it is not improbable that Anne would have chosen to relinquish Gondal writing by this time.

At present, then, Emily accounts for herself in the light of a happy and normal woman who is following a natural bent for writing. The family were aware that only in certain circumstances was Emily happy and normal: perhaps no-one, least of all Emily, was clear as to the precise nature of these circumstances. But it amounted to the practical result that Emily could not take a job. The proposal for setting up a school of their own had, however, met with Emily's pleasure. It was not, therefore, parting from Haworth which appalled Emily; nor was it exactly school life. What made certain situations intolerable to her seems to have been an instinctive antipathy towards applying her mind to an imposed system, within an environment governed by strangers. Presently Charlotte was in negotiations with Miss Wooler for taking over her school. The good lady showed hesitation. Charlotte did not wait, but plunged straightway into a new scheme. She would equip herself with a knowledge of French and German before setting up school. This would mean a period of study abroad. "I longed to go to Brussels; but how could I get there?" she wrote, "I wished for one, at least, of my sisters to share the advantage with me. I fixed on Emily. She deserved the reward, I knew. How could the point be managed? In extreme excitement I wrote a letter home, which carried the day." A few days later, Charlotte addressed a letter to Emily: "Dear E.J.—You are not to suppose that this note is written with a view to communicating any information on the subject we both have considerably at heart . . ."

The plan had been agreed. The question now was only to find the school. Did Emily welcome the prospect of attending school as cheerfully as she had anticipated starting one? "The subject we both have considerably at heart" writes Charlotte in a curious round-about way, as if the plan were a secret, which, as we have seen, it was not. Maybe Charlotte phrased herself thus in order to sound Emily's true feelings in the matter. A little further on she puts in, "Grieve not over Dewsbury Moor (Miss Wooler's school). You were cut out there to all intents and purposes, so in fact was Anne; Miss Wooler would hear of neither for the first half-year."

"Anne seems omitted from the present plan" Charlotte continues, "but if all goes right I trust she will derive her full share of benefit from it in the end. I exhort all to hope. I believe in my heart this is acting for the best; my only fear is lest others should doubt and be dismayed. Before our half-year in Brussels is completed, you and I will have to seek employment abroad. It is not my intention to retrace my steps home till twelve months . . ."

So Charlotte announces her intentions and lets it be known that doubt or dismay in others is her only fear. Charlotte was the great promoter of the Brontë sisters. She initiated their every encounter with the world during their life-time, she stage-managed their posthumous reputations. Yet it is possible that without Charlotte's activities we might never have heard of the Brontës. It was she who started their books on the way to publishers; it was probably Charlotte who inspired Emily and Anne with the desire to write marketable books—novels. But for Charlotte, the younger sisters might have spent their talent on adding fabulous material to the sprawling Gondal saga. Charlotte's bossiness sometimes betrays a sort of desperation. She was desperately keen to achieve something in life, she was desperately forceful when she greatly desired anything. So, in this matter, she declares, not only her intentions, but her assumption that Emily's acquiescence is of course beyond doubt. Emily however, regretted that negotiations with Miss Wooler over her school at Dewsbury Moor, had come to an end; this had been the last hope for the project which had so delighted Emily. Charlotte does not appear to have considered whether Emily's disappointment over this might not indicate a disinclination to attend school at Brussels. "You and I" states Charlotte "will have to seek employment abroad." "It is not my intention . . ." she continues, without enquiring Emily's intentions.

From Brussels, in May 1842, Charlotte reported their progress at Mme. Héger's school. Charlotte herself was happy; "My present life is so delightful, so congenial," she writes, "to my own nature, compared with that of a governess. . . ." She even enjoyed the wrath of "M. Héger, the husband of Madame . . . very choleric and irritable in temperament; a little black being. . . ." And Emily?—"Emily and he don't draw well together at all. When he is very ferocious with me I cry; that sets all things straight. Emily works like a horse, and she has great difficulties to contend with, far greater than I have had."

Emily had less knowledge of French than Charlotte; this was a drawback. Also, she had apparently little genuine interest in acquiring these educational advantages. Charlotte's interest came from the heart; she marvelled at herself being a schoolgirl at the age of twenty-six; she was able to enter into the spirit of the thing, and cry when appropriate. Also, she was a practised student. But Emily was in this situation from necessity; and she was not used to studying under the direction of professional teachers. She could not share Charlotte's pleasure, and at the same time, she had to work harder than her better-informed sister. Emily so well applied herself to study, that she was soon said by Charlotte to be "making rapid progress in French, German, music and drawing". "Monsieur and Madame Héger", Charlotte adds, "begin to recognise the valuable parts of her character, under her singularities."

To the Hégers, the "valuable parts" of Emily's character appear to have been her determined capacity for hard work, and her special ability in music. They were impressed by Charlotte's competence, and offered to take her as an English teacher, affording her opportunities for further study in French and German. They included Emily in this arrangement, offering to employ her, "some part of each day in teaching music to a certain number of the pupils". Charlotte accepted this offer. Emily's singularities, now mentioned for the first time in Brontë correspondence, were possibly the outward signs of some inward reluctance to participate in the Brussels transaction.

Up to this time, Emily had not shown persistence in any activity which did not come naturally and easily to her. On this occasion, however, she made a considerable effort to give her mind to systematic instruction and study. The results were curious, so far as they are represented by allusions to Emily, made by Charlotte and others. In the first place we find Emily not getting on with M. Héger. Less than a year ago, to judge by her birthday note, Emily had given the impression of being exceptionally agreeable by nature. This is the first time, indeed, that there is any hint of Emily being at odds with anyone.

A letter from Charlotte's former schoolfellow Mary Taylor, who was then in Brussels, informs Ellen Nussey of a meeting with Charlotte and Emily one evening, on which occasion Emily spoke only once or twice. Emily, in fact, was responding to unfavourable conditions in which she had reluctantly placed herself, with natural resentment. But further comments upon her at this time give us an aspect of Emily which shows she was not simply sulking because she could not have her own way.

We have to realise that those observations of Emily recorded by Charlotte approximate somewhat, if not exactly, to reality. We have cause to question Charlotte's information only where she gives it from memory. Charlotte's view of Emily at any given period during Emily's lifetime was informed by a lifelong experience of her sister in a variety of circumstances; she often, perhaps, misunderstood Emily; but Charlotte was in a position to interpret her sister's current reactions in the light of a general familiarity with her sister. But the impressions of comparative strangers have not undergone this interpretive process; and for that reason, they are both less true, and more telling, than are Charlotte's. Two people unfamiliar with Emily presently offered passing impressions of her at Brussels: Mary Taylor and M. Héger. As we shall see, the effect she had on them varies, but the common assumption is that she was difficult to get on with, not very likeable. Remarks to this effect are of insignificant value as definitions of Emily's true nature; but they are meaningful factors when we are concerned with the feelings which caused Emily to present herself in this light.

Meantime, Charlotte and Emily returned to Haworth in November 1842, summoned by the death of their aunt. William Weightman had died a few weeks before. The four Brontës were gathered in the Parsonage once more, with their father.

The sisters were provided, by their aunt's will, with a modest degree of independence. Her money was divided equally between Charlotte, Emily, Anne, and a fourth niece from her Cornwall family. Her personal belongings were variously distributed amongst the Brontës. One is tempted to wonder if their aunt had deliberated about the special suitability of the respective articles she named for each recipient. Charlotte had "my Indian workbox"; Emily was specified for "my workbox with a china top" and also "my ivory fan"; to Branwell, her "Japan dressing-box"; to Anne, "my watch with all that belongs to it" : practical treasures, amongst which the ivory fan bears a suggestion of feminine fancy. Maybe the fan had previously delighted Emily, or perhaps it was merely thrown in to make up for a workbox inferior to the one bestowed on Charlotte. Since Emily was later described as masculine in type, however, it may be worth noting this triviality; their aunt would, at any rate, hardly choose to bestow her fan on the sister least likely to appreciate it.

Early in October their father received a letter from M. Héger, urging him to send Charlotte and Emily back to Brussels. Their master praised them jointly and with Gallic courtesy, for their industry and perseverance; he expressed sadness at the loss of pupils for whom he felt an affection almost paternal, sorrow that their education remained uncompleted. "In a year" he proclaimed, with engaging confidence, "each of your daughters would have been quite prepared for any eventuality of the future."

Then M. Héger commends them separately: "Miss Emily was learning the piano, receiving lessons from the best professor in Belgium, and she herself already had little pupils. She was losing whatever remained of ignorance, and also of what was worse—timidity; Miss Charlotte was beginning to give lessons in French and to acquire that assurance, that aplomb so necessary to a teacher; only another year and the work would have been completed, and well completed. Then we should have been able, if convenient to you, to offer to your daughters, or at least to one of them, a position according to her taste."

There is little doubt that M. Héger genuinely admired the sisters' determined application to the work they had gone to Brussels to do. He could not have been unaware that they had unusual gifts, and as he was a man with a real vocation for teaching—one who took an interest in comparative methods—he would have found such pupils stimulating.

His reservation, in making a guarantee of employment to the sisters—"or at least to one of them"—may be taken to imply the probable exclusion of Emily. (The rest of his sentence assumes only one of the sisters—"a position according to her taste, and that pleasant independence so difficult for a young person to find"; which appears to imply that there was really no question of both being employed.) Charlotte, more accomplished than her sister, would naturally be preferred. But obviously he was not thinking of Emily merely in the comparative sense—as the sister who would be less useful for his school. He gives a definite impression of Emily, as he had first observed her: he had found a degree of ignorance and timidity in her; she was now losing this, he said.

In the academic sense, his impression of Emily's ignorance was perhaps justified; her timidity, too, may have been real enough. But it is curious that M. Héger should have introduced these somewhat disparaging terms in a letter which is otherwise brimming with tact. As we know from Charlotte's report, Emily did not get on with her master at first. It is probable, both from this and from an episode later revealed,[1] that he disliked Emily. In his patriarchal style, he might well have made his comments purposely to put her in her place.

Emily was generally unpopular during her stay at Brussels (as even the posthumous reports of a family called Wheelwright can be seen to confirm). She had previously met

[1] See Appendix, page 266.

Charlotte's friend, Mary Taylor, at Haworth. Mary Taylor, meeting Emily again in Brussels, had remarked on her lack of conversation. After Charlotte had returned, alone, to Brussels, Mary Taylor mentions Emily once more, in a letter to Ellen Nussey: "I have heard from Charlotte since her arrival; she seems *content* at least, but fear her sister's absence will have a bad effect. When people have so little amusement they cannot afford to lose *any*"; from which sharp thrust, it is clear that Mary Taylor regarded Emily's social qualities with some contempt, she also displayed curiosity about Emily, about whom Ellen Nussey had evidently written. "Tell me something about Emily Brontë." Mary Taylor writes, "I can't imagine how the newly acquired qualities can fit in, in the same head and heart that it occupied by the old ones. I imagine Emily turning over prints or 'taking wine' with any stupid pup and preserving her temper and politeness!" We have to read into this some idea of what impression Ellen Nussey had gained of Emily since her return from Brussels. Ellen had paid a visit to Haworth before Charlotte's lone departure. Ellen had observed, at least, that Emily was changed. In the gossip of her letter Ellen had apparently suggested that Emily had acquired some continental polish, humorously speculating, no doubt, that before long Emily would be keeping choice company. From Mary Taylor's reply, we can see at least, that she had a sense of Emily's intelligence.

The reactions of these people are of course immaterial except for the purpose of illuminating the question of how Brussels affected Emily. That she provoked a variety of new reactions, shows either that a side of her nature which was hitherto not reported is now revealed, or that she underwent a noticeable change at Brussels. Most probably the true situation combines both alternatives. Charlotte refers to Emily's "peculiarities" as if they were known to her correspondent. And then, the fact that she was so generally difficult to get on with at Brussels, posits the probability that Brussels brought out these "peculiarities" with unprecedented force. More important, however, is the nature and cause of this new aspect of Emily which emerges.

Her "peculiarities", so far as we have seen, are normal ones, inherent in people with a strong sense of vocation. In her person Emily was amiable, hopeful and in vigorous spirits when she was pursuing her vocation along certain lines, which excluded the discipline of formal scholarship. At Brussels, she got down to systematic study; she exerted her will towards acquiring knowledge; her amiability vanished, she was no longer friendly with the world; far from being able to control her distaste for the whole proceeding, she could not conceal it.

Emily Brontë may have been quite conscious of her reasons for this obvious horror of being "educated", or some instinctive process may have moved her, of which she was unaware. The question arises, was she justified? The answer rests with her work, and may be elaborated by the critics of her work. It is, however, clear that the element of choice, at this time, existed for Emily: she was not incapable of response to that systematic ordering of her mind which she so definitely wished to reject. The 'ignorance and timidity' of M. Héger's attribution is misleading. Five essays are in existence written in French by Emily Brontë under his direction.[2] Most of these are unlike anything else she is known to have produced, not only in genre, but in their rational content. They represent what are probably her first attempts to formulate her own philosophy, bringing her view of life to consciousness. Until this work had been forced upon her, the same philosophical attitudes which these essays make explicit, were concealed and implicit behind the imaginative fabric of her poems. These tenets more markedly inform *Wuthering Heights*. Her essay, *King Harold on the Eve of the Battle of Hastings,* for example, proclaims in fervent, undeniable tones, her delight in the concentrated power of the mighty romantic hero

[2] *Five Essays written in French by Emily Jane Brontë,* translated by Lorine White Nagel (University of Texas Press, 1948), from which quotations following are taken.

who is a species unto himself. Heathcliff of *Wuthering Heights* is the same thing in another guise, a fictional tributary to the rising cult of the superman. Not everyone who rejoices in *Wuthering Heights* would rejoice in the principles by which, in this brief and in many ways absurd essay, Emily takes her stand. Not everyone will care for her clear unflinching presentation of Nature in its destructive cruelty, which she offers in her pieces, *The Cat* and *The Butterfly*. She reproduces in her creative work much of the thought which forms the theme of these essays. But the very act of creating a work of art is a kind of reparation for the most perverse theme. The nearer the work approaches perfection, the more has the principle of order prevailed against whatever chaos produced it.

Therefore it is not unlikely that Emily had a real fear of conscious enlightenment through study, because this would inevitably push her working hypotheses to their logical extremes. It is not unlikely that she feared the conclusions to which rational formulation would force her. Moreover, her intellect was capable of grasping the moral implications of her creative work; this is clear from her essays, in which her argument proceeds by induction; her proposition is contained in specific examples, upon which her generalisations follow.

It is not unlikely that Emily wished, consciously or otherwise, to avoid reaching conclusions, because they played a harsh moral searchlight upon the fruits of her untrained contemplative mind. She may have been justified; if she had entirely subjected her mind to training, and her work to moral censorship, there might have been no further fruits. Her attitude was, perhaps, self-protective. She was subject to her own poetic and inner discipline; all other discipline was foreign to her.

In her essay *The Butterfly*, there may be a hint of self-justification on this question, allegorically expressed. She describes a forest scene, and soliloquising upon the "natural order", finds not order but insanity. "Life exists on a principle of destruction; every creature must be the relentless instrument of death to the others, or himself cease to live . . . the universe appeared to me a vast machine constructed only to bring forth evil . . . " Then, "like a censuring angel sent from heaven, there fluttered through the trees a butterfly with large wings of gleaming gold and purple . . . here is a symbol of the world to come—just as the ugly caterpillar is the beginning of the splendid butterfly, this globe is the embryo of a new heaven and a new earth whose meagrest beauty infinitely surpasses mortal imagination . . ." She employs this traditional illustration towards its theological conclusion: "God is the God of justice and mercy", suffering is seed for a divine harvest. Possibly, this essay has also a bearing upon her own desire to create harmony out of material which was, only too apparently, chaotic. But this is no more than a possibility; her concern here is not directly aesthetic.

1842—1848

Emily was not tempted to return to Brussels. Any pressing fears for her future had been removed by her aunt's small legacy. It is notable that within the first few weeks after her return from Brussels she gave Ellen Nussey the impression that she was changed into a more sociable being: quite the opposite impression to that formed by her acquaintances in Brussels. But this is understandable if, in her new-found release, her manner blossomed with unusual benevolence and grace. Most likely, she was particularly pleased with herself during the first weeks of freedom. Moods, up and down, were her "peculiarities".

Had she, then, acquired nothing from her nine months in Belgium? She seems to have deliberately rejected the whole experience from her conscious mind. Brussels has no place in her writings.

But she was too intelligent to fail to appreciate the mental process which had been initiated there. She had been forced

The Brontë "Gun Group".
(Emily, Charlotte, Branwell and Anne are represented from left to right.)
Drawing by Branwell Brontë.
(By courtesy of Walter Scott, Bradford. Copyright The Brontë Society)

The scene of *Wuthering Heights* (including the original farmhouse).
(By courtesy of Walter Scott, Bradford)

to organise her thought during that period; few people capable of deep and sustained thought can stop the process at will; it has its own attractions. There is no evidence that Emily was, at this period, engaged in philosophical speculation, but there are indications, in later years, that she had gradually become more of what is called a "thinker".

Emily was alone with her father at Haworth from the beginning of 1843. After the holidays Anne had returned to the Robinsons, her employers. Branwell had gone to join her as tutor to the Robinson boys. Charlotte was back in Brussels, being more or less in love with M. Héger.

"All appears to be going on reasonably well at home," Charlotte wrote to Branwell in May, "I grieve only that Emily is so solitary. . . ."

Emily does not appear to have grieved. She produced comparatively little verse, but we learn that the Gondal destinies, worked out mainly in prose, were to claim her attention for some years to come. When she was obliged, during May, to write to Ellen Nussey, she did not write the letter of a person suffering from loneliness, when we might expect a certain loquacity. She is cheerful and brief; it is the letter of a busy woman; and half-apologetic Emily adds, "The holidays will be here in a week or two and then, if [Anne] be willing, I will get her to write you a proper letter, a feat that I have never performed—with love and good wishes . . ." The ending is typical of the letters of authors at times when they are deeply occupied: a hint that further correspondence is not to be expected; an absent-minded 'Love and best wishes'.

Charlotte sent long letters to Emily bewailing her lot. Her second stay with the Hégers was turning out badly. Mme. Héger, she was convinced, did not like her, which is not surprising in view of Charlotte's subsequent letter to M. Héger. The latter, Charlotte complained, was under the influence of the former. Emily knew nothing of Charlotte's passion for her master; "I hope you are well and hearty. Walk out often on the moors" : Charlotte's advice may seem strange, considering

Emily's proverbial craving for the moors; but Charlotte probably was aware that Emily was wont to sit long hours at her desk.

In October, Charlotte, in a fit of homesickness, inserted in her letter one of those Parsonage 'scenes' from which we learn so much of the daily life at Haworth.

> "Dear E.J.—This is Sunday morning. They are at their idolatrous 'messe', and I am here—that is, in the *refectoire*. I should like uncommonly to be in the dining-room at home, or in the kitchen, or in the back kitchen. I should like even to be cutting up the hash, with the clerk and some register people at the other table, and you standing by, watching that I put enough flour, and not too much pepper, and, above all, that I save the best pieces of the leg of mutton for Tiger and Keeper, the first of which personages would be jumping about the dish and carving-knife, and the latter standing like a devouring flame on the kitchen floor. To complete the picture, Tabby blowing the fire, in order to boil the potatoes to a sort of vegetable glue! How divine are these recollections to me at this moment! . . . *You* call yourself idle! absurd! absurd! . . . Write to me again soon. Tell me whether Papa really wants me very much to come home, and whether you do likewise. I have an idea that I should be of no use there—a sort of aged person upon the parish. I pray, with heart and soul, that all may continue well at Haworth; above all in our grey, half-inhabited house. God bless the walls thereof! . . . Amen."

Charlotte returned to Haworth in January 1844. She could not bear inactivity; at once she organised the sisters into discussing a new school project. Their father could not be left alone. Haworth Parsonage would be the school-house. They had a circular printed advertising the Misses Brontës' Establishment. For months they wrote to the mothers of likely pupils, sent the circular far and wide, waited to hear the results of Ellen Nussey's endeavours on their behalf. Charlotte explained the plan in one of her letters to M. Héger. "Emily" she informed him, "does not care much for teaching, but she would look after the housekeeping, and, although something of a recluse, she is too good-hearted not to do all she could for the wellbeing of the children." In other words, Emily had made it plain that so far as she was concerned there was nothing doing. She would look after the housekeeping, as usual, but she wanted her mind to herself. Charlotte reflected, no doubt, that, when it came to the bit, Emily was, after all, 'too good-hearted' not to do all she could for children. Emily was never put to the test. (Nor was the information volunteered years later by a former pupil of Emily's at Law Hill, thus refuted: Emily was alleged to have told her class she preferred her dog to themselves.) No mama of their acquaintance wanted to send her daughters across the bleak moorland to the lonely parsonage. Anne remained at the Robinsons. Charlotte paid periodic visits to Ellen Nussey. Emily saw to the housekeeping, her pets and her work.

In the middle of 1845, Branwell was dismissed from the Robinsons. He gave out a story which not one of the sisters doubted: he had fallen in love with Mrs. Robinson, and she with him. Mr. Robinson had discovered their secret, and threatened to shoot Branwell should he send so much as a message. Branwell became an object of wonder, pity, contempt, despair, and everything except mirth, to the household. The truth of the story is obscure; there were certainly many discrepancies between Branwell's tale and the facts which came to light after the Brontë children were dead. It may be that he had simply made a nuisance of himself by making unwelcome overtures to his employer's wife; perhaps she encouraged him a little at first, until he became too serious. Branwell, however, was a trifle mad. The story which depicted Mrs. Robinson pining for him and he for her, true lovers separated by a cruel husband, consoled him for whatever his real misery was; whether hurt pride or simply boredom. His misery, however, was real; he drowned it daily at the local tavern. The sisters, awed, frightened, impressed, contemptuous, and a little thrilled, looked on and sighed when the creditors came to the door. Charlotte gave Ellen a running commentary on his condition, lamenting the unprotected upbringing of young men as compared with that of young ladies.

Anne had already decided not to return to the Robinsons after the holidays; she had not disclosed anything she knew of Branwell's affairs, which had probably prompted her decision. At the end of July, Anne and Emily composed two more birthday journals. Emily writes:

> Haworth, Thursday, July 30th, 1845.
>
> My birthday—showery, breezy, cool. I am twenty-seven years old to-day. This morning Anne and I opened the papers we wrote four years since, on my twenty-third birthday. This paper we intend, if all be well, to open on my thirtieth—three years hence, in 1848. Since the 1841 paper the following events have taken place. Our school scheme has been abandoned, and instead Charlotte and I went to Brussels on the 8th of February, 1842.
>
> Branwell left his place at Luddenden Foot. C. and I returned from Brussels, November 8th, 1842, in consequence of aunt's death.
>
> Branwell went to Thorp Green as a tutor, where Anne still continued, January 1843.
>
> Charlotte returned to Brussels the same month, and after staying a year, came back again on New Year's Day 1844.
>
> Anne left her situation at Thorp Green of her own accord, June 1845.
>
> Anne and I went our first long journey by ourselves together, leaving home on the 30th June, Monday, sleeping at York, returning to Keighley Tuesday evening, sleeping there and walking home on Wednesday morning. Though the weather was broken we enjoyed ourselves very much, except during a few hours at Bradford. And during our excursion we were, Ronald Macalgin, Henry Angora, Juliet

Angusteena, Rosabella Esmaldan, Ella and Julian Egremont, Catharine Navarre, and Cordelia Fitzaphnold, escaping from the palaces of instruction to join the Royalists who are hard driven at present by the victorious Republicans. The Gondals still flourish bright as ever. I am at present writing a work on the First War. Anne has been writing some articles on this, and a book by Henry Sophona. We intend sticking firm by the rascals as long as they delight us, which I am glad to say they do at present. I should have mentioned that last summer the school scheme was revived in full vigour. We had prospectuses printed, despatched letters to all acquaintances imparting our plans, and did our little all; but it was found no go. Now I don't desire a school at all, and none of us have any great longing for it. We have cash enough for our present wants, with a prospect of accumulation. We are all in decent health, only that papa has a complaint in his eyes, and with the exception of B., who, I hope, will be better and do better hereafter. I am quite contented for myself: not as idle as formerly, altogether as hearty, and having learnt to make the most of the present and long for the future with the fidgetiness that I cannot do all I wish; seldom or ever troubled with nothing to do, and merely desiring that everybody could be as comfortable as myself and as undesponding, and then we should have a very tolerable world of it.

By mistake I find we have opened the paper on the 31st instead of the 30th. Yesterday was much such a day as this, but the morning was divine.

Tabby, who was gone in our last paper, is come back, and has lived with us two years and a half, and is in good health. Martha, who also departed, is here too. We have got Flossy; got and lost Tiger; lost the hawk Hero, which, with the geese, was given away, and is doubtless dead, for when I came back from Brussels I inquired on all hands and could hear nothing of him. Tiger died early last year. Keeper and Flossy are well, also the canary acquired four years since. We are now all at home, and likely to be there some time. Branwell went to Liverpool on Tuesday to stay a week. Tabby has just been teasing me to turn as formerly to 'Pilloputate'. Anne and I should have picked the black-currants if it had been fine and sunshiny. I must hurry off now to my turning and ironing. I have plenty of work on hands, and writing, and am altogether full of business. With best wishes for the whole house till 1848, July 30th, and as much longer as may be,—I conclude. Emily Brontë.

Gondal was still flourishing. Had they considered the possibility of winding up the affair. If so, they had decided that Gondal should continue as long as it delighted them. The two young women, aged twenty-seven and twenty-five, played at Gondal throughout their excursion to York. Emily thought this a better idea than the school scheme, the abandonment of which she is glad to announce. "I don't desire a school at all," she declares. Why should they work when they were not in need? "We have cash enough for our present wants, with a prospect of accumulation." This picks up a motif in her previous paper: cash—this meant security, leisure, freedom to write, to keep up Gondal. She cannot understand why the rest of the family has a sense of dissatisfaction. "I am quite contented for myself: not as idle as formerly, although as hearty." Emily had, during Charlotte's absence abroad, written to tell of her "idleness". That had been, perhaps, a period of reflection. But there is the indication of things she had planned to achieve, as in her previous note. She knows now that she cannot do all that she wishes. But life, she suggests, would be more tolerable if everyone could be as unconcerned, "as comfortable", "as undesponding", as herself. Not everyone in the household had the temperament for taking life so easily.

During this year, all four Brontës happened to describe themselves in various documents. Anne, in her birthday note, admits to having had "some very unpleasant and undreamt-of experience of human nature" during her stay at the Robinsons. "E and I have a great deal of work to do. When shall we sensibly diminish it? . . . We have not yet finished our *Gondal Chronicles* that we began three and a half [years] ago. When will they be done?" Anne betrays some weariness with Gondal; she seems to have had enough of it, and may even have hinted as much to Emily. But Gondal delighted Emily. And Anne writes, she was looking forward to hearing Emily's latest Gondal-piece. But she is altogether weary in her note. Emily is "hearty"?—"I for my part, cannot well be flatter or older in mind that I am now" declares Anne.

Three months later, Branwell describes himself in a letter to an old friend, "I have lain during nine long weeks utterly shattered in body and broken down in mind. The probability of her becoming free to give me herself and estate never rose to drive away the prospect of her decline under her present grief. . . . Eleven continuous nights of sleepless horror reduced me to almost blindness. . . ."

And Charlotte, too, gives her self-portrait, in terms not dissimilar from her brother's. To M. Héger she confides, "Day and night I find neither rest nor peace. If I sleep I am disturbed by tormenting dreams in which I see you, always severe, always grave, always incensed against me."

Against these personal testimonies of the restless inner lives of Anne, Branwell and Charlotte, Emily alone is seen to be collected and even smug. No wonder she wishes they could be comfortable and undesponding like herself. Tormented by unquenchable passions or chilled with melancholy, the three sufferers must have found Emily infuriating at times, she was so contented.

In her birthday note, Emily refers to the "prospects of accumulation" which apparently adhere to their cash. Emily had been left in charge of the investment of their aunt's legacies, and she considered she had done well by the family, having placed the money in railroad shares. Then came one of those national crises which are dotted all along the nineteenth century: a Panic. Charlotte wrote to Miss Wooler "I have been most anxious for us to sell our shares ere it be too late. . . . I cannot, however, persuade my sisters to regard the affair precisely from my point of view." Anne stood by Emily, apparently. Besides, Charlotte recalled that Emily had undertaken the business single-handed. "I feel I would rather run the risk of loss than hurt Emily's feelings. . . . I will let her manage still and take the consequences. . . . Disinterested and energetic she certainly is, and if she be not quite so tractable or open to conviction as I could wish, I must remember perfection is not the lot of humanity."

This is the first occasion on which Charlotte is known to have hinted, even with qualifications, that Emily was difficult at times. Emily had been tractable enough to accompany Charlotte to Brussels. Since her return, however, she had taken her own line, first about the school, now about the railroad shares; they did not fail until after Emily was in her grave.

At this period Charlotte was pushing ahead with another project. A selection of the poems by the three sisters was to be printed at their own expense, under the pseudonyms, Currer, Ellis and Acton Bell. These poems appeared in July 1846. It is said that only two copies were sold. Few papers reviewed the book, but *The Athenæum* of July 1846 printed a notice which places Emily's poems far above the others. This critic detected

> an inspiration, which may yet find an audience in the outer world. A fine quaint spirit has the latter [i.e., Emily], which may have things to speak that men will be glad to hear—and an evident power of wing that may reach heights not here attempted. . . . How musical he can be, and how lightly and easily the music falls from his heart and pen. . . . He is no copyist. There is not enough in this volume to judge him by—but, to our mind, an impression of originality is conveyed, beyond what his contribution to these pages embody.

This critic dismisses Charlotte and Anne briefly; he was a

wise man, even though banal; he was original enough to spot Emily Brontë as soon as she appeared in print. She must have been enormously encouraged by this review.

The sisters had meantime written a novel apiece. *The Professor* by Charlotte, *Agnes Grey* by Anne, *Wuthering Heights* by Emily. While they wrote the books, Branwell was rapidly deteriorating, and so it is sometimes claimed that Emily and Anne drew upon their brother for "copy", reproducing him in their novels. This seems unlikely; they actually saw too much of Branwell to use him effectively in this way. There was no mystery in Branwell to be worked out in their novels. Had they suspected the truth of his story, they might have found his very deception worth exploring. As it was, he could be neither a dissipated villain nor broken-hearted hero; he had no magnitude either way, for he was drunk half the time. "A hopeless being" said Emily. That was pronounced on a day when he had given more trouble than usual. On the whole, they were not unsympathetic to their brother; even now, he invites pity. Only Charlotte was inclined to be hard on him; but then she had been hard on herself, she had stopped writing to M. Héger.

Wuthering Heights and *Agnes Grey* were accepted by a publisher, T. C. Newby, on their subsidising the book, which contained both works, to the extent of £50. They were obviously keen, now, to get their work published, and entertained high enough hopes to feel justified in speculating this sum. Emily was perhaps especially hopeful, on the strength of *The Athenæum's* review. Charlotte had to write another novel before she found a publisher, Smith & Elder. This firm was so prompt with the publication of *Jane Eyre* that it came out some months before the novels of Emily and Anne appeared.

In the meantime, Branwell's old employer and enemy, Mr. Robinson, died. Branwell gave out that Mrs. Robinson's reason for failing to fly into his arms was that her husband's will left her totally unprovided for, should she resume the least communication with Branwell.

The publishers of *Wuthering Heights* and *Agnes Grey* seemed in no hurry to fulfil their promise. Some proof sheets were received in August 1847, and the return of these was followed by another period of waiting. Meanwhile *Jane Eyre* by "Currer Bell" was published, and was an immediate success. This encouraged the publisher of "Ellis and Acton Bell" to bring out their long-delayed book, and to give out that Ellis and Acton were one and the same with Currer, author of *Jane Eyre*.

Their literary ventures were kept secret from their friends. "Currer Bell's" fame was high; Charlotte was embarked on a new life of letter-writing. Her principal correspondent now was W. S. Williams, a reader for her publishers; she also began exchanging letters with well-known literary people who wrote to her. "Currer Bell" was still her signature. The sisters had agreed to preserve their privacy; the Brontës of Haworth were not to be displayed to the world.

Between her birthday in the July of 1845 and the publication of *Wuthering Heights* in the December of 1847, we hear remarkably little about Emily. Between these dates, her poems had appeared in the sisters' joint volume, and she had written *Wuthering Heights* and a very few poems (that we know of). The novel had been completed in the first half of 1846. She wrote one long poem in September of that year, and thereafter apparently nothing until she started to redraft the same poem in May 1848. Almost two years are therefore unaccounted for by any of her writings. It has been suggested that she had started another novel, which she subsequently destroyed.

References to Emily are infrequent at this period. Charlotte's remark to Miss Wooler, early in 1846 that Emily was "not quite so tractable or open to conviction as I could wish", indicates that Emily's attitude to Charlotte, at least, had changed a little, since the time when she was merely the useful stay-at-home sister. This from Charlotte may be taken in conjunction with Emily's statement in her birthday paper,

"I am quite contented for myself . . . seldom or ever troubled with nothing to do, and merely desiring that everybody could be as comfortable as myself and as undesponding, and then we should have a very tolerable world of it"; Charlotte found her intractable, Emily found the whole family too fussy and querulous. Emily was then beginning to assert herself. Charlotte regretted the fact, but gave way. She was, perhaps, a little surprised that Emily, so amenable all her life, was now taking her own stand in some matters. And Charlotte had also been surprised by Emily's poems, which she never failed, in her letters to Mr. Williams, to rate high.

These circumstances may combine to account for a gradual change in Charlotte's tone in her references to Emily; and this becomes more pronounced as Emily entered the last years of her life. Charlotte is not always approving, but she respects Emily in a new way; her bewilderment grows into curiosity; later becomes awe, a recognition of Emily's literary power and of some newly-awakened personal power. This, it could be argued, may signify a development in Charlotte's faculties of perception; it need not mean that Emily's personal development follows the course charted by Charlotte's reactions. But Charlotte does not betray any unforeseen facet of her own personality in her other relationships; her reactions to life at this stage do not lead us to suspect that Charlotte herself became more or less sympathetic or observant; her writing and her success exhilarated her, but this naturally aroused more self-interest than interest in her sisters. On the other hand, we know that Emily's personality in her last three years is not consistent with the personality she herself expressed in her 1845 birthday note. Still less is there constancy in the earlier and later delineations of Emily accepted by her family and their friends: Emily's earlier 'usefulness' in the house, her willingness to fall in with whatever was agreed by the family, are no longer the items which specially signify her character; instead, Charlotte unconsciously selects more subtle manifestations of Emily's personality, when writing of her; Emily has become more important. The legendary aspect begins to appear. As though speaking of some enigmatic celebrity, Charlotte writes (in September 1847) to tell Ellen Nussey exactly with what facial expression Emily had received a gift. "Emily is just now sitting on the floor of the bedroom where I am writing, looking at her apples. She smiled when I gave them and the collar to her as your presents, with an expression at once well satisfied and slightly surprised . . ."

In October 1847, Emily is mentioned by Anne in the course of a dutiful letter to Ellen Nussey. Anne begins with the weather: "Happily for all parties the east wind no longer prevails. During its continuance [Charlotte] complained of its influence as usual. I too suffered from it in some degree, as I always do, more or less; but this time, it brought me no reinforcement of colds and coughs which is what I dread the most. Emily considers it a very uninteresting wind, but it does not affect her nervous system." Charlotte and Anne had a recurrent dread of the east wind; the Brontës had weak chests. Apparently, a bout of the east wind would get on their nerves. Not so Emily, who, to emphasise her unconcern, declared the very wind "uninteresting". Is this a foretaste of that lofty contempt for physical frailty towards which she was rapidly moving? But perhaps she meant simply that the east wind failed to evoke a response from her. Within three months, however, Anne reports that Emily has been down with influenza as a result of "this cruel east wind".

When Emily's novel was published, Charlotte was anxious for opinions on it. We do not have her friend Mr. Williams' view, but we have Charlotte's reply: "You are not far wrong in your judgment . . . Ellis has a strong, original mind, full of strange though sombre power. When he writes poetry that power speaks in language at once condensed, elaborated, and refined, but in prose it breaks forth in scenes which shock more than they attract. Ellis will improve, however, because he knows his defects." Emily's defects, from this account, are the more violent scenes in *Wuthering Heights,* those which shocked Charlotte and many other readers, and which are, in fact, the scenes most typical of the book. "He knows his defects"; does this mean that Emily had analysed her work? Possibly she had "shocked" even herself with *Wuthering Heights.*

Charlotte almost certainly had read *Wuthering Heights* on its completion in the first half of 1846, if not during its composition; she had known of Emily's poems since the autumn of 1845. These helped to form the view of Emily's "strong, original mind, full of strange though sombre powers", but this is being implied only now, at the end of 1847. Charlotte's style when referring to Emily, from this time onward, automatically slips into rhetoric, which adds to the effect of awe. And that this was not due only to an increasing appreciation of Emily's work, but also to her daily observation of Emily herself, is most likely; if Emily had remained a constant factor, familiarity would have tended to accustom Charlotte to the genius her sister had displayed in her poems and novels; nor was there any new work of Emily's, so far as we know, to fill Charlotte with wonder. There now existed a real dichotomy between the present and the past impressions of Emily.

Where we do find constancy, and to a high degree, is in the development of Emily's poems, which converge towards *Wuthering Heights.* It was submitted earlier, that the tone and character of the poems did not evidently absorb the concurrent experiences of her conscious life. The poems were not ultimately untrue to the character of Emily Brontë, but their themes were not progressively identical with her personal development. Not only did the poems represent features of her mind which she did not reveal to others, and which, indeed, were concealed from herself, those features were not then fully distinguishable. That the poems lead up to *Wuthering Heights* does not mean they could not possibly have led to anything else, with an equally inevitable appearance.

In Emily Brontë's last years we see her personal behaviour

approximating more closely to the character of her work; we recognise the author of *Wuthering Heights* and of the mystical poems in the manner in which she responded to her last illness. Previously, the Haworth Parsonage scenes depicted by herself and Charlotte, have not shown her as the living equivalent of the death-impassioned, earth-enamoured poems she was writing. The inescapable conclusion is that Emily had, in a short time, become conscious of the practical implications of her work; she had begun to realize principles which were dormant in her mind. This is not, of course, an unusual course of development in an artist; but the process of interpretation and reflection is normally gradual; otherwise, it can impede the practise of art. It has been observed that Emily seems to have wished instinctively to avoid this very process, in her repeated rejection of schooling.[1]

The experience at Brussels did, in fact, exercise her capacity for philosophical reflection; she was forced, there, to reflect upon principles and ultimates, where before she had contemplated them. Or, rather, she forced herself. From all accounts, it was by a tremendous effort of will that Emily complied with Charlotte's conception of her duty. This was the first occasion, so far as we know, on which Emily had asserted her will with any degree of determination. There is nothing like the sustained exercise of will in meeting unpleasant demands to bring about an apparent change of character. In Emily this change was as swift as her effort was powerful, and it is apparent where she is observed to be asserting her personality increasingly from this time forward; and she directed this new-roused faculty towards defining, in terms of action, the principles which, in the years that followed, she came to recognise in her work. Emily Brontë is never so much a child of the Romantic Movement, as in this. The Romantic poets tended to express in personal conduct, the hypotheses underlying their creative writings. It was as if the principles involved in their work amounted to beliefs so passionately held, that

[1] See also Appendix, page 266.

it seemed necessary to prove them to others by putting them to the test of action. The result was not always satisfactory, so far as the life of the poet was concerned.

In February 1848, Charlotte presented Mr. Williams with the aspect of Emily which was next to emerge; her correspondent had suggested that the "Bells" should visit London. "Ellis, I imagine, would soon turn aside from the spectacle in disgust. I do not think he admits it as his creed that 'the proper study of mankind is man'—at least not the artificial man of cities. In some points I consider Ellis as somewhat of a theorist: now and then he broaches ideas which strike my sense as much more daring and original than practical; his reason may be in advance of mine, but certainly it often travels a different road. I should say Ellis will not be seen in his full strength till he is seen as an essayist."

For some reason, perhaps because she is trying to understand her own feelings, Charlotte is anxious to convey an impressive idea of Emily when she mentions her. Emily as a theorist . . . "ideas which strike my sense as much more daring and original than practical . . ." Charlotte feared the practical issues of Emily's ideas, as she had every reason to do. In July, Charlotte and Anne went to London to prove that they were separate authors. Anne's publisher, T. C. Newby, had attempted to further his interests in America by claiming that *Wuthering Heights, Agnes Grey, Jane Eyre* and Anne's new novel *The Tenant of Wildfell Hall,* were all the production of one author, Currer Bell. The two excited sisters turned up at the city offices of Smith & Elder, and though it had long been suspected that the "Bells" were women, Charlotte's explanation, "we are three sisters" was received with due surprise and pleasure. This admission was regarded differently by Emily, when they returned to Haworth after being subjected to rapid and exhausting hospitality by Charlotte's publisher. "Permit me" writes Charlotte from the sober light of Haworth, "to caution you not to speak of my sisters when you write to me. I mean, do not use the word in the plural. Ellis Bell will not endure to be alluded to under any other appellation than the *nom de plume*. I committed a grand error in betraying his identity to you and Mr. Smith. It was inadvertent—the words 'we are three sisters' escaped me before I was aware. I regretted the avowal the moment I had made it: I regret it bitterly now, for I find it is against every feeling and intention of Ellis Bell . . ." In answer to his suggestion that they should see something of "London society", she admits there would be great advantage in it, "yet it is one that no power on earth could induce Ellis Bell, for instance, to avail himself of."

Charlotte's next criticism of *Wuthering Heights* shows that she was uneasy about the moral significance of the character Heathcliff: she observes his "naturally perverse, vindictive, and inexorable disposition"; kindness might have made of him a human being, but under tyranny and ignorance he becomes a demon. "The worst of it is" Charlotte continues, displaying her misgivings about the health of the book, "some of his spirit seems breathed through the whole narrative in which he figures . . ." Which was an unconscious tribute to the author, none the less.

In September, Charlotte's publisher took over the book of poems from their previous publisher. Once more she eulogises Emily's poems. "They stirred my heart like the sound of a trumpet when I read them alone and in secret. . . . I was sternly rated at first for having taken an unwarrantable liberty. This I expected, for Ellis Bell is of no flexible or ordinary materials. But by dint of entreaty and reason I at last wrung out a reluctant consent to have the 'rhymes' as they were contemptuously termed, published. The author never alludes to them; or, when she does, it is with scorn. But I know no woman that ever lived ever wrote such poetry before. Condensed energy, clearness, finish—strange, strong pathos are their characteristics. . . ."

There are phrases and words used here to describe Emily, which have become almost key-words to a long line of comment upon her: "Of no flexible or ordinary material";

"Contemptuously", "with scorn". Emily, contemptuous, scornful, inflexible, and made of superhuman material, has come down to us. The phrases date from this last year of Emily's life, when Charlotte was becoming ever more fervent in dramatising her sister. Does this tendency in Charlotte, then, reflect something of how Emily appeared at the time?

We know Emily had been theorising—delivering herself of ideas which, to Charlotte, were daring and original, but not practical. If Emily had worked out a philosophy from her own work, if she had evolved a system which was the logical equivalent of that in which her writings were placed, then Charlotte was right. It was not practical. If it were put into practice, in fact, it would be highly dangerous, for its principles were destructive.

Many factors already mentioned tend towards the conclusion that Emily had begun to dramatise, in her own person, the aspirations expressed in her work. If she saw herself, in the end as the hero and cult of her own writings, we may expect to find more or less what we do find, a copy of her self-image; enlarged by the details her friends supplied after her death.

It is clear that Emily had gone sullen; she is described as inflexible, contemptuous and scornful of her own work, who, in her birthday notes had expressed herself in terms which suggest she was highly satisfied with her writing activities; far from being inflexible, she had appeared singularly accommodating. The human consummation of Gondal was the cult of the supreme hero; son of a special race; a being who recognised no law but that of Nature; one powerfully raised above the common destiny of man; in the world, a courageous stoic; in essence mystically united with Nature; amoral, ruthless. Such a being would partake of the extremes of passion, primitive in action, mystically remote in contemplation. In other words, he would be absurd.

Fortunately, Emily Brontë never got so far as this. She had envisaged one aspect of such a being in her short essay (in

French). *King Harold on the Eve of the Battle of Hastings.*

> . . . a multitude of human emotions awaken in him, but they are exalted, sanctified, made almost divine. His courage is not temerity, nor is his pride arrogance. His anger is justified, his assurance is free from presumption. He has an inner conviction that by no mortal power will he be defeated. Death alone can gain victory over his arms. To her he is ready to yield, for Death's touch is to the hero what the striking off his chains is to the slave.

The reverse side of this paragon is Heathcliff in *Wuthering Heights,* where Heathcliff's passions, instead of being "exalted, sanctified, made almost divine", are degraded, accursed, made almost daemonic.

Emily's fatal illness, in her 31st year, accentuated any tendency she possessed to play out the part in her life. The illness itself, consumption, was inherent. It is not to be assumed that an early death was part of the heroics Emily had identified herself with, except in so far as she would be bound to meet death in a manner appropriate to her role, whenever it should come her way. It may, of course, be argued that inherent consumption predisposed her to prepare for her death in this way, but this is a question which even those who understand the psychology of consumptives would perhaps be indefinite about. For the purposes of biographical accuracy, Emily's death was not willed by herself. She caught a cold at her brother's funeral, Branwell having submitted his tortured soul to more dissipation than the Brontë constitution could stand.

Charlotte records the bitter progress of Emily's last weeks, sometimes to Ellen Nussey, at other times to her publisher.

To Ellen, at the end of October, she confided,

"Emily's cough and cold are very obstinate at present. I fear she has a pain in the chest, and I sometimes catch a shortness in her breathing, when she has moved at all quickly. She looks very, very thin and pale. Her reserved nature occasions me great uneasiness of mind. It is useless to question her; you get no answers. It is still more useless to recommend remedies; they are never adopted."

To W. S. Williams, a few days later:

"She is a real stoic in illness: she neither seeks nor will accept sympathy. To put any questions, to offer any aid, is to annoy; she will not yield a step before pain or sickness till forced; not one of her ordinary avocations will she voluntarily renounce. You must look on and see her do what she is obviously unfit to do, and not dare say a word —a painful necessity for those to whom her health and existence are as precious as the life in their veins."

Mr. Williams recommended homeopathy. Charlotte handed Emily the letter "taking care not to say a word in favour". Emily's response was that "Mr. Williams' intention was kind and good, but he was under a delusion: Homeopathy was only another form of quackery." Not only would she not have quackery, she would not see any doctor; Charlotte repeats it again and again; "She has refused medicine, rejected medical advice; no reasoning, no entreaty, has availed. . . ."

One day Charlotte read out a notice of *Wuthering Heights* from the *North American Review,* to amuse Emily and Anne.

"As I sat between them at our quiet but now somewhat melancholy fireside, I studied the two ferocious authors. Ellis, the 'man of uncommon talents, but dogged, brutal, and morose', sat leaning back in his easy-chair, drawing his impeded breath as he best could, and looking, alas! piteously pale and wasted; it is not his wont to laugh, but he smiled, half-amused and half in scorn, as he listened."

To Ellen, on 23rd November:

"I told you Emily was ill, in my last letter. She has not rallied yet. She is *very* ill. I believe, if you were to see her, your impression would be that there is no hope . . . Her pulse, the only time she allowed it to be felt, was found to beat 115 per minute. In this state she resolutely refuses to see a doctor; she will not give an explanation of her feelings, she will scarcely allow her illness to be alluded to. Our position is, and has been for some weeks, exquisitely painful. God only knows how all this is to terminate."

Charlotte had latterly felt an overwhelming love for Emily. In fact, it seems that the worse Emily treated her elder sister, the more did Charlotte love her. "I think Emily seems the nearest thing to my heart in this world", she wrote.

Anne's relationship with Emily at this time is not known. The Gondal alliance had probably ended at the end of 1846. During 1847, as we know, Emily had written nothing which is left to us. Anne wrote only personal poems from 1847 onward. If it is true that Anne had wanted her release from Gondal, she may have taken advantage of her occupation with novels to bring it about. But Emily, too, may have tired of the game.

Anne was an orthodox Christian and a moralist: she would disapprove of Emily's manner of meeting her death; but she as well as Charlotte, would suffer none the less from the torture of watching Emily die unalleviated. They had long prepared themselves to lose Branwell; the death of a sad, wrecked being is not so tragic, in the dramatic sense, as that of a proud and intelligent spirit. It was in the dramatic light that they saw Emily, for that was how she presented herself.

One wonders why Mr. Brontë, the 'Papa' on whom the whole family looked as to a final authority, did not insist on Emily seeing a doctor. Did he too fear her? "My father shakes his head", writes Charlotte tersely, "and speaks of others of our family once similarly afflicted . . . who are now removed where hope and fear fluctuate no more . . ."

Emily would not disclose anything of her motives. "I *do* wish" Charlotte exclaims, "I knew her state and feelings more clearly." All she could do was to pester Emily to see a doctor. "No poisoning doctor" was to come near her, said Emily. Desperately, Charlotte wrote out a careful description of the symptoms and sent them to a doctor recommended by her friend the publisher. The doctor sent some medicine "which she would not take. Moments so dark as these I have never known. I pray for God's support to us all . . ." This was written on Tuesday, 19th December.

To Ellen, December 23rd.

"Emily suffers no more from pain or weakness now. She will never suffer more in this world. She is gone, after a hard, short conflict. She died on *Tuesday,* the very day I wrote to you. I thought it very possible she might be with us still for weeks; and a few hours afterwards she was in eternity. Yes; there is no Emily in time or on earth now. Yesterday we put her poor, wasted, mortal frame quietly under the church pavement. We are very calm at present. Why should we be otherwise? The anguish of seeing her suffer is over; the spectacle of the pains of death is gone by, the funeral day is past. We feel she is at peace. No need now to tremble for the hard frost and the keen wind. Emily does not feel them. She died in a time of promise. We saw her taken from life in its prime . . ."

Anne also died of consumption, within five months, having taken much trouble to find a cure.

Charlotte lived another six years, the Rev. Patrick Brontë another twelve.

GENERAL CONSIDERATIONS

When all the afterthoughts, rumours, elaborations, legendary anecdotes and pure inventions which gradually clustered round Emily's posthumous reputation have been set aside, there still remains the recognisable outline of the Emily Brontë familiar to biography. This is not, however, the complete picture. The information which is so eagerly offered when anyone becomes posthumously famous is valuable, particularly where it gains wide credence. There seems to be an instinctive process of selection, whereby essential, if not literal truths attach themselves after a time to a reputation. So that the recent biographer who asserted of Emily in her earlier days that she showed pity and contempt for Anne, cannot be ignored, only corrected. There is not a scrap of evidence to support the statement; there is much evidence to refute it. Still, the biographer comes in a long line of commentators who have said as much; thousands of people believe it. *Securus judicat* . . . It is not literal truth, of course, but the statement carries an essential truth: it may be interpreted to mean "Emily had it in her to show contempt and pity for Anne. Anne had it in her to evoke pity and contempt". It is part of a biographer's business to show what the subjects had it in them to do and be. But it is also necessary to show at what stage they notably did and were anything; it is necessary for the purpose of tracing the development of character.

What was of tremendous interest to everyone who wrote about Emily when she became the fashion, was her 'stoical' death; not only was this ennobled beyond all its most plain deserts, but from it were drawn adulatory conclusions which, to the less romantic temperament, distort her into a kind of daemonic monster. The first promoter of her reputation on this score, Charlotte, more or less admitted she was obsessed by Emily's death, when she wrote to Ellen Nussey. "I cannot forget Emily's death-day. It becomes a more fixed, a darker, a more frequently recurring idea in my mind than ever. It was very terrible. She was torn, conscious, panting, reluctant, though resolute, out of a happy life." Charlotte was even further carried away in her *memoir* prefixing an edition of *Wuthering Heights* and *Agnes Grey,* but already we can detect more alliteration than accuracy. What does she mean, "reluctant, though resolute"? We know Emily had been reluctant to ease her pain and to save her sisters' grief, we know she had been resolute to avoid medical care and to endure a somewhat spectacular illness with stoicism. But at the moment of her death, for what was she reluctant—life or death? She was, it seems, reluctant for death. "Resolute" suggests that she forced herself to die, against her natural instincts; almost that she could live or die at will. This is a prevalent theme in Emily Brontë comment; the implication that Emily's illness and death were willed by herself is frequent. This, no doubt, is what she herself wished to believe; but it was not so. Emily Brontë succeeded on the whole in conveying to posterity the idea that she was superhuman.

It may be that Emily was, from 1847 onward, unbalanced in mind, and that this disaster fell more severely upon her during her last months. It does seem that she really believed herself to be superhuman, and in some way free to will or not to will death from a fatal disease. Of course it is said that consumption has an optimism of its own; but Emily does not give the impression of optimism. Her refusal of medical care, of any assistance, and her agonised attempts to move about as usual, show rather an effort to combat the *fact* of her illness; she appears to have felt that it only existed if she acknowledged it; if she ignored it, the infection would disappear. Nor does the manner of her death convey the idea of death-wish. Such a condition would not call forth those dramatic qualities which she displayed; she was the centre of attention during her illness; she attracted the silent horror of her sisters at her persistent refusal of any kind of help or alleviation; she knew they were aghast at this perverted martyrdom; these factors do not lend themselves to interpretation of a wish for death; rather, a distorted wish for life—a wish to be observed as an autonomous, powerful sufferer.

As she was the author of this daily spectacle, we must conclude either that her mind was exceptionally tortured, or that it was exceptionally perverted. We have no grounds for thinking that Emily was a daemonic or vicious woman. She was latterly, it seems, "possessed"—not with daemonic possession, but with delusions of her own powers, perhaps the early symptom of some more serious mental disease. This is not incompatible with the employment of rational powers; it was the more bewildering to the sisters as she did not speak of delusions, she enacted them. Branwell may perhaps have suffered from a similar calamity; in his case he wove stories around himself.

Charlotte, puzzled by Emily's conduct, seems to have tacitly accepted the situation as it was presented. Emily was more than human; she was some strange rugged monolithic mystic. In *Shirley,* Charlotte gives a somewhat nauseating example of what presumably she considered to be Emily's mysticism; Emily herself did it better, in verse. Did Anne, like Charlotte, take Emily seriously? Anne makes no direct comment, but since the character Shirley is cited as an accepted picture of Emily, it may not be out of place to cite a poem by Anne. It should be said that Anne's verse, apart from her Gondal pieces, was unfeignedly autobiographical. And so when we read a poem by Anne we may assume she refers to some time or place or person within her present experience.

In the poem, which is dated August 1811 and entitled *The Three Guides* Anne addresses three Spirits in turn: of Earth, of Pride, and of Faith. This is a strangely-juxtaposed set of personifications; one wonders why Earth and Pride, a concrete and an abstract concept, should stand together as significant alternatives to Faith. But conventionally she rejects first the Spirit of Earth, then the Spirit of Pride, and finally accepts the Spirit of Faith. It is a very long poem, and a few stanzas must suffice to indicate the tone. The style so resembles Emily's, and is employed towards demolishing a theme so typical of Emily, that one cannot avoid the conclusion that Anne was guying Emily in more ways than one.

Spirit of Pride! thy wings are strong,
Thine eyes like lightning shine;
Ecstatic joys to thee belong,
And powers almost divine.
But 'tis a false destructive blaze
Within those eyes I see;
Turn hence their fascinating gaze;
I will not follow thee!

. . . .

(*Spirit of Pride* replies)

Cling to the earth, poor grovelling worm;
'Tis not for thee to soar
Against the fury of the storm,
Amid the thunder's roar!
There's glory in that daring strife
Unknown, undreamt by thee;
There's speechless rapture in the life
Of those who follow me!

(The poet speaks)

Yes, I have seen thy votaries oft,
Upheld by thee their guide,
In strength and courage mount aloft
The steepy mountain-side;
I've seen them stand against the sky,
And gazing from below,
Beheld thy lightning in their eye,
Thy triumph on their brow.

Oh, I have felt what glory then,
What transport must be theirs!
So far above their fellow-men,
Above their toils and cares;
Inhaling Nature's purest breath,
Her riches round them spread,
The wide expanse of earth beneath,
Heaven's glories overhead!

But I have seen them helpless, dashed
Down to a bloody grave,
And still thy ruthless eye has flashed,
Thy strong hand did not save.

. . . .

What shall they do when night grows black;
    When angry storms arise?
Who now will lead them to the track
    Thou taught'st them to despise:

It needs no elaborate method of detection to see Emily and her heroes in this. Anne, it is to be feared, disapproved strongly of Emily in the last two years of her life: she recognises her sister's remote brooding, her "speechless rapture", her scorn, her assumption of "powers almost divine"—she saw these attitudes together as "a false destructive blaze", the self-consuming sin of pride. There is no other reason why Anne should choose this particular manifestation of pride, unless she had Emily in mind. It was certainly right along the lines of Emily's thought and, from what we see, her conduct. But Anne could not have lacked sympathy with her life-long friend in her last illness. We learn of her "silent grief" after Emily's death.

It is doubtful if there was much element of choice for Emily if she had become obsessed by the ideology of her work. Theorising probably did her untold harm, as she had instinctively guessed when she did all she could to avoid having her mind organised in school life. She shows all the symptoms of such an obsession in her last months; Anne's earlier moralizing seems beside the point in so tragic an affair. Something corrosive had laid hold of Emily's being, and it seems most likely that if she had not died of consumption, she would have died mentally deranged. For she lacked the equilibrium of the pure mystic.

It might be worth noting that, if Anne's poem was an allegorical account of her experience of Emily in her later years, the "pity and contempt" which Emily is wrongly said to have bestowed on Anne all her life, was amply forthcoming at the later date, towards the whole household.

Most of Emily's early biographers believed, with Charlotte, in Emily's self-styled superwomanism. It was enough, for

Charlotte and her successors to know Emily as a 'stoic', to be filled with admiration and awe. But while it is true that nobility of character may be an element in pure stoicism, it does not at all follow that stoicism, in its accepted sense of mere physical endurance, is in every circumstance noble. Anne's orthodox ethics would, of course, reject stoicism as a self-reliant rule of conduct, although in fact she herself displayed in her illness the virtues of 'Christian stoicism'. But even as a purely social ethic, it was as incorrect to ascribe to the stoicism demonstrated by Emily the nobility proper to the true stoical spirit, as it would be to call a man who tied himself to the stake, and himself lit the faggots, a martyr. Before any gesture or attitude can partake of glory, the circumstances are the decisive factor. Nobility is not the automatic attribute of stoicism. Was Emily Brontë's tormented and tormenting procession to the grave a noble death? It was not; neither was it an ignoble death, since, whichever way one looks at it, Emily Brontë was a woman distracted in her later days, by a torturing self-image, a fantastic unattainable ideal. Her spirit suffered under this affliction, infinitely more than did her body under disease.

Her former days were happy. She was the least neurotic of the sisters (it is sometimes said that neurotics are not the most likely to end insane). The impression given by Emily up to 1845 is that she held, understandably, an image of herself as a creative writer; and towards this image she continually struggled. She had not only genius, she had the will to write; and not only the will to write, the desire to profess creative writing—to follow a recognised vocation. That she concealed her work from Charlotte does not mean she did not intend to reveal any of her work to the world. Anne, for one, was privy at least to her Gondal writings. Emily seems to have been a severe critic of her own work, since she presumably destroyed the bulk of it. Her reluctance to produce her poems in 1845 may simply indicate that she did not consider her work ready for publication.

What is so striking about Emily in comparison with her sisters is her single-mindedness in connection with her writing. All her "peculiarities" and prejudices and domestic considerations are explicable only if her work is placed in the centre of her existence. She would, in her birthday papers, grow lyrical over hard cash: because it meant leisure to write. She was unhappy when sent to school in her late teens: because the type of work she desired to do was not possible to a rationally-trained mind. She revolted against her teaching job: because she was there, again, subject to a discipline alien to her work. She accepted the first plan for the Brontë school: because it was the easiest way to economise freedom, and hence to do her work in peace. The Brussels school she deliberately did not reject; but she revolted bitterly against her own acceptance of it: because her mind would be directed away from its proper path. Against the second plan for the 'Misses Brontës' Establishment', Emily did not even trouble to revolt, she simply declared she would not teach; she was financially independent, and did not see the need to employ herself other than with her writing and her household tasks. She suggested that she could not understand why the others did not feel the same. When Charlotte proclaimed Emily's devotion to the moors, there is no doubt this was true; of course she loved the moors, her dog, her sisters, her home; but she loved her work most.

The further question frequently arises, whether Emily was ever in love. Now, both Anne and Charlotte were, at various times, interested in men as potential husbands. Both fell in love; both pined for the return of love from the men concerned. Their feelings towards these men were not outside the normal conditions of love, with the exception of Charlotte's first passion for M. Héger, which differed from her more cautious attachment to her publisher, George Smith, in that she could not include within her aspirations, marriage with M. Héger. Otherwise, love as known to Anne and Charlotte, included the elements of marriage, sex, companionship, children, womanly status and many others, combined, as one emotion—love; and as one desire—to be loved in like manner.

Emily had no understanding of this at all. It was not because she had no experience of it: the mere potentiality for an experience makes for understanding; a lesser imagination than Emily's could have grasped the essentials of love between man and woman, given the potentiality. Emily had none. Her work reveals this lack of understanding, and in fact she substitutes for normal love, a different type of attachment which helps to give her writings their impressive distinction. So far as Emily herself is concerned, she appears to have been a born celibate. This is not to repeat what has somewhere been suggested, that she was sexless, far less is it to suggest she was some kind of freak. It is questionable if there is such a phenomenon as a sexless human being; there are people of either sex and there are hermaphrodites. Emily was definitely of the female sex. A few people remembered, after her death, that she had masculine qualities, but this seems to be pure myth, build up from an overlying impression of *Wuthering Heights*. Her latter-day 'stoicism' possibly contributed to this idea, although in fact, her final gestures were more feminine than masculine.

One thing strikes one about Emily Brontë's relationship with people: she had no apparent desire for any company outside her family, and in particular, Anne. This may be evidence of her single-minded absorption in her work. But she did not therefore have an opportunity to realize her potentiality for the type of love she did understand, and which is apparent in her poems and in *Wuthering Heights*. It is a type of love peculiar to the natural celibate, and is a relationship which the current usage of the term 'Platonic' does not altogether describe. It is not a passionless friendship. It is a passionate and in many ways mystical union; and is described in early writings to the effect that the individuals are so closely united that they share as it were a single soul, without losing personal identity, not a common state, but not a freakish one. The partners were nearly always of the same sex, and that such a relationship pre-supposes celibacy (not merely continence) will make clear its great distinction from homosexuality. Such mystical intimacies were of course more frequent in the middle ages than they were in Emily's time. In the nineteenth centry, the celibate man or woman was looked upon as one who had renounced the 'desires of the flesh'. The question whether the type of natural celibacy described above was conditioned by, or conditioned a desire for the relationship with which it is invariably associated, is probably unanswerable. The important factors are that such unions are not uncommon to earlier history, and that some people were celibates, as it were, by special calling. Along with this, is found a common desire for an Absolute in one sense or another.

From the evidence of the love relationships which Emily depicts in her work, it appears that this was the type of love she could understand. In *Wuthering Heights,* of course, there is no conjoining Absolute to give us the sense that Cathy and Heathcliff are involved in any system more significant than each other. To that extent they appear as lost souls. Most likely, the only type of love she could have become personally engaged in, was that of a mystical union, but she was unlikely to find a celibate soul-mate at Haworth, indeed she did not look. Desire, either to possess or to be desired by, another of such nature, is not the motive of this type of union. Desire for the Absolute, which Emily possessed in passionate quantity, is seen as the motive. In an earlier age, Emily Brontë would most possibly have thrived in a convent. (Charlotte compared her to a nun). Emily was, perhaps, somewhat born out of time in this respect.

To a post-Freudian age, it is difficult to convey, without giving rise to scepticism, the nature of the type of celibate it is suggested Emily was, in the context of the term 'passion' which rightly adheres to her name. The most precise definition might be that she was a passionate celibate; (and it should be clear that a frustrated spinster is not meant). So far as this affected her life, it is unlikely that Emily would have been an 'unfulfilled' woman. The later dissatisfaction and disintegration in her life, arose from her shift of apprehension of the Absolute; she shifted it from an objective, to a subjective position. She became her own Absolute; so that she would be forced to expend passion, adoration, worship, contemplation, on herself—a destructive process, since sources of replenishment are not self-generated. Emily's inspiration would dry up; her whole being would be thrown into disorder. But formerly, she had all the forces of her "passionate great genius" as Swinburne expresses it, to expend upon the universe at large, from which she also drew nourishment.

To the extent that she universalised every relationship between man and woman which she touched, she was unrealistic. But her genius was most positively manifest, in its most distinctive forms, when she offered these universalised forms of love. "I *am* Heathcliff" cries Cathy in *Wuthering Heights,* the proposition may not appeal to us, for the reasons already described: the lovers are not really significant enough, they have not the magnitude, to convince us that such a rare relationship is in any way justified; for they have no purpose beyond their mutual love, to measure by. However, Cathy's is a definitive statement; the men and women in Emily's work are apt to meet each other on the grounds of passionate mutual identity, which excludes sexual union: we are not told this, but it is a generally observed fact that Emily's men and women appear to be 'sexless'.

"She died in a time of promise", Charlotte said. Not exactly: the time of promise was past. But there had been a time of tremendous promise, so great that Emily's work represents a very small fulfilment of it. And this work is by no means negligible. Much of Emily's promise was in fact fulfilled. It is tempting to wonder if the promise might have been more richly fulfilled, and, what is more important, if Emily could have maintained her equilibrium, had she stood out against Charlotte and refused to go to school at Brussels. To fix on the Brussels episode as the one decisive factor in Emily's misfortunes may be unwise; it may be almost superstitious. It does not, however, seem to have been a very lucky move, and Charlotte, acting for the best all round, certainly did not see any connection between taking Emily to Brussels, and her helpless daily watch over her dying sister. And in the end, even had Emily's genius flowered for a longer period, there was still to be faced the early death common to the Brontë children, whom Emily had once said were "all stout and hearty".

Appendix to Biographical Study

Emily Brontë's stay in Brussels presents one of the most puzzling aspects of her career. She was seen there in a new light, which is reflected in the remarks made by those with whom she came in contact. These have been considered in their context; but since Emily's encounter with M. Héger at Brussels has also seemed to the present writer to have marked a turning-point in Emily Brontë's development, the following account by M. Héger might prove illuminating. This account was given by him to Mrs. Gaskell some fifteen years after Emily's stay in Brussels. It compares strangely with the remarks he made on Emily at the actual time; but although he shows a new respect and admiration for the now-famous novelist, there is also some moral censure which is new. In particular, we get a picture of Emily, far from "timid" as he at first described her, defiant and resentful towards his teaching methods; we see her speaking her mind. We cannot entirely rely upon M. Héger's testimony; moreover, against his first statement we must place the fact that he made it to her father, and would thus hardly enlarge upon her supposed shortcomings; against his second account, we must weigh the intervening fifteen years, during which period Emily's work had become known.

Although, therefore, the following report of what M. Héger said cannot be taken as direct evidence, the reference to Emily Brontë's open resistance to his methods of teaching can be seen to support the conclusions independently arrived at in the preceding essay.

(From Mrs. Gaskell's *Life of Charlotte Brontë* [1857])

> M. Héger, who had done little but observe, during the few first weeks of their residence in the Rue d'Isabelle, perceived that with their unusual characters, and extraordinary talents, a different mode must be adopted from that in which he generally taught French to English girls. He seems to have rated Emily's genius as something

even higher than Charlotte's; and her estimation of their relative powers was the same. Emily had a head for logic, and a capability of argument, unusual in a man, and rare indeed in a woman, according to M. Héger. Impairing the force of this gift, was her stubborn tenacity of will, which rendered her obtuse to all reasoning where her own wishes, or her own sense of right, was concerned. 'She should have been a man—a great navigator', said M. Héger in speaking of her. 'Her powerful reason would have deduced new spheres of discovery from the knowledge of the old; and her strong, imperious will would never have been daunted by opposition or difficulty; never have given way but with life'. And yet, moreover, her faculty of imagination was such that, if she had written a history, her view of scenes and characters would have been so vivid, and so powerfully expressed, and supported by such a show of argument, that it would have dominated over the reader, whatever might have been his previous opinions, or his cooler perceptions of its truth. But she appeared egotistical and exacting compared to Charlotte, who was always unselfish (this is M. Héger's testimony); and in the anxiety of the elder to make her younger sister contented, she allowed her to exercise a kind of unconscious tyranny over her.

After consulting with his wife, M. Héger told them that he meant to dispense with the old method of grounding in grammar, vocabulary, etc., and to proceed on a new plan —something similar to what he had occasionally adopted with the elder among his French and Belgian pupils. He proposed to read to them some of the master-pieces of the most celebrated French authors (such as Casimir de la Vigne's poem on the "Death of Joan of Arc," parts of Bossuet, the admirable translation of the noble letter of St. Ignatius to the Roman Christians in the *Bibliothèque Choisie des Pères de l'Eglise, etc.*), and after having thus impressed the complete effect of the whole, to analyse the parts with them, pointing out in what such or such an author excelled, and where were the blemishes. He believed that he had to do with pupils capable, from their ready sympathy with the intellectual, the refined, the polished, or the noble, of catching the echo of a style, and so reproducing their own thoughts in a somewhat similar manner.

After explaining his plan to them, he awaited their reply. Emily spoke first; and said that she saw no good to be derived from it; and that, by adopting it, they should lose all originality of thought and expression. She would have entered into an argument on the subject, but for this, M. Héger had no time.

If these are Emily's words, they support, too, the conclusion that Emily thought of herself consistently as a writer. A young woman training to be a governess would hardly have gone to such trouble to protect her "originality of thought and expression" from outward discipline.

Part Two

CRITICAL

by

DEREK STANFORD

INTRODUCTION

Alone, perhaps, of the great English writers, Emily Brontë's fame has survived without the keen preservative of a cool discriminative criticism. Of every other kind of attention her work has received a plenary measure. She has had her biographers and topographers, editors, bibliographers, and general researchers. She has had—less popularly—her psycho-analysts; and, finally, her life and work have been blessed with a great host of professional sympathisers, writing with endless affirmation on her.

On top of the labours of these commentators, there exists also a collective body for the remembrancing of the work of Emily, her family, friends, and relations. This organisation, The Brontë Society, has proved itself piously dutiful in discovering and studying many facts concerned with the Haworth circle; but its function—by intention, no doubt—has not led to a searching criticism and evaluation of the Brontë authors, any more than has the composition of the greater part of Brontë literature.

To suggest, of course, that no criticism, objective, balanced, and serious in tone, has ever been written about Emily would be to state the situation wrongly. Excellent words, sentences, and pages have been penned by a number of critics, to instance only the opinions of Swinburne, Arthur Symons, Sir Herbert Read, and Lord David Cecil. But many of the most pertinent judgments upon Emily and her work have been discharged in the form of essays rather than in full-length studies of her writing. This has meant that the statements on her work, by critics as eminent as these, have been generalised to a high degree. They have been the result of intuition, or of some single-minded conception of the subject, rather than deductions drawn from a thorough sieving of literary material.

Thus, in the space of a few thousand words, Swinburne has endeavoured to show Emily in the light of an epical spirit, the great tragédienne of the English novel. In a similar way, the other critics mentioned have been occupied with interpreting their subject according to some dominant theory. Arthur Symons' notion was that Emily provided the perhaps unique paradox of "passion without sensuousness" as a force behind creation. Sir Herbert Read advanced the idea of Emily as a psychic hermaphrodite, whilst Charles Morgan concentrated upon the mystic side of her genius.

The only exception among these critics was Lord David Cecil who devoted a long essay to *Wuthering Heights* in his book *Early Victorian Novelists*. Besides providing a unifying theory about the nature of this novel, he also considered its separate aspects: characters, background, narration, and structure. But within the scope of thirty-five pages (in the *Pelican* edition of his book) analysis was naturally curtailed. And above that, too, in the plan of such a volume, there could be no place for an examination of Emily's poems—no postscript body of writing.

True, there has been other work upon Emily not limited to essay-length and still largely critical in tone. Two of the best of these are Phyllis Bentley's *The Brontës* (in the Home and van Thal *English Novelist* series), and Laura Hinkley's *Charlotte and Emily*. But the second of these is primarily biographical, and the first sets out to cover both biography and criticism, in even proportions, in a very short book. Then, too, although there are many admirable critical *dicta* to be found in these two works—especially in Phyllis Bentley's little volume—the treatment tends towards the eulogistic, which is almost the norm for Brontë criticism. This *a priori* favourable approach is perhaps no very perverse matter, when we remember that the biographer or the novelist by nature inclines more to hero-worship than does the more abstract-minded critic. But when we observe this distinction, we find that we have to apply it to nearly every book about the Brontës; for nearly every book upon them (their work as well as their personalities) has been the product of occasional writers, professional biographers, or novelists.

Now it is clearly right and natural that a family of innate genius and talent, remotely situate from any common nexus of culture and society, should fascinate or hypnotise the biographical mind. Natural, too, is the attraction that the mind of the novelist must feel in regarding the three inborn novelists of Haworth—talents that ripened outside the orbit of literary equipment and encouragement. So that both the biographer and the novelist should be expected to contribute their warm homage is something we can take for granted. But what, though still natural, is not so satisfactory, is that our opinion of Emily's work should largely be the result of pronouncements by people not primarily concerned with the value and status of a novel or a poem.

Perhaps it may seem that my conception of the biographer or novelist is narrowly exclusive. Indeed, we all know of certain exceptions where the biographer has been the critic, and the example of Henry James stands boldly up to rebuke the idea that the novelist must lack the critical mind. But considering these separate literary vocations in a purely functional manner, we must admit that all call forth distinct and individual mental disciplines. Thus, the biographer acts the critic by selecting, ordering, and emphasising the details in the life-story of his subject. Similarly, the role of critic is exercised by the novelist upon the substance of his own imagination, by urging and restraining his own creative powers. But neither of them, in the course of their function, are called upon to assess the excellence of language and thought in a novel or a poem, and compare that excellence with the excellence of others. And where the novelist or biographer *is* called upon to perform this last function, we must remember that he performs it marginally and incidentally, and that it can never be his first concern.

When, then, I repeat that the disquieting fact about the assessment of Emily's work, in anything like a systematic fashion, is that it is the result of pronouncements by people not primarily literary critics, I would not have the reader infer that I am lamenting the number of books upon her by biographers and novelists. What I do regret, when I consider the formation of opinion about Emily's work, is that *all* the books on her have been written by biographers and novelists, and *none at all* by critics.

This disproportionate treatment and assessment is, necessarily not a crime we can lay at the door of her biographers. The sin is chiefly a sin of omission; and if any party is to be held responsible it must be the reluctant literary critic.

Imagine, for example, how we should think and feel about such poets as Keats and Wordsworth if studies upon them were limited to picturesque reconstructions of their lives, in which the biographers drew upon the poems as so many colourful diary-entries, or as two- or three-line texts to verify and heighten their sober researches in the subject's daily living. That has largely been the position with Emily as far as critics are concerned. Time and again, in endless volumes, they have seen the prose and verse of Emily used by the biographer as a kind of book-mark inserted in the account of her days. They have seen passages in her poems and her novel used to prove such and such a point about Emily's person, about Emily's existence. And on those rather rare occasions when her writing has been treated in and for itself, it has generally been bathed in the enthusiastic beams which biographers, quite properly, emit in the presence of their subject. Perhaps it is this no-uncertain lack of impartiality which has scared off the critics. Perhaps with their passion for objectivity—that is, ideally speaking—they have been frightened away from a subject which seems to be one of the strongest preserves of partiality in our literature. Then, too, I do not pretend that the serious critic is so bashful a person unless he deem it partly in his own interest. Now the 'cosy' note so often struck, when Emily is introduced, is a powerful deterrent to the critic who takes his own role more or less in earnest. He observes, among the writers upon her, a natural or deliberate restriction of range. Emily's work is compared and re-compared with that of Charlotte, Anne, and Branwell; and her father's prose and verse may possibly be dragged in, in order to establish the family tone. That Emily's appropriate peers—with whose work parallels would prove truly fruitful—are ever to be sought outside the bounds of a rather limited northern village seldom seems to have occurred to her biographers. The family circle at Haworth Parsonage or the somewhat wider radius of the Héger Pensionnat appears, to these students of domestic detail, to provide an ample circumference of reference. Emily being, at her best, one of those few poets whose thought can put a girdle round the earth in sixty seconds, the critic no doubt finds himself doubly dismayed at this unwavering parochiality.

Such circumscript placing of Emily's work has had the unfortunate result of conferring upon her the status of a great middle-brow classic. Among 'Brontë-lovers' it is not the fashion to question, evaluate, or reflect on Emily's work. Her novel and her poems are not located in the great body of English letters, and the even vaster body of European thought. They are read, dwelt, and enthused upon within the confines of a local culture. Her readers are inclined to form a sort of invisible 'home circle', in which all that can be labelled 'made at Haworth' requires from them no further guarantee.

All this is apt to depress the literary critic. He sees the subject assuming shape, attaining to a figure of judgment, not in the ambience of the best thought and known, but surrounded by provincial rumour and chat. Or, when this is not the case, the works of Emily are presented in the white-hot glow of personality worship. Either way, the relative approach—in terms of literary standing—is eschewed.

Perhaps no other novelist save Jane Austen has received such narrowing and levelling treatment. And with the latter the abrogation of her fame by genteel, style-mongering, belles-lettrist critics has not been without some justification. Unlike Emily's, her tone and thought is sociable and keyed to a study of manners; indeed, one may say, largely so limited. Then, too, her letters and private life reveal a flair for social living, for a pleasing practice of the sociable virtues totally foreign to Emily. Even within the precincts of the family, Emily's reserve was almost notorious. To place such a being within the circumference of common domestic relationship is clearly more unwise than to treat Jane Austen as solely a drawing-room phenomenon.

My attempt to remove the works of Emily from such environing circumstances, in the following pages, will doubtless prove unpopular. A case in point of the zealousness with which the 'civil and genteel' school of critics defend their proprietary authors occurred but recently to forewarn me. A Californian critic had chanced to write a book upon the novels of Jane Austen, and had been so crude as to mention such subjects as Marxism and the New Criticism. Aware that this most lady-like figure was being extracted from her vicarage frame-work—though possibly aware of little else—the English reviewers sprang to arms.

Now I do not cite this incident to express my approval of the Californian critic, so much as to show our native fear of larger treatment for certain of our classics. Jane Austen, though no profound intelligence, is a shrewd and agile enough author to stand up to other canons of thought, even though belonging to fields remote to her. Her sensibility and perception can match the economist's analysis of facts. But this her custodians would forbid. Her sponsors deliberately curtail her sphere of reference.

Despite which intimidation, I intend to let the light in on Emily a little. True, such illumination as I can provide will not be of the hard Sophoclean order; and its diffusion will prove, I am afraid, of a fragmentary uneven nature. Yet, to the best of my ability, it shall, I promise, be critical.

At this juncture it becomes me to state what I mean by my shibboleth. But first, I would like to assure the reader that it is not a social-revolutionary standpoint. What I am *not* going to do, is to try and show that Emily was an unconscious socialist, a socialist in disguise, or a socialist manqué; nor am I going to attempt to demonstrate that she would have been better had she been one. As will transpire in the course of these pages, I believe her thought was the weaker for not sufficiently exercising itself within the context of a traditional society. But such conclusions can bide their time and the evidence I can muster to prove them.

For the moment, I propose to attend to what I mean by 'critical', and the kind of criticism I wish to apply to the poems and novel of Emily.

Briefly, and with apologies to its eminent American proponents, I intend these pages as a modified essay in the New Criticism. That the sobriquet is undeserving here, I shall readily enough allow; and, indeed, it would probably be more correct to describe my endeavour as an example of the Much Older Criticism. But as the judgment on Emily's work obviously stands in need of a corrective, and that corrective is of an order which the New Criticism could best provide, I hope to be permitted a run of its armoury though I do not avail myself of all its many weapons.

By saying I desire to subject Emily's work to assessment by the New Criticism, I am really saying very little—though that, I hope, in the right direction. Namely, an attempt to concentrate upon her novel and her poems, and evaluate them in their own right, and not as biographical extensions. I wish, then, to try and determine the merits of her novel and her poems both as modes of literary expression and as statements of thought and belief. And when I have arrived at certain individual judgments, I desire to present a general impression of her capacity as verse- and prose-writer, and her capacity as a thinker. In the course of this task, I shall expect to compare her work with the work of other poets, novelists, and thinkers, and locate her in relation to them.

How much this modest, direct, and simple programme would have, in theory, the approval of the New Critics themselves, I cannot guess. Apart from the omission of biographical matter—to which my colleague, Muriel Spark, is attending—my method (allowing for my own limitations) is perhaps more related to that of Johnson than of the new American school. If, therefore, as I suggested, I had called my effort an essay in the Older Criticism it would possibly have been more precise. Baring the consideration of some propositions which Johnson took for granted, but which in our time it is difficult to do, I feel it is his concerns I am assuming; particularly, maybe, the moral concern. Again, I do not propose to myself the creation or adoption of a special terminology which the American New Critics favour. It is possible I may find myself requiring a few new epithets for descriptive purpose, but I do not anticipate the need for such a host of neologisms as John Crowe Ransom, for example, can marshall; nor for the fresh categories of 'literary parsing' which Yvor Winters manfully shoulders. In part, I think, this does not spring from any essential disagreement with these writers, as from the limits I accept in this study. Sensing in myself an inability for sustained analysis, such as they take on, I shall restrict my own considerations to representative passages and problems. Of itself, this would render the completer apparatus of the New Critics pretentious here, as well as showing up my own failings. But, as I have hinted, Emily stands in need of a freshly-focussed cultural publicity; and this is most advantageously obtained for her under the ægis of the New Criticism.

Before proceeding with my examination, it is necessary to speak of two matters that ought to receive preliminary attention. These—which I feel to be the principal obstacles to a critical assessment of Emily's work—are the opinions and reports of critics who have subscribed to the 'Emily cult', and whom I hope to show as the villains of the piece, and what I shall call the red herring of Gondal (the literary game which Emily and Anne played first as children together and perpetuated into their full adult years). Having traduced the Brontë commentators from the start in this study, as I have done, it is right that I should offer the reader some evidence for what, elsewise, may appear mere prejudice.

As touching the second interest, I realise that I shall be opposing a concern more formidable, if such can be imagined, than the New Criticism; that is, American scholarship and research. I realise, too, that while the current of 'cosy' comment and criticism is well over fifty years old, and may therefore be expected to be flowing without its first fine impetus, the Gondal research movement is of later extraction, and comparatively still in powerful spate. Not being a scholar, however, and therefore unfearful of a passage-at-arms in which I must have proved defeated, I shall take courage by remembering that what I have to do with is not scholarship in its own right, but rather the effect of scholarship upon literary criticism and public opinion.

When I have established my relationship to these two matters, and the relationship of these two matters to Emily's work, I hope the field will show the clearer, and that its proper boundaries be already in sight.

1

IMPEDIMENTS

The False Baptists

In commentaries upon the Brontës, by authors who have combined the roles of biographer and literary critic, two distinct tones are generally to be distinguished. These are, 'the tabby' and 'the tigerish', and various modifications upon each; though both evince and seem to spring from an element of feline possessiveness.

The trouble began with the original recorder of the Brontë story, Mrs. Gaskell, who, in her *Life of Charlotte Brontë,* acted as their first hagiographer. Here is the last bar of her swan-song, as devoid of particularity as it is modulated to a praiseful lament:

> "But I turn from the critical, unsympathetic public—inclined to judge harshly because they have only seen superficially and not thought deeply. I appeal to that larger and more solemn public, who know how to look with tender humility at faults and errors; how to admire generously extraordinary genius, and how to reverence with warm, full hearts all noble virtue. To that Public I commit the memory of Charlotte Brontë."

In the grave-side oration of her prose—which tells us nothing about Charlotte, and could be employed to fit the occasion of any decease of unusual talent—there are certain points to be observed. Note, first, the flattering capital awarded to a non-critical 'Public'. Then, next, how the critical is equated with the superficial in feeling and thought. Thirdly, criticism is apparently harsh; whilst what is not critical would seem to be solemn.

That criticism attempts to arrive at anything like an objective view-point nowhere seems to be considered. Criticism, as Mrs. Gaskell sees it, has solely a destructive denigrative function.

One further confession will probably indicate the tasks that Mrs. Gaskell preferred to shelve. Speaking of Charlotte, she writes, "I cannot measure or judge of such a character as hers. I cannot map out vices and virtues, and debatable land". In other words, 'I cannot see my subject in a normal human perspective, as a being beset, like all mortality, by certain failings off-set by certain graces'. This fashion of conceiving one's subject by ignoring the debits and credits of behaviour, I term the heroic mode of biography. But properly speaking, by definition, it is something even more far-flown; for even the hero has his Achilles' heel, that undoing ounce of *hubris* in his nature. If we call it, then, the hero-worship school, we shall be, biographically, nearer the mark; and if our subject is a woman, and the school therefore becomes the heroine-worship school, we see that a new factor of chivalrous feminism may be introduced.

This is especially noticeable when the subject is a woman and the author one also; and when we get the enhanced situation of Mrs. Gaskell's *Life of Charlotte Brontë* introduced by May Sinclair the tension is increased triple-fold. This latter author, besides being one of the foremost champions of female mental emancipation, is mistress of a heightened style and statement which we may describe as the superlative sublime.

> "It is", she writes of Mrs. Gaskell's biography, "impossible to put the book down. It holds you with the grip of life and death. Time never dulls the poignancy of the grim and powerful narrative. The passages which forced tears from you when you read them in your childhood are as unbearable, as unapproachable almost, now as then. You know that they are coming and you shrink from the pain. But the book carries such profound conviction of its reality that you would not have it otherwise."

This is the real blue-stocking's heart-throb, which makes all further comment pointless.

But in adding the name of May Sinclair to that of Mrs. Gaskell, I have introduced the chief exponent of the 'tigerish tone' in Brontë criticism. More than the 'tabby tone' of Mrs. Gaskell (to another of whose disciples, Clement Shorter, I return later), the tigerish tone commands our attention by reason of its greater intelligence, its greater trenchancy, and fierce enthusiasm. But almost always it is an intelligence deflected from objective concentration on account of its utter possessiveness, its emotional identification with its subject.

Here is May Sinclair, in her book *The Three Brontës,* asserting one aspect of her Emily cult: the utter uniqueness, as she sees it, of Emily's artistic powers in *Wuthering Heights.* She will not even hear of any comparison:

> ". . . this book stands alone, absolutely self-begotten and self-born. It belongs to no school; it follows no tendency. You cannot put it into any category. It is not 'Realism', it is not 'Romance', any more than *Jane Eyre*: and if any other master's method, De Maupassant's or Turgeniev's, is to be the test, it will not stand it. There is nothing in it you can seize and name."

In other words, it is all settled and final, when indeed nothing is settled at all; and in the fact that things are not settled (—note the challenging finality of her last statement—), May Sinclair appears to proudly rejoice, 'I have explained *Wuthering Heights',* she seems to say, 'by explaining that it cannot be explained'. And this exclusiveness of her subject—its incommunicability—exalts her greatly. That previously she had shown how the character Heathcliff in *Wuthering Heights* had received its first draft in a Gondal poem, and how there existed a relationship between the Gondal poems and Byron's poetry, is something she has evidently forgotten.

The *nonpareil* note, which May Sinclair perfects, sounds again in this passage on Emily:

> "You may call her what you will—Pagan, pantheist, transcendentalist, mystic, and worshipper of earth, she slips from all your formulas. She reveals a point of view *above* good and evil. Hers is an attitude of tolerance that is only

not tenderness because her acceptance of life and all that lives is unqualified and unstinting. It is too lucid and too high for pity."

And too lucid, apparently, for definition.

But if we read on, we shall see that May Sinclair does not quite mean what she says; or means it only rhetorically. What she really infers is, in fact, the very opposite.

"Heathcliff and Catherine exist", she continues, speaking of the characters of *Wuthering Heights*. "They justify their existence by their passion. But if you ask what is to be said of such a creature as Linton Heathcliff, you will be told that he does not justify his existence; his existence justifies him.

Do I despise the timid deer,
Because his limbs are fleet with fear?
Or, would I mock the wolf's death-howl,
Because his form is gaunt and foul?
Or, hear with joy the lev'ret's cry
Because it cannot bravely die?
No! Then above his memory
Let Pity's heart as tender be.

After all it *is* pity; it is tenderness."

Well, self-contradiction and having it both ways have ever been female prerogatives; but perhaps they do not make for trustworthy criticism, even when presented through the agency of an innocuous rhetorical device.

Nor can I feel that May Sinclair's judgment of character is any sounder than her judgment and summary of Emily's thought.

"But", she writes, with a touch of Hollywood flaunting in her adjective before the days of films, "—and this is what makes Emily Brontë's work stupendous—not for a moment can you judge Heathcliff by his bare deeds. Properly speaking, there are no bare deeds to judge him by. Each deed comes wrapt in its own infernal glory, trailing a cloud of supernatural splendour."

The infernal glory, one presumes—to take but one example

—of Heathcliff's hanging of Isabella's small dog, by suspending it by a handkerchief from a hook. If actions of such adolescent nastiness as this seem, to May Sinclair, to be "trailing a cloud of supernatural splendour", one fears both for her metaphysics and her ethics. Or has she, in the excitement of her prose, simply overlooked this deed of Heathcliff? Either way, we are led to mistrust her critical balance.

But my purpose here is not to catalogue my many disagreements with this novelist (for which there will be some occasion later), as to suggest the tone of her criticism: its vehement, trenchant, yet illogical nature. Charles Morgan, a more tolerant critic than myself, has himself commented on her "sweeping statement" and her "strangely irrelevant twinge of feminism"; so I hope my own citations of her 'this-is-final' manner will not be interpreted by the reader as a retaliatory misogyny on my part.

I quote the passage in which he advances the first of these charges against her. The reader may note how it also bears out my general accusation against Brontë commentators.

> "Here", Charles Morgan writes, of the relation between Emily's life and her mystic experience, "we are on dangerous ground—dangerous because no theory about Emily Brontë's inner life is capable of final proof, doubly dangerous because, in many minds, the Brontës are an obsession which, while it lasts, attaches to them the privileges and penalties of Cæsar's wife. We know that they were passionate writers, and that Emily was the most passionate. We know, or should know if we have remarked elsewhere the fruits of imaginative genius, that to infer from this alone that Charlotte was in love with Héger or that Emily experienced the satisfactions or even the desires of the flesh is unwarrantable. But Miss Sinclair, writing in 1911, went too far. She was violently scornful of those who then accepted the possibility of Charlotte's having been in love with Héger, she regarded the suspicion as an attempt to belittle the genius of a woman novelist; she said that

Charlotte, being 'pure, utterly pure from all the illusions and subtleties and corruptions of the sentimentalist', was incapable of 'feeling in herself the possibility of passion'; and, following Mrs. Gaskell, the only source then available, she quoted a fragment of one of Charlotte's letters to Héger in support of the conception of her heroine as a "fiery-hearted Vestal'. Two years later this letter and three others were published in full in *The Times* (July 29, 1913). It was seen that Mrs. Gaskell, who must have been shown the originals by Héger, as Mr. Benson[1] supposes, but who more probably worked from a copy or copies retained by Charlotte, had been discreetly selective. That Charlotte loved Héger was established. The indignant rhetoric of Miss Sinclair was seen to have been thrown away, for the artist's repute was not touched; and all but those who had believed that a virginal soul was a necessary support to an impassioned imagination wondered what all the fuss had been about.

The incident would not be worth its place here if it were not that rhetoric of the same colour has been, and is still being, used in defence of Emily's absolute chastity of act and wish, and that the publication of new material might at any moment cause this rhetoric to perish. Someone may dare to say that Emily too, was in love. 'But we shall at least know that he has made it up', says Miss Sinclair. 'And even so, it will have been better for that man if he had never been born. He will have done his best to destroy or to deface the loveliness of a figure unique in literature.' What an obsession is this! Who would feel that anything essential in the woman was defaced if it was proved that she had loved a man, or whose adoration of her genius be lessened? It is true that fiery genius is extremely rare in women who lack sexual impulse, and there may exist, in some minds, a wish to preserve so great a rarity, but this is not a good reason for saying, with Miss Sinclair, that 'when Emily wrote of

1 *Charlotte Brontë*, by E. F. Benson, 1932.

passion, she wrote of a thing that, as far as she personally was concerned, not only was not and had not been, but could never be.' There is none but speculative evidence for this sweeping statement. There is at present none but speculative evidence against it. In each reader's knowledge of women and in his biographical interpretation of the works, the subject may be allowed to rest until new evidence is forthcoming."

To Charles Morgan I again resort for comment on Clement Shorter, a popular practitioner of the tabby tone, and author of *The Brontës and their Circle,* and *The Brontës*: *Life and Letters*.

"It is an instance", observes Charles Morgan, "of Shorter's obtuseness in all things relating to Emily Brontë that he should have written: 'It is certain that her own letters to her sisters, and particularly to Anne, must have been peculiarly tender, and in no way lacking in abundant self-revelation.' If by abundant self-revelation, Shorter meant no more than chatter about dogs and birds or domestic details that he might have hastened to publish in a domestic journal, he may have been justified. Emily had two lives. It was the essence of her genius that they were distinct."

Upon this comment I need remark but little. Emily's reserve and aloofness, in all things touching her deepest thoughts and feelings, is now become almost a by-word. Indeed, it always was the one trait we knew of; so that the most casual reader of even a single Brontë biography (or, for that matter, of the Prefaces that Charlotte wrote for Emily's work) will realise Clement Shorter's error. But what is important to point out, is that only a mind ignoring the facts, and calmly setting the objective aside in the name of some more intimate vision, could have come to commit this mistake. And just this setting-aside of the objective in the name of some more intimate vision is the failing to which authors of the tabby tone are prone.

But if the tabby and the tigerish tone could claim no further exponents than Mrs. Gaskell, Clement Shorter, and May Sinclair the situation would not be so bad. But still quite bad enough, since *The Life of Charlotte Brontë, The Brontës and their Circle,* and *The Three Brontës* are probably the three most popular books ever written on Emily and her sisters. In addition, however, to forming a picture (and that, a highly proprietary one) of Emily, Anne, and Charlotte in readers' minds, they have, between them, set the fashion for subsequent books upon the Brontës.

And so, I opine, these three must stand as the prototypal false baptists of the Brontë dispensation: firstly, the soulful, sentimental Mrs. Gaskell; secondly, the sedulous collector of often indifferent facts, the obtuse Clement Shorter; and, thirdly, that virago of virginity, the high-pitched and high-handed May Sinclair.

That the effects which these three have wrought are out of all proportion to their intentions, I shall readily allow; but that the posterity of their works must stand as a guilty influence in the light of what it has begotten, I yet hold to and advance.

Until we make an effort to see Emily's poems and novel outside the fug of small domestic thinking, as represented by the tabby-toned authors, and as free from the protective superlative hedging which the tiger-toned writers erect about her, we shall only be engaging in repetitive labours, or in minute tasks which the scholar delights in but which do not make up the critic's province.

Emily, I say, can well stand up to the relative-minded quizzing of her work; for if, as I believe, she has much to lose in such a process, there is much that she undeniably retains; and that with a greater enumeration of her specific merits than she has yet enjoyed.

IMPEDIMENTS

The Bogus Background

As children the Brontës were given to the elaboration of imaginative games. The characters and incidents of their creation were not, like those of many children, enacted by themselves in person, but recorded on paper in chronicle-fashion.

To the time when Charlotte, the eldest, went away to school at Roe Head early in the year 1831, they played, under her leadership, a game called Angria, from the name of the country which its protagonists—the Angrians—inhabited. The two chief impressarios of the Angrian legend had been Charlotte and Branwell, and when Charlotte left Haworth Parsonage to attend school at Roe Head, the imaginative leadership fell upon Branwell. He then became the principal organiser of the Angrian fortunes, their inspirer and administrator—a status that Emily and Anne were apparently not prepared to allow him.

Rebelling against his desire to organise them, they started a new game of their own—the Gondal game, which both continued to play, together or alone, until their deaths.

The very barest outline of this story, I give in the words of Miss Fannie E. Ratchford, the cardinal authority on Gondal research, and librarian of the special collections in the University of Texas.

> "Its setting", she writes, in a preface to C. W. Hatfield's edition of *The Complete Poems of Emily Jane Brontë*[1], was Gondal, an island in the North Pacific, a land of lakes and mountains and rocky shorelines, with a climate much like Emily's native Yorkshire. Its people were a strong, passionate, freedom-loving race, highly imaginative and intensely patriotic. Politically, Gondal was a confederancy

[1] Published 1941.

of provinces or kingdoms, each governed by a hereditary ruling family. Between the House of Brenzaida, in the kingdom of Angora, and the House of Exina existed a deadly rivalry which gave direction to the developing play.

When the hardy, far-ranging Gondalan mariners discovered Gaaldine, a large tropical island in the South Pacific, princes of these two great families were foremost among the adventurers who explored, conquered, and partitioned it into the kingdoms and provinces of Alexandria, Almedore, Elseraden, Ula, Zalona, and Zedora. Old rivalries and hates went with them, and a goodly number of Emily's poems have to do with the wars and conquests waged by Julius of Brenzaida, against his Exina neighbours in Zalona."

These are the principal dramatic and geographical facts relating to the Gondal legend, but, as Miss Ratchford continues:

"Emily's and Anne's extensive prose literature, constituting a full and detailed background for their somewhat cryptic poems, has been lost, and their verse now stands alone, scantily supplemented by a short journal fragment signed by both girls when they were about fifteen and sixteen; the notes they exchanged on Emily's birthday in 1841 and 1845; and Anne's list of Gondalan place names and personal names."

Yet in spite of the gaping spaces which yawn in the walls of an edifice never completed, Miss Ratchford and Miss Laura Hinkley (to instance but two present Brontë commentators) have both attempted the work of reconstruction. That this task is about as difficult as would be that of reconstructing Shakespeare's plays (supposing them to have perished) from the snatches of songs they included, has not deterred these determined scholars.

My comparison, of course, is exaggerated; but that there can be no certainty about the lines of this rehabilitation is accepted by both of the authorities quoted. This must needs lead to vague conjecture, as when Miss Ratchford writes, in her preface to the Hatfield edition of the poems:

"A study of Emily Brontë's poems . . . reveals that the majority, perhaps all of them, pertain to an imaginative country called Gondal."

But this hopeful and sanguine note requires to be modified by the time she arrives at the end of her preface.

"The long period through which the epic grew", she admits, "makes occasional inconsistencies and even contradictions inevitable. Yet, despite these several difficulties, approximately one-half of the one-hundred and ninety-three poems and fragments printed by Mr. Hatfield, including the larger and more important pieces, take their places in the Gondal pattern."

Miss Hinkley, whose reconstruction of the Gondal theme in her book *Charlotte and Emily* (1945) came four years after Miss Ratchford's preface and the fuller study of this subject in her work *The Brontës' Web of Childhood*,[2] is moderate in her claims, realising from the start the limitations of certitude in this field. Here is her numerical account of the position:

"One hundred and ninety-four of Emily's poems are known. . . . In February, 1844, a month or more after Charlotte came home from Brussels, Emily began to transcribe what she evidently considered her best work into two notebooks, one for general verse, one entitled *Gondal Poems*. In the first notebook are thirty-one poems, in the Gondal notebook forty-four. Forty-one more poems are definitely Gondal as shown by subject, reference, proper name, title, or signature. Of the remaining thirty-one many are probably Gondal though without clear identification as such."

In addition to the factual indecisiveness concerning what are and what are not Gondal poems, Miss Hinkley concedes further points to the sceptical reader of these childish sagas.

"As a clue to Emily's 'inner life' ", she writes, "the Gondals have proved as misleading as they were alluring"; and again:

"The Gondals' tragic destinies have invoked as much

[2] Published 1941.

misunderstanding of Emily's temperament as of her experience";

followed by:

> "The Gondal story is difficult to disentangle, principally because neither the order in which Emily wrote the poems, nor that in which she transcribed them in the Gondal note-book, gives any reliable clue to the order in which events are supposed to have happened."

Perhaps it is the difficulty of assembling this jig-saw which has provided the chief inducement. For, after all Miss Hinkley's modest disclaimers as to what the Gondal writings can establish for us, and what we can establish of them for ourselves, she goes ahead and does her best in half a whole chapter and an appendix.

Unlike Miss Hinkley, who accepts the fact that the Gondals must be studied for themselves rather than as sure biographical clues, Miss Ratchford in her preface is insistent upon their double roles as biographical and critical interpreters.

> "Thus," she writes, "Emily Brontë's own voice turns into nonsense the hundreds of pages of Brontë biography based on the subjective interpretation of her poems."

What Miss Ratchford does not consider is that Emily and a Gondal character could speak together in the same poem; that Emily could speak through a Gondal mouthpiece; and that this mouthpiece could offer her what she sometimes might have needed—a mask.[2a] I do not, in any way, wish to suggest that this would invariably be the case, but that it might sometimes be so—(that, indeed, from our evidence of the poetic mind with its strongly oblique and secretive side, in all probability, now and again, would)—is something we have at least to be prepared for.

That Miss Ratchford, in her preface, does not give heed to the possibility of such a mode of personal expression, makes us doubt her biographical understanding of poetry, as much

2a W. B. Yeats in his *Autobiographies* remarks that, "As I look backward upon my own writing, I take pleasure alone in those verses where it seems to me I have found something hard and cold, some articulation of the Image, which is the opposite of all that I am in my daily life, and all that my country is."

as her second statement makes us wary of her critical appreciation of it.

> "The following outline of the reconstructed epic of Gondal", she writes in the last paragraph of her preface, "incomplete as it is, and liable to error where gaps in the documents have to be bridged by inference, is submitted to Brontë lovers for their greater understanding and enjoyment of Emily's poems."

Miss Ratchford's last words are the key-terms here: "a greater understanding and enjoyment of Emily's poems". How far does our knowledge of Gondal increase this?

The answer to this may best be come at by, first of all, asking a general question: what sort of knowledge about a poem adds to our enjoyment of it? Now in my answer I am going to reply in terms approved of by the New Critics, because I believe that they supply the best short answer to irrelevancies. And the answer is, 'such kind of knowledge as helps us to read the words on the page as a self-sufficient pattern of language and thought'. By this, I mean such kind of knowledge as assists us in enjoying a poem as a poem, and not as a piece of 'verse' biography or some other thing than a literary composition. I know, of course, that other enjoyments deriving from a poem are possible; but these are not given in the nature of its being, and their existence is strongly adulterate. Thus, facts about the writer or writing of a poem may add to our enjoyment of a lyric, let us say, a dramatic interest not inherent in it. The external facts about the writing and the writer provide a stage and background for the poem, and what we enjoy is not the composition in its complete and present state,[3] but in its past, its origin, its birth—a re-creation of its own creation. This, we may admit to be a complex and civilised form of pleasure, and not an entertainment that ought to be deplored. And this is so, unless such a mode of entertainment intervenes between us and our enjoyment of the poem in its own pure state.

[3] Goethe has a good phrase for this state. He terms it "the eternal present" of art.

With Emily, this is certainly the case. Her poems are encrusted with biographical barnacles, and have yet to be looked at for themselves.

And so I return to my previous position, and ask 'what kind of knowledge will help us to read Emily's own words on the page as a self-sufficient pattern of language and thought?' And the answer is: only such knowledge as assists us in our first assumption about the poem. If it is a lyric, we wish to so read it. If it is dramatic, we would like to know who the speaker is, and what part he is playing; and if it is narrative, we want to be informed as to who is telling us the story, and learn of any points referred to but not given.

In theory, then, a knowledge of Gondal—its characters, incidents, and localities—should increase our literary enjoyment of the poems. But in this instance an unbridgeable gulf opens up between theory and practice.

One way of describing this discrepancy is to say that what is good in Gondal is incidental and irrelevant to it, whilst what is most successfully designed as part of a whole is generally bad. Another way of putting it, is to say that the lyrical beauty of expression, the fervour and profundity of thought in these poems is out of all proportion to the ramshackle structure and childish melodramatic plots. Reading the best of Emily's poems against the background of the Gondal myth is like suddenly hearing some exquisite and Shakespeare-moving eloquence on the lips of some ridiculous ranting character out of a 'ham' Ruritanian play. It is like discovering some impossible prince or count from a novel by Anthony Hope speaking lines as compelling as a passage from *Hamlet*. There is no correspondence between the words they utter, the ludicrous roles they take upon themselves, and the worthless situations in which they speak them.

Speaking of Shakespeare's heroines, Ruskin once observed how a power to confer appropriate and indicative names upon the characters of one's creation, is a faculty reserved for imaginative genius. This literary christening he sees as a process which validates and crowns genuine character-creation. Now the consummating stroke, the imaginative accolade, which—on the bestowal of a name—brings the character galvanically to life, is something Emily and Anne could not perform when they named their Gondal creations. And the absence, here, of this magic nomenclature is the more significant in that Emily possessed it when she came to name the places and people of her novel. Wuthering Heights, Thrushcross Grange, Heathcliff, Hindley, Hareton Earnshaw: the names are a pipe-roll of the real, an inventory of verisimilitude!

With the earthy individuality of these, compare the wretched histrionic pollysyllables of the Gondal *dramatis personæ* (there are "forty-two persons mentioned by name or initial", as Miss Hinkley points out, and others in the story who go unnamed). The hero, Julius Brenzaida, who is the Emperor of Gondal, enjoys other Ruritanian distinctions: he is Prince of Angora, and King of Almedore. But the heroine improves on this, for she is known, severally, as "Augusta Geraldine Almeda, A.G.A., Rosina of Alcona, A.S., 'Sidonia's deity', and Gondal's Queen".[4]

A list of other names taken at random lack authenticity in just the same fashion: Fernando de Samarna; Alexander, Lord of Elbe; E. R. Gleneden; Angelica; Claudia; Julian M.; and A. G. Rochelle. One notes the foreign and exotic colouring. There are Latin names, French names, German names, and Scots names; but nothing like a native English name, unless one permits the romantic-operatic Claudia to pass muster.

And when we come to the names of places, the prospect is even worse: Ula, Zalona, Zedora, Elseraden, Aspin Castle, and the Gaaldine Prison Caves. If the place-names in *The Prisoner of Zenda* had been taken from hints out of Blake's *Prophetic Books,* the unlikeliness of them all could not be worse!

For the kind of situations we find in Gondal, and the

[4] this roll-call has been worked out by Miss Ratchford.

atmosphere in which these occur, I refer the reader to Miss Hinkley's Appendix, in her book *Charlotte and Emily*. Here she has arranged eighty-six poems to form a consecutive Gondal story, indicating the pieces by their first line, and offering a prose resumé of the situation from which the poem sprang.

The tone and temper of these situations can be swiftly assessed by our glancing at the matters which compound them. As an example, I will quote the background which Miss Hinkley reconstructs to the poem, "I've seen this dell in July's shine":

> "Augusta grows up beautiful and alluring, with her father's energy, courage, and magnetism, her mother's tenderness, and a capacity for poetry and passion beyond either. As Julius's elder child and a possible claimant to the chief throne of Gondal, she becomes a centre of intrigue among the ambitious and discontented nobles. Augusta's girlhood friend is Angelica, whose sweetheart, Amadeus, transfers his passion to Augusta. His devotion involves him in one of the intrigues going on about her in which he is caught and sentenced to exile. In spite of his passionate pleas the sentence is enforced. Angelica goes with him, and 'under a foreign heaven' they plunge into 'a 'wildering scene of frenzied crime'. Together they commit a murder for which Amadeus pays with his life. Angelica escapes, blames Augusta, and lives for revenge.
>
> Augusta is absorbed in the first great love of her life. Alexander of Elbe (which lies in Alcona on the southern shores of Lake Elderno) returns Augusta's passion—but he is already married. They become lovers and the parents of an infant daughter. Since Augusta's royal rights would be forfeit should the existence of an illegitimate child become known, Alexander decrees it must not live. The concealed birth and death occur in the mountains near Augusta's girlhood home. Disguised as a man, Augusta takes the infant out in a snowstorm and abandons it."

The 'cardboard sublime' of the Gondal structure and its wire-pulled puppets is apparent in this passage. And the poem which precedes it—according to Miss Hinkley's reckoning—is about as undistinguished as poetry, as these events are shoddy as drama. Here are some representative verses:

> But I'll not fear—I will not weep
> For those whose bodies lie asleep:
> I know there is a blessed shore
> Opening its ports for me and mine;
> And, gazing Time's wide waters o'er,
> I weary for that land divine.
> Where we were born—where you and I
> Shall meet our dearest, when we die;
> From suffering and corruption free,
> Restored into the Deity.

What we notice about these verses is not only their conventional frigid badness read with an eye to the language, but the assumption of a 'formal' pious tone utterly foreign to Emily at her best.

Another good reason for taking no account of the Gondal story in our attempt to assess Emily's poetry is: that, besides providing a structure of theatrically sham material—a structure totally inadequate to bear the intense verbal beauty and profound and feeling thought which emerges from it in many superb detachable poems—it encouraged the writing of much bad verse. To this facile metrical scribbling, Emily was particularly prone when inspiration did not move her. Thus, of one of her most famous poems, Charles Morgan has the following observation:

> "The opening of *The Prisoner,* telling how narrator and jailer visit a dungeon and speak with a female prisoner confined there is evidently fictitious, probably Gondal,[5] and, like all Emily's work, when written deliberately and not dictated by the spirit within, second-rate."

> About her lip there played a smile of almost scorn:
> "My friend," she gently said, "you have not heard me mourn;
> When you my kindred's lives, my lost life, can restore,
> Then may I weep and sue—and never, friend, before!"

[5] identified as such both by Miss Ratchford and Miss Hinkley.

"No genius", continues Charles Morgan, "was needed for the composition of that", and then goes on to comment upon a poem which suddenly, unexpectedly, from being a dreary exercise in a then-outmoded style of Gothic gloom, buds out into one of the greatest statements of mystical experience in English verse.

Well, that, we see, is what one is up against: the ridiculous weakness of the Gondal dramatic structure, its bevy of incredible characters; and the unreliability of a Gondal guarantee as to whether we might expect a good or bad poem.

In the next chapter, in which I shall begin to look at Emily's poems in and for themselves, the burden of most that is bad in Gondal will find itself laid at the door of Byron's verse. In the course of apprehending the guilty party, I shall quote from several more Gondal poems, so that readers who require further proofs of my contention will find my further evidence therein.

And now, in concluding this present chapter, I should like to repeat the plea that we try to forget the Gondal cycle as a source of useful knowledge in our appreciation of Emily's poems. That they are often narrative in form and dramatic in incident must be accepted. Normally, such poems would benefit from further information about the speaker, the role he played, and the affairs in which he and others were implicated. But in the case of the Gondal poems, the dramatic background, as we have seen, cannot be relied on to provide an adequate commensurate explanation. Between the Gondal whole and the Gondal parts (as represented by the best poems in the cycle), there is no spiritual intellectual correspondence.

If we find a theory useful at this juncture, we can say that perhaps the Gondal structure of characters and incidents represented a conscious creation on the part of Emily and Anne; and that this conscious framework acted as a magnet, a call-boy, to Emily's unconscious mind. On such occasions, possibly, we get the enduring individual poem that rises, head and shoulders, above the dramatic compost in which it seems rooted. And when it does so, the poem starts to speak, not in the voice of a Gondal coloured-cut-out, a trashy operatic-Byronic 'ham', but in a voice which is highly individual, and which we sometimes feel is Emily's, referring to her own thoughts and emotions; or in tones which appear to transcend the personal, seeming to speak for all mankind. But whether this transcendence results in an expression which we describe as personal or cosmic, individual or universal, there can be no doubt as to when it *does* occur. To the reader with an ear for compulsive language, or a mind susceptible to fresh vigorous thought, its presence is immediately registered.

And when, as in *The Prisoner* which Charles Morgan quotes, the transmission from the false conventional voice to the individual/universal voice is made in the course of a single poem, the difference becomes more startlingly apparent. To illustrate my point I will print the first twenty-four stanzas of the poem:

JULIAN M. and A. G. ROCHELLE

(1) Silent is the House—all are laid asleep;
One, alone, looks out o'er the snow wreaths deep;
Watching every cloud, dreading every breeze
That whirls the 'wildering drifts and bends the groaning trees.

(2) Cheerful is the hearth, soft the matted floor;
Not one shivering gust creeps through pane or door;
The little lamp burns straight, its rays shoot strong and far;
I trim it well to be the Wanderer's guiding-star.

(3) Frown, my haughty sire; chide, my angry dame;
Set your slaves to spy, threaten me with shame:
But neither sire nor dame, nor prying serf shall know
What angel nightly tracks that waste of winter snow.

(4) In the dungeon crypts idly did I stray,
Reckless of the lives wasting there away;
"Draw the ponderous bars; open, Warder stern!"
He dare not say me nay—the hinges harshly turn.

(5) Our guests are darkly lodged," I whispered, gazing through
The vault whose grated eye showed heaven more grey than blue.
(This was when glad spring laughed in awaking pride.)
"Aye, darkly lodged enough!" returned my sullen guide.

(6) Then, God forgive my youth, forgive my careless tongue!
I scoffed, as the chill chains on the damp flagstones rung;
"Confined in triple walls, art thou so much to fear,
That we must bind thee down and clench thy fetters here?"

(7) The captive raised her face; it was as soft and mild
As sculptured marble saint or slumbering, unweaned child;
It was so soft and mild, it was so sweet and fair,
Pain could not trace a line nor grief a shadow there!

(8) The captive raised her hand and pressed it to her brow:
"I have been struck," she said, "and I am suffering now;
Yet these are little worth, your bolts and irons strong;
And were they forged in steel they could not hold me long."

(9) Hoarse laughed the jailer grim: "Shall I be won to hear;
Dost think, fond dreaming wretch, that I shall grant thy prayer.
Or, better still, wilt melt my master's heart with groans?
Ah, sooner might the sun thaw down these granite stones!

(10) "My master's voice is low, his aspect bland and kind;
But hard as hardest flint the soul that lurks behind;
And I am rough and rude, yet not more rough to see
Than is the hidden ghost which has its home in me!

(11) About her lips there played a smile of almost scorn:
"My friend," she gently said, "you have not heard me mourn;
When you my parents' lives—*my* lost life, can restore,
Then may I weep and sue—but *never,* Friend, before!"

(12) Her head sank on her hands; its fair curls swept the ground;
The dungeon seemed to swim in strange confusion round—
"Is she so near to death?" I murmured, half aloud,
And, kneeling, parted back the floating golden cloud.

(13) Alas, how former days upon my heart were borne;
How memory mirrored then the prisoner's joyous morn:
Too blithe, too loving child, too warmly, wildly gay!
Was that the wintry close of thy celestial May?

(14) She knew me and she sighed, "Lord Julian, can it be,
Of all my playmates, you alone remember me?
Nay, start not at my words, unless you deem it shame
To own, from conquered foe, a once familiar name.

(15) I cannot wonder now at ought the world will do,
And insult and contempt I lightly brook from you,
Since those, who vowed away their souls to win my love,
Around this living grave like utter strangers move!

(16) "Nor has one voice been raised to plead that I might die,
Not buried under earth but in the open sky;
By ball or speedy knife or headsman's skilful blow—
A quick and welcome pang instead of lingering woe!

(17) "Yet tell them, Julian, all, I am not doomed to wear
Year after year in gloom and desolate despair;
A messenger of Hope comes every night to me,
And offers, for short life, eternal liberty.

(18) He comes with western winds, with evening's wandering airs,
With that clear dusk of heaven that brings the thickest stars
Winds take a pensive tone, and stars a tender fire,
And visions rise and change that kill me with desire—

(19) "Desire for nothing known in my maturer years
When joy grew mad with awe at counting future tears;
When, if my spirit's sky was full of flashes warm,
I knew not whence they came, from sun or thunderstorm;

(20) "But first a hush of peace, a soundless calm descends;
The struggle of distress and fierce impatience ends;
Mute music soothes my breast—unuttered harmony
That I could never dream till earth was lost to me.

(21) "Then dawns the Invisible, the Unseen its truth reveals;
My outward sense is gone, my inward essence feels—
Its wings are almost free, its home, its harbour found;
Measuring the gulf it stoops and dares the final bound!

(22) "Oh, dreadful is the check—intense the agony
When the ear begins to hear and the eye begins to see;
When the pulse begins to throb, the brain to think again,
The soul to feel the flesh and the flesh to feel the chain!

(23) "Yet I would lose no sting, would wish no torture less;
The more that anguish racks the earlier it will bless;
And robed in fires of Hell, or bright with heavenly shine,
If it but herald Death, the vision is divine."

(24) She ceased to speak, and I, unanswering, watched her there,
Not daring now to touch one lock of silken hair—
As I had knelt in scorn, on the dank floor I knelt still,
My fingers in the links of that iron hard and chill.

"Suddenly", remarks Charles Morgan, on the entry of a new current into this poem, "suddenly, with so violent a flash that I am inclined to wonder whether the connection between the earlier and the later sections of the poem is not an editorial error,[6] Emily Bronte speaks

'Still, let my tyrants know . . .' "[7]

[6] not according to the latest Brontë scholarship·

[7] This line, quoted by Charles Morgan, from an earlier edition of the poems of Emily, is now corrected in Hatfield's 1941 edition to "Yet tell them, Julian, all, I am not doomed to wear".

The transition is abrupt, is spiritually a cleavage. There is no mistaking this tone when we hear it.

But this is not the only dislocation of tone and language which the poem contains; for in the version to which Charles Morgan refers us, the first three stanzas are omitted. Now these three stanzas, without possessing the vigour of thought and expression which informs stanzas 18-22, have their own authenticity of speech, as different as possible from the lumber-room language of stanzas 4-17. Note, for example, the alliterative force of the fourth line of stanza 1 ("That whirls the 'wildering drift and bends the groaning trees"), and the way in which a monosyllabic verb is twice employed and twice followed by a three- and two-syllable present participle, suggestive of the eddying results of a swift directly-passing action. Note, too, the contrast which stanza 2 provides to the last line of stanza 1. The stillness of the interior is heightened by our passing to it from the wild movement of wind and snow; and our sense of this is brought splendidly home in the third line of the stanza ("The little lamp burns straight, its rays shoot strong and far"), where the quiet vertical direction of the flame contrasts with the mazy "'wildering" motion of the snow and wind outside.

The language in the first two stanzas is realistic and evocative in a natural and unforced fashion; and the last line of stanza 3 ("What angel nightly tracks that waste of winter snow") substantiates with a note of mystery the note of human curiosity in the reference to "the Wanderer's guiding-star" (who is this Wanderer?).

But after this, till stanza 18 the vividness of language suffers an eclipse. All the out-worn epithets of poetic incarceration are paraded: "dungeon crypts", "jailer grim", "chill chains", "damp flagstones", ponderous bars", and "hinges" that turn "harshly". Nor is the description of the captive any more authentic in touch. In spite of her Byronic defiance and generally challenging manner ("About her lips there played a smile of almost scorn"), we learn that her face was "soft and mild, as sculptured marble saint or slumbering unweaned child". Apart from the unlikeliness of a heroine of iron will (not to mention her experience in the amorous field, referred to in stanzas 13 and 15), having so unfledged and flower-like an appearance, we note the unmatching double simile. To equate the looks of "sculptured marble saint" with those of a "slumbering unweaned child" seems to me utterly incorrect. About the former there is surely a certain coldness and setness of features expected which better resemble an actual death-mask or the face of some dead adult than a child's.

In a like manner, after stanza 22, the language descends from the elevation it manifests for five stanzas, and drops back into the tawdry common-place; so that by stanza 24 we have comfortably returned to such platitudes as "iron hard and chill", "dank floor", and "silken hair". This anti-climax of speech is then continued to the length of another fourteen stanzas.

Verbally, we see that this poem does not exist on one level, either of excellence or demerit. The language reveals an intermittence of power which comes and goes, then again comes and goes. And this, almost to the point where one can extract from its thirty-eight stanzas two self-sufficient poems of three and five stanzas respectively.

Confronted thus with the results of a close 'verbal' reading of the poem, the inadequacy of the Gondal structure to explain it poetically becomes the more obvious. Here is Miss Ratchford's construction of the background to this poem:

> "The strangest case is that of Lord Julian M. who discovers among the Republican prisoners in the dungeons of his father's castle a girl, who had been his childhood playmate, now hoping for death. Touched by the memory and her plight, by her loveliness and the strange spiritual beauty of her character, Julian becomes her jailer and nurses her for thirteen weeks, enduring, though proud and brave, the taunts of his family and friends for not going to war. After Rochelle dies he continues to endure the taunts, remaining

at the castle, tensely wooing her spirit to return to him every night."

It tells us nothing that we need to know for the enjoyment of the poem, simply because some thirty stanzas out of a total of thirty-eight *are not to be enjoyed as poetry,* unless we enjoy them as samples of bad verse; and of the remaining eight stanzas, no further information is needed. Poetically, they are two self-descriptive compositions.

Whatever our affections for the Gondals, we need not cherish them on the pretext that they succour our understanding of the poems. When Emily speaks as we would have her do, we do not require the fantastic masks of Julius Brenzida and his dreary like, to help us to appreciate what she is saying.

I have spoken of the Gondal myth as the sham background to Emily's poems. Factually, no doubt, its credentials have existence, but poetically speaking its bearing is irrelevant.

THE POEMS

Geneology

In 1846 there appeared a 'slim volume of verse' which sold two copies. With the title *Poems of Currer, Ellis and Acton Bell,* it represented the first venture[1] of the Brontë sisters into publishing, and contained twenty-one poems by Emily. A further eighteen[2] by her were published in the 1850 volume which Charlotte edited after Anne's and Emily's deaths.

Since then, larger and ever larger editions of Emily's poems have made their debut, culminating in C. W. Hatfield's *Complete Poems of Jane Emily Brontë* which appeared in 1941 and included one-hundred and ninety-three pieces, either complete or in fragment form.

But when I contemplate the number of these editions, I admit to being filled with a dismal gratitude towards the scholarship which has been exerted, together with a fear that this conscientious labour may not have been for the best after all. Perhaps my doubts have now and then entered the minds of those engaged in compilation; for, modestly enough, in his Introduction to the *Complete Poems of Emily Brontë* (1910), Clement Shorter, whose collection included some one-hundred and seventy-seven pieces, suggested that no one could deny to his fresh acquisitions "a certain bibliographical interest". Another Brontë specialist, Sir William Robertson Nicoll, wrote, deprecating any over-evaluation of this edition: "It is not claimed for a moment", he assured the reader, "that the intrinsic merits of the verses are of a special kind." Yet still the work of collection went on.

Latest of all, C. W. Hatfield, in the Introduction to his definitive edition, carefully avoids evaluative comment, and limits

1 Anne had had verse by her published in *Chambers' Journal,* and Charlotte had published, anonymously, some translations of French poems in a periodical. Emily had published nothing.

2 seventeen of which were found in manuscript.

himself for the main part to distinguishing the provenance of the poems. This, it would seem, is the best procedure; or, if not the best, at least the safest. For the fact of it is, that Emily's poems cry out for presentation three times as stridently as Wordsworth's poems appeared to Matthew Arnold to do.

The best editions, after Charlotte's are—like Charlotte's—choice and small. By best editions here, I mean such volumes as manifest in their selection and in their introductory comment a feeling for what is poetically the finest and for what this fineness consists in. My idea of a best edition, then, is not the scholar's but the critic's idea. Emily's work, for purpose of research, needs to be presented quantitatively; but for the purpose of poetic enjoyment it requires qualitative and critical presentment. This it has fortunately obtained at the hands of Philip Henderson and Muriel Spark, whose respective editions[3] of Emily's poems help to counter-balance the bull-dozing effect of the scholars who lump good and bad verse cheerily together.

And, truth to tell, there is plenty of the latter; some examples of which I must briefly touch on, before progressing to consider the more durable aspects of Emily's poetry.

Perhaps one of the reasons why Brontë authorities have not come out properly into the open over that large body of bad verse which Emily certainly composed, is due to the slow-dying belief in Emily as a self-tutored genius. Being seen too exclusively as a mind removed from all the effects and reverberations of literary tradition, Emily has appeared as an isolated figure, as a type of creative independence, unfed by currents of thought and language which help to nourish the majority of writers. This, of course, is largely in some measure true; and it is a rule among 'Brontë-lovers' that all that is native to the sisters is best. Therefore, if Emily wrote much verse, composing it solely on her own initiative, then all that she did must be accepted. To think otherwise about such a matter would be to show lese majesty.

3 *Emily Brontë Poems* (Lawson & Dunn, 1947).

A useful step in the other direction has been taken by Muriel Spark who tells us, in her Introduction to the poems, "that Emily Brontë is perhaps best seen as a part of the tradition of English poetry". She then goes on to locate the relationship which Emily's work bears to other English poets: to the Border Balladists, to Burns and Scott, to Cowper, Wordsworth, and the seventeenth-century poets. But although she mentions Emily's reading of Byron, she does not discourse upon its effect. Now here, it seems to me, we have the clue to all that is bad in the Gondal structure and most that is bad in Emily's poems.

By the time that Emily started writing verse, the Byronic vogue had been superseded by the fashion for reading and writing like Shelley. But Emily, at Haworth, was a good decade behind, so that Byron remained her starting-off point.

Already, by 1834, twelve years before Emily's first poems were published, Sir Henry Taylor[4] had analysed the corrupting effect which Byron and his followers were having upon English verse. Speaking of the Byronic school as a whole, this much-underrated poet and critic declared that,

> "These writers had, indeed, adopted a tone of language which is hardly consistent with the state of mind in which a man makes use of his understanding. The realities of nature, and the truths which they suggest, would have seemed cold and incongruous if suffered to mix with the strains of impassioned sentiment and glowing imagery in which they poured themselves forth. Spirit was not to be debased by any union with matter in their effusions, dwelling, as they did, in a region of poetical sentiment which did not permit them to walk upon the common earth or to breathe the common air."

This passage well defines the state of mind which Emily attributed to her Gondal creations. These beings are never shown as making use of their understanding. They never reason or appeal to logic, but declaim and plead to the

[4] in the preface to his poetical drama, *Philip van Artvelde.*

emotions. Their speeches are not arguments but rhapsodies —"effusions":

> Patriots, no stain is on your country's glory;
> Soldiers, preserve that glory bright and free.
> Let Almedore, in peace, and battle gory,
> Be still a nobler name for victory.

(And note, in passing, the surplus nature of the inverted epithet "gory". When have battles not been so?)

Sir Henry Taylor proceeds to consider certain characteristics of Byron's poetry, the focal-centre of those writers "whose appeal is made so exclusively to the excitabilities of mankind", and whose own example "undoubtedly gave the strongest impulse to the appetite for it". After remarking on Byron's misanthropy (which, as he says, was "not practical, but merely matter of imagination, assumed for purpose of effect"), Sir Henry Taylor gives his attention to the poet's notion of what constitutes a hero. As the Gondal characters answer so well to this description, I shall quote it in its entirety:

> "These imperfections of Byron's thought are especially observable in the portraitures of human character (if such it can be called) which are most prominent in Lord Byron's works. There is nothing in them of the mixture and modification—nothing of the composite fabric which Nature has assigned to Man. They exhibit rather passions personified than persons impassioned. But there is yet a worse defect in them. Lord Byron's conception of a hero is an evidence not only of scanty materials of knowledge from which to construct the ideal of a human being, but also of a want of perception of what is great or noble in our nature. His heroes are creatures abandoned to their passions, and essentially, therefore, weak of mind. Strip them of the veil of mystery and the trappings of poetry, resolve them into their plain realities, and they are such beings as, in the eyes of a reader of masculine judgment, would certainly excite no sentiment of admiration, even if they did not

provoke contempt. When the conduct and feelings attributed to them are reduced into prose and brought to the test of a rational consideration, they must be perceived to be beings in whom there is no strength except that of their intensely selfish passions—in whom all is vanity; their exertions being for vanity under the name of love or revenge, and their sufferings for vanity under the name of pride. If such beings as these are to be regarded as heroical, where in human nature are we to look for what is low in sentiment or infirm in character?

"How nobly opposite to Lord Byron's ideal was that conception of an heroical character which took life and immortality from the hand of Shakespeare:

> Give me that man
> That is not passion's slave, and I will wear him
> In my heart's core; aye, in my heart of heart."

"But, continues Sir Henry Taylor, in all fairness to the poet, "Lord Byron's genius . . . was powerful enough to cast a highly romantic colouring over these puerile creations, and to impart the charms of forcible expression, fervid feeling, and beautiful imagery, to thoughts in themselves not more remarkable for novelty than for soundness. The public required nothing more."

But what Byron could do, Emily could not. Her heightened colouring is seldom convincing.

Here is just one instance of a Gondal character proudly proclaiming herself as "passion's slave":

> I flung myself upon the stone,
> I howled and tore my tangled hair,
> And then, when the first gush had flown,
> Lay in unspeakable despair.

From the poetry of 'temperament' to the poetry of tantrums, there is merely one step, and Emily often takes it.

The man who is "passion's slave", and has the free vent of his passions denied him, becomes the perfect misanthropist. The Gondals are full of such temperamental creatures

—the Giaours and Laras of a mind mistakenly working in an alien convention:

Angelica, from my very birth
I have been nursed on strife:
And lived upon this weary Earth
A wanderer, all my life.
The baited tiger could not be
So much athirst for gore:
For men and laws have tortured me
Till I can bear no more.[5]

"I have not loved the world, nor the world me", wrote Byron in his *Childe Harold;* and other poets took up this cry, with greater stridency and less style. What was, at best, in Byron a poetry of rhetoric became in his followers a prosody of ranting. Among such disciples, Emily must be counted. See how she echoes in the following stanza the theme of Byron's high-pitched attractive poem, *The Destruction of Sennacherib*. Here is the original:

Like the leaves of the forest when Summer is green,
That host with their banners at sunset were seen:
Like the leaves of the forest when Autumn hath blown,
That host on the morrow lay withered and strown.

And here is Emily's 'copy':

King Julius left the south country
His banners all bravely flying;
His followers went out with Jubilee
But they shall return with sighing.

It is hardly necessary to remark upon the descent in quality. The colour and imagery of Byron is absent; and we are left with a flat statement, in itself most infelicitiously worded ("Jubilee" for an army going to the wars or advancing into battle seems clumsily unusual, and "sighing" for the distressed expression of defeated troops both tame and inept).

But Byron himself could write bad verses as well as encouraging others to write them:

Upon his hand she laid her own—
Light was the touch but it thrilled to the bone,
And shot a chillness to the heart,
Which fix'd him beyond the power to start.

[5] It is worth while to notice that a hatred of the law is linked in Emily's Byronic heroes with a hatred of their species. To misanthropy is added antinomianism.

he writes in *The Siege of Corinth,* with a fourth line as maladroit as one might ever expect to discover. Matthew Arnold, in his essay on Byron, has listed some dozen further examples of the poet's bad diction and gauche syntax; and a writer capable of such faults as these must always be a dangerous example to the tyro.

By far the greater element of corruption in Byron, however, is the general tone and temper of his world, the atmosphere which his poems set out to generate:

> Know ye the land where the cypress and myrtle
> Are emblems of deeds that done in their clime?
> Where the rage of the vulture, the love of the turtle,
> Now melt into sorrow, now madden to crime!

Like many young poets writing after Byron's death, Emily set herself to evoke the same heated mental climate. Scene and characters are often exotic, with a kind of pastiche exoticism:

> Palm-trees and cedars towering high
> Deepened the gloom of evening's sky;
> And thick did raven ringlets veil
> Her forehead, drooped like lily pale.

But relations and parallels between Emily's and Byron's poetry become the more numerous when one studies them together. The obvious debt which the Gondal hero, Douglas,[6] with his blighted "basilik charm", owes to the Byronic prototype has been remarked upon by commentators. A less noticeable likeness undoubtedly exists between Emily's poem *The Prisoner* and Byron's *The Prisoner of Chillon*. Apart from a similar charnel-house depiction of the dungeons which both poets share, there is also the character of a mild and forgiving prisoner common to both. Needless to say, in the two authors this mildness is exaggerated, just as their ferocities are over-emphasised.

Other themes from Byron prolifically appearing in Emily's verse are the love of social freedom and the military attempt

[6] Douglas is the character described in the poem "And now the house-dog stretched once more" according to Miss Ratchford.

to obtain it. But in Emily there are no mountains that look on Marathon; and the verse in which she celebrates liberty or its loss are like blasts on a tin trumpet. Her politics are those of a child, and her poetry of liberation[7] just so much pseudo-martial rubbish:

Has Almedore in battle bled?
Have slaves subdued the free?

she writes. But liberty or tyranny—it is all the same in Emily's verse: it is all an occasion for unoriented ranting:

"Woe for the day; Regina's pride
Regina's hope is in the grave;
And who shall rule my land beside,
And who shall save?

"Woe for the day; with gory tears
My country's sons this day shall rue.
Woe for the day; a thousand years
Cannot repair what one shall do.

"Woe for the day." Mixt with the wind,
That sad lament was ringing;
It almost broke my heart to hear
Such dreary, dreary singing.

Indeed, when Emily's poetry deals in a localised and specific fashion with Gondal characters and events, so that no under- or over-tones, addressed to the general world of men, are able to reach the reader's ear, the net result is so often the same—"Such dreary, dreary singing", as she herself puts it. One of the few repudiations of this tendency is to be found in the following stanza, where Emily's sense of her own environment, the reality of the moor-lands around her, serves to correct the fake exotic setting which her fantasy had been bent on maintaining:

O how the hearts of the voyagers beat
To feel the frost-wind blow!
What flower in Ula's gardens sweet
Is worth one flake of snow.

But one single snow-flake, however treasured, does not

[7] As always, with Emily, we must distinguish between her collective and individual expression of a thought. Briefly, her poetry of subjective liberation is as interesting as thought and verse, as her collective expression of the same passion is puerile.

suffice to make a winter; and, for the most part, the technicolour sets and buskined Byronic melodrama prevail.

I know, of course, that psychologically, nothing is easier to excuse than Gondal. The game began as a 'teen-age diversion, soon growing into a mode of escape that held its founders to it right through their adulthood. But, then, I am not concerned with causes, but with their effects—their poetic effects. And of late years so much attention has been given to Gondal research that we are tending to see the poems through it, or to see the many first-rate poems in the light of other often worthless compositions that have recently been discovered and edited. Emily's poetic opus has been found to be nearly five times larger than was originally thought.[8] But in finding further poems, we have tended to lose sight of the original poet. I have therefore stressed the necessity of 'de-Gondalising' Emily's verse in order to come at what is of value. In the same way, I think it important for us to 'de-Byronise' the poet in Emily; since I believe that she found in Byron's work no real clue to her own personality nor to her vocation as an artist. If ever there was an example of a poet taking to himself the artistic personality of another poet, and then proceeding to speak out of that ersatz-personality, such an example was Emily. That its effects were not so far-reaching as to destroy the possibility of any truly original expression is something for which we must be thankful.

Perhaps I incline to over-estimate the danger. Perhaps Emily's personality was such that portions and aspects of her thought must always have retained their integrity intact against the seduction of any poet. None the less, there can be no denying that the poems of Emily which evince a Byronic influence show a high mortality-rate.[9] There is hardly one of them we should call a good poem.

But Emily, in her role as poet, possessed—besides her own personality—other resistants to the Byronic epidemic. These

[8] During Emily's life, and immediately after her death, (in the volume that Charlotte published) forty poems were printed. C. W. Hatfield prints one-hundred and ninety-three, complete or in fragments.

[9] In another chapter I shall be examining the repercussion of Emily's Byronic fantasy upon her novel, *Wuthering Heights*.

were her readings of the works of other poets, certain of whose qualities she assimilated into her own poetry. This assimilation was a more subtle matter than the influence of Byron upon her. It is harder to discover its traces in her work than the bare and lurid foot-prints of Byron. Sometimes, we may hazard, this reading of the poets did not percolate through to show in her verse, but merely served as counter-forces which prevented the attraction for Byron having its own way entirely with her poems.

And which were the poets that Emily read? This is a subject very little studied, in any but a most cursory fashion. We know some of the titles of books read by the Brontës from letters that Charlotte wrote to friends. A list of the books that were present on the shelves of the Keighley Mechanics' Institute (to which the Brontës regularly resorted) is another addition to our knowledge. But which books Emily, or the others, borrowed from the Institute we generally do not know; nor do we know what other books they were able to obtain, by loan or purchase. And then, to read a book is one thing: to make it a part of one's sensibility, so that its essence can be reproduced in the work one writes, is quite another. And of this positive influence of reading very little has been made (except by special pleaders).[10]

Muriel Spark, in her edition of Emily's poems, reckons the influences principally seven: the Border Balladists, Cowper, Burns, Wordsworth, Byron, Scott, and the seventeenth-century lyricists. *Douglas's Ride,* she thinks, owes a deal to Cowper's *John Gilpin* and possibly *Tam O'Shanter,* but remarks that it is "so technically and suggestively indebted to the earlier forms, even in its conventional fireside opening, that it is, in fact, an excellent piece of ballad *pastiche*". Again, of the ballad influence, she writes:

"It would be difficult to believe that the author of the lines,

[10] Mrs. Humphrey Ward's theory, for example, that *Wuthering Heights* derives from the *Tales of Hoffman,* or the more fanciful notion of Malham-Dembleby that *Wuthering Heights* was written by Charlotte, largely influenced by a work entitled *Gleanings in Craven, or The Tourists' Guide,* whose author was one Frederic Montagu.

> Is he upon some distant shore
> Or is he on the sea
> Or is the heart thou dost adore
> A faithless heart to thee?

> or of *Douglas's Ride,* was not acquainted with the border ballads. Scott, whom we know to have been a favourite source of reading in the Brontë household, had done much, with his *Minstrelsy of the Scottish Border,* to revive during the first part of the nineteenth century the interest aroused earlier by *Percy's Reliques.*"

To the "ballad tradition" Muriel Spark also attributes "Emily Brontë's prototypal warriors and defiant female figures", an ascription I do not quite agree with. Emily's figures, it seems to me, differ from those of the border ballads through lacking that authentic touch of nature which the earlier poets generally imparted. Or say, they are rather ballad figures which have lost the human touch by coming to us via the artificial heat of Byron's Gothic conservatory.

Further evidence of the ballad influence is to be seen in the poem, "The night was dark yet winter breathed". The first stanza does not show the marks of the ballad style clearly, if at all, and the ballad touch and atmosphere seems to fluctuate throughout the poem. Unlike *Douglas's Ride,* it cannot be considered as a ballad exercise or *pastiche,* since the poem possesses no over-all style. But in the sixth and seventh stanzas, the ballad spirit seems to take command, with an influx of assonance, internal rhyme, effective archaism, and a pervasive sense of magic:

> It was about the middle night,
> And under such a starless dome
> When, gliding from the mountain's height,
> I saw a shadowy spirit come.
>
> Her wavy hair, on her shoulders bare,
> It shone like soft clouds round the moon;
> Her noiseless feet, like melting sleet,
> Gleamed white a moment, then were gone.

There is possibly the influence of Coleridge here as well.

The reaction of Wordsworth on Emily's verse is probably the next in order of importance after that of Byron and the Balladists. One example of this which Muriel Spark gives is Emily's line, "The violet's eye might shyly flash", which—as she says—suggests the Lakeland poet's precision. Other instances of close observation, occasionally among the minutiæ of nature, are to be found in such lines as these:

> The damp stands in the long, green grass
> As thick as morning's tears.

and

> Only some spires of bright green grass
> Transparently in sunshine quivering.

and

> How sweet it is to watch the mist
> From that bright silent lake ascend,
> And high o'er wood and mountain crest
> With heaven's grey clouds as greyly blend.

and

> The blue ice curdling on the stream.

Much of this may be attributed to Wordsworth, but Crabbe and Cowper are by no means without the image-detecting eye.

Another factor in Emily's culture that may have exercised her optic sense was her prosecution of the study of drawing and painting under Charlotte's tutelage.[11] Charlotte, in this art, as we know, was particularly given to the detailisation of natural objects correctly copied, and Emily may have learned to look at things partly in this close descriptive manner.

But whatever training in visual perception Emily received from Cowper and Crabbe would probably be small in comparison with what Wordsworth offered her—for in his poetry Emily found not only a clue to exact observation, but also an imaginative doctrine of nature. Just how far Emily's own thought was derived from, or related to, Wordsworth are questions I reserve for a future chapter. But that there are traces of Wordsworth's beliefs, sometimes in a crude,

[11] A habit no doubt accentuated by Charlotte's painful short-sightedness.

undigested state, to be uncovered in Emily's poems is a fact we can easily verify. Here is one passage in which she combines Wordsworth's faith in nature as the sovereign remedy along with the ideas that inform his *Ode on Intimations of Immortality*. One may catch, too, in the third and fourth lines the rhythm of Wordsworth's last line in his sonnet on *Westminster Bridge* ("And all that mighty heart is lying still"):

> Is it not that the sunshine and the wind
> Lure from itself the mourner's woe-worn mind;
> And all the joyous music breathing by,
> And all the splendour of that cloudless sky,
> Re-give him shadowy gleams of infancy,
> And draw his tired gaze from futurity.

The flat side of Wordsworth, which partly resulted from his self-enforced simplicity, is also at times to be found in Emily's verse. George Darley—a poet deriving from Shelley—used to speak slightingly of the Lakeland author's *"Simpletonian system"*—all "Go-carts and Girandolas". The following poem by Emily would certainly justify Darley in his statement that Wordsworth had a bad effect upon young authors. But if it is flat, jejune, and banal, at least it lacks the ridiculousness of Emily's strident Byronic pose. Sheep buried by snow-drifts, peasants, and moorlands were items in Emily's everyday: adulterous princesses and dungeons were not.

> It was night, and on the mountains
> Fathoms deep the snow-drifts lay;
> Streams and waterfalls and fountains
> Down in darkness stole away.
>
> Long ago the hopeless peasant
> Left his sheep all buried there:
> Sheep that through the summer pleasant
> He had watched with fondest care.
>
> Now no more a cheerful ranger
> Following pathways known of yore,
> Sad he stood a wildered stranger
> On his own unbounded moor.

Muriel Spark discovers "something of Cowper's handling of the classical couplet . . . eminently suited to narrative" in the poem, "And now the house-dog stretched once more"; but beyond this, and her already-mentioned suggestion of *John Gilpin* in *Douglas's Ride,* I detect little of Cowper's influence. Much as his verse was in favour with her Evangelical sister Anne, one feels that the poet of *The Sofa* was too sedentary and social for Emily, the ambulatory and aloof.

A further debt to Scott that Muriel Spark remarks on is "the Marmionesque sense of chivalry, the recognition of family loyalties which take precedence over private friendships" in *Come, the Wind may never again,* a poem "reminiscent of Scott's tenor of thought".

With Muriel Spark's opinion that Emily's verse was also influenced by the seventeenth-century poets, I find it hazardous to agree. Lamb, Hazlitt, and Coleridge had already done much to recreate a taste for Elizabethan, Jacobean, and Caroline poetry. But whether such a fashion had caught on outside the ranks of the epigoni is rather doubtful. Anthologies of such poetry (of the lyrics even more than of the dramas) were by no means plentiful or easy to come by, and I find no record of such books in the library of the Keighley Mechanics' Institute. But, of course, this does not constitute positive evidence against her having read them. Emily might have come across such works elsewhere; and at least she would be acquainted with the lyrics contained in Shakespeare's plays. And in defence of Muriel Spark's contention, it must be admitted that the lines she quotes,

> Fall, leaves, fall; die, flowers, away
> Lengthen night and shorten day

do most undeniably echo the seventeenth century.

Perhaps it was a case of "music in the air"—a prevailing mood or kinship of mind which made it possible for Emily to echo the verse of certain poets she had never read. In much the same way, she might have been able to anticipate poets who had not as yet written. "Why do I hate that lone green dell" (dated 1838) seems to look forward to Tennyson's *Maud* (written ten years later); and such repetitive effects as we find in the fragment, "All hushed and still within the house", and such funereal suggestive lines as these from the fragment, *Old Hall of Elbë,*

> House to which the voice of life shall never more return;
> Chambers roofless, desolate, where weeds and ivy grow

seem to achieve what Poe was achieving, largely unknown to the English public, on the other side of the Atlantic.

But, here, we tread much on the ground of conjecture—a fascinating but uncertain soil. What I, for my part, find more significant, is that in Emily's best poems—her half-dozen pieces which must be classed as major poems of the English language (such compositions as "There let thy bleeding branch atone", "Cold in the earth, and the deep snow piled above thee!", "Death that struck when I was most confiding", and "No coward soul is mine"), she speaks in so assimilated a style that any foreign influences seen fused together in it, presenting an accent, a rhythm, thought, and diction, peculiarly and personally her own.

This is not to belittle the notion that Emily, largely unconsciously, employed herself as a poet within the currents of poetical tradition. For every poet who ever develops a verbal sensibility of value, the written word must always mean much; and the idea of Emily as a cultureless recluse, writing solely out of a *farouche* imagination certainly needed counteracting. But if the sound poet stands in need of the written word for nourishment in his time of growth, a certain type of romantic poet seems to dispense with this criterion in the most personal moments of his work. Instead of adding, say one new element, to a given number of poetic characteristics (which is what the classical poet does), he smelts down all his inheritance, his literary acquisitions from around him and the past, and creates a poem that appears new throughout.

Such a poet I take Emily to have been.

4

THE POEMS

The Background Theme

So far, in this book, I have been led to act as counsel for the the prosecution. To be able, at this point, largely to take over the role of counsel for the defence is something which affords me a sense of relief; a relief in which the reader may possibly participate. Of course, the part of *enfant terrible* guarantees to its performer a limited amusement. But to carry it off successfully requires an absence of that objective vision which the critic cultivates and prizes above all. With my own conservative inclinations, I admit to a feeling of pleasant security in returning to fields of consideration where I can once again affirm. It is, then, from this vantage-point that I would ask the reader to look back on what is written, regarding it not as a work of destruction but as a preliminary task of spring-cleaning.

What I should next like to attempt is a general survey of Emily's poetry: a quick delineation of its various aspects—its characteristic styles and structures, its diction, interests, and themes. This cross-sectional presentation will prepare the way for our concentrating on Emily's totally fulfilling achievement—her half-dozen major pieces. Consideration of these poems, however, must wait its turn in some future chapter. By first taking her other compositions, I shall later hope to show how their motifs and 'directions' were utterly attained in her six great successes; and how this body of—for the main part—good or interesting minor verse was spiritually related to her consummating poems. By this method, I believe, the single-mindedness of Emily's poetic vocation will become more abundantly clear, and the monuments she raised to it more bathed in meaning.

Before the Gondal research caught on, with Clement Shorter's edition of Emily's poems way back in 1910, Emily was taken for a nature poet; and, as late as 1926, Sir Herbert Read had written that her poems show "the most intense rendering of the embodied presence of nature that anywhere exists in English literature".

If by nature poet, we mean a writer whose thoughts and feelings are enacted against a natural background (which, in turn, is evoked in the poem) then the ascription defines her field of working. But with the exhumation of the Gondal corpse, an inferior body of verse was brought to light. The background to these poems was often artificial—life in exotic palaces and cities or on tropical islands unmentioned on the map. This fictitious background was the more unconvincing in that Emily, by her own experience, had never come across anything *like* it. But along with the fake exotic drop-scenes, the Gondal poems also resorted, for some of their incidents and adventures, to natural backgrounds which were based on the natural scenes round Haworth that Emily knew.[1] The fact that of the Gondal poems which employ natural scenery as their background, those which resort to descriptions of nature that tally with nature about Haworth are best, whilst those which employ an exotic scenery foreign to Emily are the worst, is a proof of the degree in which Emily's thought found in nature a starting-point.

But if by the term 'nature-poet', one were to imply the kind of writer whose work is 'all about nature', then Emily must not be made to wear the cap. For unlike Clare, she does not give us a *catalogue raisonné* of natural life and objects. Her verse is not a kind of illustrated calendar, a metrical almanac of the seasons. I say 'unlike Clare', because the body of his work provides us with descriptive poetry; but I might have written 'like Clare at his greatest', for at his greatest Clare is not a depictive poet writing about nature, but an intensely subjective poet, expressing himself against a natural background.

[1] In this survey I do not distinguish between any Gondal or non-Gondal poems. Those Gondal pieces written in the Byronic mode (and which I do not reckon to be 'good or interesting minor verse') I shall proceed to ignore.

In Emily, we must not look to find the mind turned outwards, scrutinising nature as the chief substance of its thought, as we do in so many of Clare's descriptive sonnets, which offer us detailed inventories of nature. There is nothing in Emily's verse quite so consistently physical—so located in a series of actual objects—as in Clare's poem ***An Autumn Morning***:

> The autumn morning, waked by many a gun,
> Throws o'er the fields her many-coloured light,
> Wood wildly touched, close tanned, and stubbles dun,
> A motley paradise for earth's delight;
> Clouds ripple as the darkness breaks to light,
> And clover plots are hid with silver mist,
> One shower of cobwebs o'er the surface spread;
> And threads of silk in strange disorder twist
> Round every leaf and blossom's bottly head;
> Hares in the drowning herbage scarcely steal
> But on the battered pathway squat abed
> And by the cart-rut nip their morning meal.
> Look where we may, the scene is strange and new,
> And every object wears a changing hue.

Yet, even so, Emily does convey the sense of some specific region, an idea of the moorlands amongst which she lived.

> "At times", wrote Arthur Symons in 1906, "the landscape in this bare, grey, craggy verse, always a landscape of Yorkshire moors, with its touches of stern and tender memory, 'The mute bird sitting on the stone', 'A little and a lone green lane' has a quality more thrilling than that of Wordsworth. There is none of his observation, and none of his sense of a benignant 'presence far more deeply interfused'. At first this unornamented verse may seem forbidding, may seem even to be ordinary, as an actual moorland may, to those for whom it has no special attraction. But in the verse, as on the moors, there is space, wind, and the smell of earth; and there is room to be alone."

Leaving aside such a question as the comparison with Wordsworth, this passage of Arthur Symons does give us an indication of the *kind* of topography we shall find in Emily's poems. There *is* a sense of regionality here; a sense of the

West Riding of Yorkshire; but it is not the West Riding of a cartographer or a botanist. Instead, it is a highly condensed, personal, and symbolic topography—a sort of psychic Yorkshire we discover.

By this, I mean that Emily's poems are not store-houses of local observation; are not careful transcripts of the countryside around her; but poems concerned with 'eternal verities' apprehended against a Yorkshire background.

None the less, it is truly surprising how Emily creates a feeling for her district with the barest minimum of located copied objects. Phyllis Bentley, in her monograph *The Brontë Sisters,* senses this well when she writes:

> "There are two elements in Emily's poetry whose fusion provides its special personal quality: the local and the universal. Her descriptions of her beloved moorlands have not merely a vivid pictorial but a profound emotional effect. Such lines as
>
> Where the grey flocks in ferny glens are feeding,
> Where the wild wind blows on the mountain side.
>
> or
>
> . . . in the red fire's cheerful glow
> I think of deep glens, blocked with snow;
> I dream of moor, and misty hill,
> Where evening closes dark and chill . . .
>
> evoke in the heart of those who love the moors a deep nostalgic emotion."

And again, in her book *The Brontës,* when she writes of Emily's means to this effect:

> "Her musings and her descriptions are alike expressed in grave, austere but singularly potent language. Her lines have no bright blossoms of metaphor or simile, and little glitter of epithet; they achieve, however, a wonderful verbal heather-bloom by the never-failing simplicity, strength and exactness of their expressions. Here and there a sudden choice unexpected word—unexpected but recognised when read as inevitable in its stern piercing aptness—gives a patch of brighter purple."

The secret of Emily's symbolic regionalism is, then, to be found in her combination of the local and the 'universal'; of what is singular or unique to one specific countryside, and what is common in nature to all men. Thus, along with the heather, the sheep-tracks, and the moors, she gives us a powerful impression of the more catholic side of nature: the wind, the stars, the sunlight, and the moon. Another of the ways in which she succeeds in her art of evocative impression is, by never settling down to document the natural objects which she mentions. She gives them, states them, almost casually, but with a potent short-hand of suggestion, and then passes on to other matters: to her own feelings, or those of the Gondals whose emotions and adventures are so often featured.

This we can check by taking many a poem and examining the swift transitions of its reference. *A Farewell to Alexandria* begins with a subjective impression of almost 'universalised' nature:

> I've seen this dell in July's shine
> As lovely as an angel's dream;
> Above, heaven's depth of blue divine;
> Around, the evening's golden beam.

This verse might apply to recollections of summer in almost any region of the temperate zone. There is nothing that fastens it to one rustic region; no tell-tale adjectives, no nouns that 'belong'. All words here carry with them the vaguest and widest reference. "Dell", "July", "heaven", "evening" are not to be appropriated to any portion of the map. And the large and unlocalised impression is heightened (or should we say, even more diffused) by the quite common-place simile which possesses, none the less, an exclamatory brightness: "As lovely as an angel's dream." Everything here is geographically unidentified and larger than life. The sky is clear and empty of clouds or horizon; the evening, in its ample radiance of gold, settles down on a country without maps or signposts. In all, we feel the sense of "space" which Arthur Symons spoke of; we receive the impression "there is room to be alone"

But in the next stanza Emily passes from the 'universal' to the local, from an unfocussed scene to a Yorkshire of the spirit, in one easy unpremeditated step:

> I've seen the purple heather-bell
> Look out by many a storm-worn stone;
> And oh, I've seen such music swell,
> Such wild notes wake these passes lone—

Immediately the picture forms distinct within us. Our impression is not like that which we obtain from looking at a topographical print. It is not an impression which results from perceiving a sum of small details, but rather an impression whose power over us works through one or two salient symbols. The "purple heather-bell" and the "storm-worn stone" are more evocative in their lonely content, in their unembroidered place in the poem, than would be some dozen minutiæ. As they stand in this stanza, they are merely the unadorned names of natural objects, the barest descriptions of things we might see in that vicinity of which Emily writes; and yet, so well chosen are these objects, that without any verbal ingeniousness, they become the symbols of regionality—essences of the spirit of place.

I have said that in their presentation, we find no verbal ingeniousness, but my statement needs to be qualified.

Ingeniousness, in the sense of intricacy, is not to be located here. But ingeniousness as a process of reduction, rather than one of skilful addition, has certainly played a part in the choice of epithet. "The purple heather-bell" and the "storm-worn stone" are triumphs of instinctive selection. They are both the picture which Yorkshire paints and the signature Yorkshire attaches to that picture. No swifter, more economical way of suggesting a locality could possibly be employed; and it is possible that Emily learnt much of this brevity of descriptive brush-work from the example of the ballads. But in the ballads this brevity is principally used for dramatic reasons or in order to suggest a point of character. Emily, alone of the nineteenth-century poets, seems to have used it for landscape purposes.

But in speaking of the brevity of Emily's epithets, I may have given the impression of slightness incommensurate with solidness or weight. Yet there is nothing one-dimensional, ghost-like, or meagre about them at all. Their brevity is tremendously compact, without any literary straining for effect. "Purple" in conjunction with "heather-bell" is so obvious that we may incline to discount it. But the adjective "purple" in combination with the double-barrelled noun "heather-bell" creates a unit of descriptive language which is both tight and right and dense. The impression is firm, yet entirely unaffected. The same (only more so) may be said of the "storm-worn stone" in the following line. Here it is the adjective which is double-barrelled, and the noun (which dense enough already) is single. But additional weight and precision of impression is given to the image, in that it is not "the storm-worn stone" but "many a storm-worn stone". The increase in response to this extension of the epithet may be seen to reside in the concatenation of like consonants: the 'ms' and 'ns' repeated throughout the phrase, and the switch in vowel sounds from 'a' to 'o'.

A further strengthening of the effect results from the way in which the image in the first line is indissolubly joined to that in the second. "Heather-bell" and "stone" are not disparate objects, but are linked in the relation of cause to each other, since the heather-bell is rooted in the stone or in the soil contained in its crevice or at its base. Neither is the relationship merely adumbrated, but is actually portrayed by the choice of verb, which is vividly and colloquially intransitive: "*Look out* by many a storm-worn stone".

> I've seen the purple heather-bell
> Look out by many a storm-worn stone.

Each part of this impression is right and perfect, but the parts are greater when subsumed within a whole.

The concreteness of things established by Emily in the first two lines of this stanza, she goes on in the next to evoke an effect by subjective rather than objective terms:

And oh, I've seen such music swell,
Such wild notes wake these passes lone—

Here, the tone is emotional: feeling is substituted for seeing. Note the two counters of sentiment, "wild" and "lone", and the exclamation "oh", as well as the tremulous throbbing verb, "swell". I have said that in these two lines feeling is substituted for seeing, and yet we are faced with the statement: "And oh, I've *seen* such music swell." "Seen", of course, in this context, is not quite an objectively descriptive term. Music cannot be seen: only the movement of its passage (when it is the music of the wind) can be perceived by the eye. And then, again, there is the suggestion that in having "seen" the "music swell", more is to be understood than a verbal description of the wind's visual passage: the feelings which the wind woke have, too, been apprehended, by an act which has almost made them visible.

But scenery, stated or suggested, is never Emily's foremost business. She does not elaborate upon these symbols—these potent compressed ciphers of place—which she throws out in the course of her poems, but hurries on to the main affair; in this instance, to relating how a mother abandons her child in the snow. For the next four stanzas, there are no topographical references, save a passing mention of "the green heath-sward". Apart from that, the language is subjective and emotional; or, when it speaks objectively of nature, speaks of it in a non-specific fashion, after the manner of the first stanza:

So soft, yet so intensely felt,
So low, yet so distinctly heard,
My breath would pause, my eyes would melt,
And my tears dew the green heath-sward.

I'd linger here a summer day,
Nor care how fast the hours flew by,
Nor mark the sun's departing ray
Smile sadly glorious from the sky.

Then, then I might have laid thee down
And deemed thy sleep would gentle be;
I might have left thee, darling one,
And thought thy God was guarding thee!

But now there is no wandering glow,
No gleam to say that God is nigh;
And coldly spreads thy couch of snow,
And harshly sounds thy lullaby.

Then, suddenly, eruptively, in the first two lines of the seventh stanza, the concrete local touch is back, only to depart again, without reappearance in the poem:

Forests of heather, dark and long,
Wave their brown, branching arms above,[2]
And they must soothe thee with their song,
And they must shield my child of love.

This, it would seem, is the way Emily worked, as reference to her other poems bears out. Nature—if we distinguish it as the special characteristics of a certain region—is only used by Emily for background purposes. So, in the following poem, the scene is set by the first four lines:

The linnet in the rocky dells,
The moor-lark in the air,
The bee among the heather-bells
That hide my lady fair:

But this background purpose does not preclude the use of emotional tones in speaking of natural forces and objects. Nature is not limited here to being an impersonal and unresponsive frame-work. Rather do we often receive the feeling that from this sympathetic background reverberations pass to the foreground of the poem. To show my meaning I will print the piece from which I have quoted entire:

The linnet in the rocky dells,
The moor-lark in the air,
The bee among the heather-bells
That hide my lady fair:

The wild deer browse above her breast;
The wild birds raise their brood;
And they, her smiles of love caressed,
Have left her solitude!

I ween, that when the grave's dark wall
Did first her form retain,
They thought their hearts could ne'er recall
The light of joy again.

[2] my italics.

They thought the tide of grief would flow
Unchecked through future years,
But where is all their anguish now,
And where are all their tears?

Well, let them fight for Honour's breath,
Or Pleasure's shade pursue—
The Dweller in the land of Death
Is changed and careless too.

And if their eyes should watch and weep
Till sorrow's source were dry,
She would not, in her tranquil sleep,
Return a single sigh.

Blow, west wind, by the lonely mound,
And murmer, summer streams,
There is no need of other sound
To soothe my Lady's dreams.

The last stanza, unlike the first, is entirely devoid of local colour; and yet, we observe how it seems to hark back and heighten our first impression of the scene. Part of this effect, I think, must be explained by the powerful and evocative image of "the lonely mound", which, without being a topographical figure like the "moor-lark", "the linnets", or "the heather-bells", conveys, as these do, a sense of space, of uninhabited solitary freedom. "The lonely mound", we can say, is an archetypal image of 'universal' nature, in just the same way that the "heather-bells" and "linnets" are archetypal images of a regional nature. A burial hummock (though the work of man) is as timeless and catholic a feature of landscape, as the moor-lark and heather-bells are timeless and specific. In terms of time and space, both, respectively, are archetypal.

Sometimes, as in the poem *My Comforter,* a process of nature that carries with it the hint of topographical colouring is made to serve as a metaphor for some inward force in Emily's own mind. Thus, the element of inspiration, and the place it played in Emily's life, outwardly so bleak and cheerless, is compared to a mild current of air thawing out some winter landscape:

Like a soft air above a sea
Tossed by the tempests' stir—
A thaw-wind melting quietly
The snow-drift on some wintery lea;
No—what sweet thing can match with thee,
My thoughtful Comforter?

So far, I have tried to distinguish between the imagery of 'universal' nature and regional nature in Emily's poems. I think this distinction valuable in theory, valuable as a working hypothesis, because it helps to explain the wide appeal which a purely local poet cannot depend on, and which Emily certainly achieves. But as one examines more and more of her poems, one sees how the regional and the 'universal' are blended and all-but lose separate identity. Yet still, in such instances, the regional—however minimised—seems to retain some final quintessence, and impart to the poem its own northern colour. For example, in the following poem, there is only one distinct topographical feature—the image of a "heathy sea"—and yet from its presence there emanates back, through the whole eight lines, a Yorkshire atmosphere:

The sun has set, and the long grass now
Waves drearily in the evening wind;
And the wild bird has flown from that old grey stone,
In some warm nook a couch to find.

In all the lonely landscape round
I see no sight and hear no sound,
Except the wind that far away
Comes sighing o'er the heathy sea.

In much the same way, in a poem entitled *Song by Julius Brenzaida to G.S.*, we cannot help but see the landscape through a veil of Yorkshire associations:

Wild the road and rough and dreary;
Barren all the moorland round;
Rude the couch that rests us weary;
Mossy stone and heathy ground.

But, when winter storms were meeting
In the moonless, midnight dome,
Did we heed the tempest's beating,
Howling round our spirits' home?

No; that tree with branches riven,
Whitening in the whirl of snow,
As it tossed against the heaven,
Sheltered happy hearts below—

Factually, there is nothing peculiar to Haworth and its countryside about "that tree with branches riven, / Whitening in the whirl of snow"; and yet the image, even more than the reference to heath and moorland in the first stanza quoted, seems redolent of Emily's region. The same may be said to hold good for two lines in a second poem by the same name:

The wild moorside, the winter morn,
The gnarled and ancient tree.

Such phenomena as these are not confined to Yorkshire; and yet it is in this context that we read them.

The answer, I think, is that very largely the Yorkshire of Emily's poetry is a quintessential Yorkshire; a Yorkshire of the inward eye. We notice that most of the images examined, whether specifically regional or not, have carried with them a northern suggestion—a tone of bleakness, vastness, and cold. And it is just this telling reduction to aspects and features which finally count, which finally decide the nature of a landscape, that makes Emily so evocative a poet in this field.

In his book *Reason and Romanticism,* Sir Herbert Read, writing on his country-woman Emily, has well explained her æsthetic of the moors.

"The question", he tells us, "of the immediate influence of natural scenes differs from this general evocation of the spirit of nature. There is about the moors of Yorkshire, where they yet remain, a quality that works on the mobile senses. Their sparseness and loneliness drive you to an intimacy with whatever life does exist there; a small thing like the scent of bog myrtle can kindle a strong emotion. There is a severity in the unrelieved reach of gradual hill country; the eye drifts into distant prospects, seeks the sky-line that is not a line, but a subtle merging of tones; the human mind *is* perhaps heard more distinctly in this inorganic stillness—only when, however, it has learned to think, and to express its thoughts. The moors, like any other local endowment, are merely material for observation and perception, and if into their confines there happens to enter a mind of exceptional dimensions, this mind will use its environment to some purpose. Such was the case with Emily Brontë."

But something more than this may be said, I believe, about the way in which Emily condenses and essentialises natural scenery; and this has been said (though not with reference to her) by Arthur Symons, in the Introduction to his book *The Romantic Movement in English Poetry.*

"The quality", writes Symons, "which distinguishes the poetry of the beginning of the nineteenth century, the poetry which we can roughly group together as the romantic movement, is the quality of its imagination, and this quality is seen chiefly as a kind of atmosphere, which adds strangeness to beauty. What is it in the atmosphere of an English landscape that seems at once to reveal and, in a sense, to explain that imaginative atmosphere which distinguishes the finest English poetry, and, in a special sense, the poetry of the nineteenth century, from almost all the fine poetry of the world? I was walking one afternoon along one of the slopes of Hampstead Heath, just above the Vale of Health, and I saw close beside me a line of naked autumn trees, every twig brown and separate: a definite, solid thing, beautiful in structure, sober and admirable in colour, just such branches as one would see in any clear country, where everything is distinctly visible, in Italy or in Spain. But, at some distance, on the higher edge of the heath, against the sky, there was another line of naked trees, and over their whole outline there was a soft, not quite transparent, veil of mist, like the down on fruit: you saw them and the general lines of their structure, but you saw them under a more exquisite aspect, like an image seen in a cloudy mirror. Nothing that was essential in their reality was lost, but they were no longer the naked, real thing; nature had transformed them, as art transforms nature."

This account of the manner in which English poets incline to a modified naturalism applies particularly well to Emily. "Nothing", we may say, adapting Symons' words to describe the Yorkshire images in Emily's poems, "nothing that was essential in their reality was lost, but they were no longer the naked, real thing; the mind had *condensed* them, as art *condenses* nature."

Hitherto, in this chapter, I have been employing the word 'nature' to signify landscape. In the next chapter I have to consider it as implying the sum of elemental forces, or of the separate workings of the same with reference to some universal law or plan.

As a lead-in to this consideration, I return to my earlier distinction of the regional and the 'universal' in Emily's portrayal of natural scenery. By the power of the first she became the curt descriptive poet we have seen her to be: by the power of the second, she was led to ponder the significance behind the appearance of things, the causal relationship between the diversity and recurrence of phenomena and the "eternal verities" as she construed them.

THE POEMS

The Foreground Thought

In her Introduction to Emily's poems, Muriel Spark has observed that "the metaphysical lyric achieved in her its most important development since Shelley".[1] The remark is pertinent and its terms are precise, since Emily is often spoken of as a mystical poet but seldom referred to as metaphysical. And yet she is more often to be seen as a metaphysical writer, engaged in examining the nature of things, than as a mystic affirming the presence of a revealed beatific reality.

The hesitation of past critics in describing Emily as metaphysically-minded has probably rested in the limited understanding of the key-term. The fact that metaphysical processes of mind are often as intuitive as the poetic, and that between them there needs be no clear discrepancy, was a point the nineteenth century hardly comprehended. It is true that Wordsworth, Coleridge, and Shelley, in their own verse and theorising, apprehended the organic nature of thought; but their understanding was a rare exception. Keats, certainly, was for long unable to reconcile the claims of the poetic and the metaphysical within him, and realise the two demands as one. In his inability to solve this issue, it is possible his own poetic progress was impeded; and the century as a whole, even more than Keats, failed to understand that metaphysical thinking could be an intuitive, as distinct from a ratiocinative, process. This academic fallacy led to a vogue for reflective poetry rather than for metaphysical verse. Tennyson is often reflective; indeed, sometimes most ponderously so; but metaphysical almost never. The kind of 'musings' which we associate with the late eighteenth-century 'Gothic' poets (Blair, Thomson, etc.) and with the reflective strain in Tennyson

1 One of the few critical statements which substantiates Muriel Spark's remark is that of Sir Herbert Read, who—in his book *Reason and Romanticism* (1926)—says of Emily: "Her absorption in metaphysical problems has no parallel in the poetry of her age."

differs from Emily's reflective thought as much by degree of intensity as by any other matter. Emily's metaphysical process is what we may call high-pressure thought, or "felt thought" as Sir Herbert Read terms it: the thought of these other poets is a more low-pressure affair. It is not, as with Emily, thought interfused with emotion; but thought mildly coloured by reflective sentiments upon the nature of existence and the absolute.

Sir Herbert Read, in his essay on *The Nature of Metaphysical Poetry,* has an image that helps us to make this difference plainer. Speaking of metaphysical poetry, he says that as an illustration "we might represent thought and emotion as two separately revolving pulleys: one, emotion, has a revolution a thousand times greater than the other; but by the operation of a lever the two pulleys are connected, and immediately thought is accelerated to the speed or intensity of emotion".

The same, we may say, holds good of reflective poetry, but here—in place of the pulley of emotion—we have the pulley of sentiment whose revolution is five hundred times lower, though still five-hundred times greater than that of thought.

Emily's poetry, in its metaphysical aspect, represents—to resort to the same eminent critic—"the emotional apprehension of thought"; and if it had not for so long been assumed that metaphysical poetry was the writing of metaphysics in verse—the application of the laws of metre to the contents of an academic body of knowledge—the thought in Emily's poetry would sooner have been recognised for what it was.

But these are only preparatory remarks. In a later chapter we shall be comparing Emily's metaphysical verse with that of other metaphysical poets. Here, the purpose of these introductory statements is to help us to distinguish the presence of a metaphysical element in Emily's poems, as well as the presence of the mystical with which it is too often confounded, and beneath which heading too generally subsumed.

In this present chapter we shall consider the various currents of thought which Emily entertained in her verse. These are, basically, four: stoicism, pantheism, Christianity, and a form of personal quietism; though each of these, in turn, can be divided into other dependent sections and themes. A further complication here is that in some of these poems the metaphysical and mystical are blended, while others provide us with an example of what I would call the metaphysics of mysticism. Emily's chief accomplishment, however, in the writing of mystical poetry is to be found in the six great major poems which will be examined later. For the rest, the distinction I shall observe is one that describes as mystical those poems concerned with revelation, and metaphysical those concerned with establishing the nature of first principles.

Stoicism, as applying to one aspect of Emily's complex of thought, is to be taken here in the popular rather than the academic sense. By it, in this context, then, I imply a culture of self-endurance, an exercise in training oneself how to take things, rather than any consistent doctrine deriving from the school of Zeno. It is true that the Keighley Mechanics' Institute contained a copy of Seneca's *Morals*, but Seneca was something of a populariser; and, in any case, there seems to be no knowing whether Emily ever took this volume out.

Of course, the popular conception of stoicism and that entertained by its philosophic schools are not without their points of rapport. Emily's poem *The Old Stoic* gives us an image to work on, which might have borrowed much from both hearsay and learning:

Riches I hold in light esteem
And Love I laugh to scorn
And lust of Fame was but a dream
That vanished with the morn—

And if I pray, the only prayer
That moves my lips for me
Is—"Leave the heart that now I bear
And give me liberty."

Yes, as my swift days near their goal
'Tis all that I implore—
Through life and death, a chainless soul
With courage to endure!

In this poem, there is the suggestion of more than the quality of self-dependence which hall-marks the stoic in popular thought. Beyond asking for sufficiency of will, the strength which makes one independent of hardship—

Through life and death, a chainless soul
With courage to endure!"

the poet insists on other virtues which the philosophic stoics of the schools recommended. 'Riches',[2] 'fame', and 'love' are illusions, and the only desirable condition is freedom to achieve that autonomy of self which looks to others neither to provide its good nor as a protection against the bad.[3] But about the stanza which advances this principle there seems to be a certain ambiguity.

Is "Leave the heart that now I bear/And give me liberty", addressed to "the only prayer" in its passage from the speaker's lips, implying in other words a desire to be free of all external religious formulations; or is it a wish to be free of life itself; an expression, in fact, of the instinct for death?

[2] In his *Epistles to Lucilius* Seneca writes thus *On the Contempt of Riches*: "*But you desire not*, you say, *rich beds trimmed with gold or furniture adorned with jewels.* It may be so; there is no reason you should commend yourself for this: for what virtue is there in condemning such things as are not necessary? Then it is that you may commend yourself, when you can despise even necessaries: it is no great thing that you can live without a noble and royal equipage; that you desire no wild boars of a thousand weight on the side-table; nor a dish of the tongues or red wings, and other prodigies of luxury, that disdains whole animals and only selects the nicer bits.
Then it is that I shall admire you, when you disdain not the coarsest bread; when you are persuaded that herbs and vegetables, in case of necessity, were not provided only for the beasts of the fields, but for the nourishment of man; when you shall know that the young shoots or top twigs of trees can fill the belly; which we now store with so many precious things, as if it were a treasure-house to preserve them."

[3] In the work already quoted Seneca has some pertinent remarks upon that *Happiness* [*which*] *comes from within.* "Never think a man happy", he counsels, "whose happiness is in suspense. He depends on frailty who rejoices in an adventitious good. Such joy will pass away as lightly as it came: but the joy that ariseth from within is faithful, is firm; it continually grows stronger, and holds out to the last. Other things which the vulgar admire are only good for a time. What, then, is there no pleasure or profit in them? Who denies it? But it must be when they depend upon *us*, and not we upon *them*. All things within the power of fortune may thus be made fruitful and pleasant to us, if he that possesseth them is master also of himself, and subjects not himself to his possessions.
For they are mistaken who think that what fortune can give us is either good or bad. She gives us indeed the material part of good and evil; and to her we owe the beginning of those incidents which in the issue may prove either happy or unhappy for us. But the mind is stronger than any fortune; it conducteth its own affairs, right or wrong; and is itself the cause of its own happiness or misery."

There are passages in others of Emily's poems which would substantiate either of these readings. In any case, we know that she often equated liberty both with death and independence. Whatever the stations of thought in this poem, the conclusion is clear and even commonplace. It is the oft-repeated plea for invincible resolution of spirit, a good all stoics have held in common.

But, when all is said and done, stoicism is perhaps an interim philosophy, most suitable to those stone-walling phases in the life of the race or the individual. Certainly it would appear to have been so for Emily, in whom more positive and joyous notes struck their own music from time to time.

What I wish to suggest is that Emily's stoicism expressed that part of her personality when she felt she had her back to the wall. It provided the first, but not the final, answer, to her perception of the world as the arena of fallen human nature. And when she wrote the following stanzas in her poem *How Clear She Shines,* she understood, we feel, just what the single spirit is up against in this mortal existence:

And this shall be my dream to-night—
I'll think the heaven of glorious spheres
Is rolling on its course of light
In endless bliss through endless years;

I'll think there's not one world above,
Far as these straining eyes can see,
Where Wisdom ever laughed at Love,
Or Virtue couched to Infamy;

Where, writhing 'neath the strokes of Fate,
The mangled wretch was forced to smile;
To match his patience 'gainst her hate,
His heart rebellious all the while;

Where Pleasure still will lead to wrong,
And helpless Reason warn in vain;
And Truth is weak and Treachery strong,
And Joy the shortest path to Pain;

And Peace, the lethargy of grief;
And Hope, a Phantom of the soul;
And Life, a labour void and brief;
And Death, the despot of the whole!

Elsewhere, in the same poem, she had written:

The world is going—Dark world, adieu!
Grim world go hide thee till the day;
The heart thou canst not all subdue
Must still resist if thou delay!

Thy love I will not, will not share;
Thy hatred only wakes a smile;
Thy griefs may wound—thy wrongs may tear,
But, oh thy lies shall ne'er beguile.

And in another poem, *To Imagination,* the dichotomy between the ideal and the real, the gulf between what should be and what is, is stated by her with neat antithesis:

So hopeless is the world without,
The world within I doubly prize.

In other minds, such a dual response has sometimes led to the strange combination of idealism and cynicism; an ideal treatment of the things of the spirit and a cynical outlook on worldly matters. Emily did not react in this fashion. Most often her attitude to outward affairs was one of pride and high disdain; but that her own intense inner existence did not blind her to the fact of what human history seems destined to accomplish, or fail to accomplish, is proved by the following poem:

There was a time when my cheek burned
To give such scornful fiends the lie;
Ungoverned nature madly spurned
The law that bade it not defy.
O in the days of ardent youth
I would have given my life for truth.

For truth, for right, for liberty,
I would have gladly, freely died;
And now I calmly hear and see
The vain man smile, the fool deride;
Though not because my heart is tame,
Though not for fear, though not for shame.

My soul still chafes at every tone
Of selfish and self-blinded error;
My breast still braves the world alone,
Steeled as it ever was to terror;
Only I know, however I frown,
The same world will go rolling on.

Here we have the formulation of a position of wise accep tance; mature, reluctant, and sadly knowing. It is not complicity, cynicism, or indifference; but a declaration of acceptance and endurance; an acceptance which is not acquiescence, and which does not preclude resistance; an acceptance which is merely a form of knowledge—a correct estimation of the general tenor and limitation of hum-drum humanity. But this acceptance does not exclude the aspirational urge which, here, comes out in the inward friction, the inward kicking against the pricks of crassness and injustice which Emily expresses:

My soul still chafes at every tone
Of selfish and self-blinded error;
My breast still braves the world alone,
Steeled as it ever was to terror.

But this comparative mildness in Emily is only heard when she considers what she can anticipate on behalf of the world. She recognises the fact that, collectively speaking, mankind will somehow jog along in the same moral rut as it has run in for centuries and centuries. But her haughty lenience with regard to a humanity, which numerically would appear to be damned, is very different to the attitude she adopts towards herself. Others may backslide if they will, she tells us, and seems to have no doubt that they will do so; but, for herself, the end she holds in view is one of

The long fight closing in defeat—
Defeat serenely borne—

And in this same poem, she reflects on how she must learn to face death:

Look on the grave where thou must sleep,
Thy last and strongest foe;
'Twill be endurance not to weep
If that repose be woe.

And, adding to the sense of things unaccomplished which she fears will confront her at the time of her death, she anticipates also the pull of earth, the pantheistic stirrings in her nature which would make her parting from the world the harder:

Alas! the countless links are strong
That bind us to our clay;
The loving spirit lingers long,
And would not pass away.

Yet, still, her last wish is for total disaffection, a relinquishing of all things cherished save the spirit:

The long fight closing in defeat—
Defeat serenely borne—
Thine eventide may still be sweet,
Thy night a glorious morn.

Before passing on to consider the other principal strands of thought discoverable in Emily's poems, I feel it important to stress the origin of Emily's stoicism in her own needs. It was not only her imaginative vision of the world as evil which called for such an armour, but her own personal experience of grief and frustration. Indeed, one side of her nature was emotionally prone to pessimism; and it was stoicism which seemed to offer the most practical treatment for this malaise.

Just how deeply she felt her own life to exist in a condition of darkness, we can read from the poem *Castle Wood,* dated February 2nd, 1844. That this is Emily speaking in her own voice seems fairly clear, for even Miss Ratchford has had some doubts about locating it in the Gondal cycle:

The grief that prest this living breast
Was heavier far than earth can be;
And who would dread eternal rest
When labour's hire was agony?

Dark falls the fear of this despair
On spirits born for happiness;
But I was bred the mate of care,
The foster-child of sore distress.

No sighs for me, no sympathy,
No wish to keep my soul below;
The heart is dead since infancy,
Unwept-for let the body go.

But it is hard to find in stoicism the lyrical afflatus which the poet seeks for; and perhaps we might hazard that while Emily the woman obtained certain consolations from its tenets,

Emily the poet felt that it lacked something. If the limits of stoic promise could assist her only to maintain a position in which she could merely encourage the spirit to

> . . . journey onwards, not elate
> But never broken-hearted.

then perhaps some other train of thought or feeling was necessary to her. Not to be "broken-hearted" is much, when faced with all the oppressions of existence, but the poet requires something above such a subsistence-level philosophy —the poet requires to experience elation. Where, then did Emily turn for it?

Not, I think, to Christianity. For apart from that strange undecipherable poem *There let thy bleeding branch atone* (which will be discussed hereafter), most of the references in Emily's verse to Christian thought are negatory.

Thus, in the poem *Castle Wood,* she disclaims all wishes for immortality, for redemption in heaven, or heavenly assistance and consolation while on earth:

> No star will light my coming night;
> No moon of hope for me will shine;
> I mourn not heaven would blast my sight,
> And I never longed for ways divine.
>
> Through Life hard Task I did not ask
> Celestial aid, celestial cheer;
> I saw my fate without its mask,
> And met it too without a tear.

We have seen, also, in *The Old Stoic,* how she rejects all Christian thought of prayer:

> And if I pray, the only prayer
> That moves my lips for me
> Is—"Leave the heart that now I bear
> And give me liberty.

In another poem, *O wander not so far away,* the idea of Original Sin seems to be repudiated:

> If thou hast sinned in this world of care,
> 'Tis but the dust of thy drear abode—
> Thy soul was pure when it entered here,
> And pure it will go again to God.

The notion encountered here may remind us of Wordsworth's Ode on *Intimations of Immortality*, especially of his lines

> The Soul that rises with us, our life's Star,
> Hath had elsewhere its setting,
> And cometh from afar:
> Not in entire forgetfulness,
> And not in utter nakedness,
> But trailing clouds of glory do we come
> From God, who is our home:[4]

But, even more, Emily's idea that the soul itself cannot, or does not, sin—though contained within a body that is all too prone to do so, recalls the dualistic theory of the Catharists, a heretic sect popularly associated with the Albigensian Crusade. Deriving much from the Manicheans, the Catharists believed that the soul was good since it was created by a good and just God: the body, however, they thought to be bad, since they believed it to have been created, like all matter, by the devil.[5]

Predestination, in all its forms, Emily likewise denied:

> Unless there be no truth on earth
> And vows meant true are nothing worth,
> And mortal man have no control
> Over his own unhappy soul.

Along with Anne, her sister, Emily reacted against the Calvinistic teachings of their aunt. Long before Dean Farrer had dispensed with the idea of eternal punishment for

[4] It was with this passage in mind that Pater wrote the following words on Wordsworth: "Following the soul, backwards and forwards, on these endless ways, his sense of man's dim, potential powers became a pledge to him, indeed, of a future life, but carried him back also to that mysterious notion of an earlier state of existence—the fancy of the Platonists—the old heresy of Origen."

[5] In his most interesting short work *The Holy Heretics: The Story of the Albigensian Crusade*, the late Edmond Holmes gives an excellent résumé of Catharist doctrine. Catharism, he tells us, carried the disguised dualism of the Christian religion (as formulated by the Church) to its logical conclusions. "It denied that a perfect God could have created an imperfect world; and, admitting the reality of evil, it contended that whatever is evil must have had an evil source. For the dualism of the Creator and the created world it substituted the uncompromising dualism of two Creators, two acts of creation, two created worlds. In other words, it gave full scope and a free rein to the disruptive potentiality of dualism. It rent the universe asunder, and interposed between the two dissevered worlds an abyss which in strictness could neither be fathomed nor spanned.

But how was evil to be distinguished from good? In the world of our experience the two are intermingled. What is the distinguishing mark, the "note" of each? The Catharist was at no loss for an answer to this question. Matter is intrinsically evil. Spirit is intrinsically good. The world of the good God is the world of spirits. The world of the bad God is the world of material things."

unrepentant sinners as being one of the obligatory beliefs of the Anglican Church, these two girls had impugned the conception. In the poem *Far, far away is mirth withdrawn,* we get Emily's most balanced rejection of it:

> But God is not like human-kind;
> Man cannot read the Almighty mind;
> Vengeance will never torture thee,
> Nor haunt thy soul eternally.
>
> Then do not in this night of grief,
> This time of overwhelming fear,
> O do not think that God can leave,
> Forget, forsake, refuse to hear!

Here, we note the image of God as an exacting judge (which the doctrine of eternal punishment presupposes) is not changed for a God of love or mercy (though the last two lines seem to hint at this). The larger hope, though, seems to lie in restoring to the thought of God's unknowability; to the belief that what God thinks is incommensurate with what man thinks about God, or what man persuades himself God is thinking.

But in a poem written two months earlier, Emily repudiates the doctrine much more wildly, and with a touch of italicised defiance:

> No; *that* I feel can never be;
> A God of *hate* could hardly bear
> To watch through all eternity
> His own creations dread despair.

It is rather as if Emily were saying, 'You call your God a God of love, and yet you believe that notion of Him concordant with the thought of eternal punishment. It seems to me, from your latter notion, that He is more like a God of hate; and even a God of hate wouldn't behave in the way you suggest.'

Her argument, of course, is impulsive and by no means logical. For if we conceive of a God of hate, and admit that one of any god-head's attributes is that of eternal permanence, then just such a changeless permanence of hate is what we should most properly expect. Emily's statement is, strictly, incoherent; the result of angry rhetoric; and chiefly important as a personal symptom. In any case, the poem in which this appears is disordered in thought and unruly in expression; and if artistic integrity is in some way related to sincerity of statement, then the ideas encountered here must be suspect. Indeed, something like a pure contradiction to what Emily already has said is to be met with in the last two stanzas:

He smiles and sings, though every air
Betrays the faith of yesterday;
His soul is glad to cast for her
Virtue and faith and Heaven away.

Well thou hast paid me back my love!
But if there be a God above
Whose arm is strong, whose word is true,
This hell shall wring thy spirit too.

No doubt a little equivocation could turn all the key-terms in this passage into purely harmless metaphors, making them descriptive of emotional states of merely relative and earthly duration. Thus, "Heaven" and "hell" could be interpreted as standing for conditions of contentment and misery; though this would ignore the capital letter gracing "Heaven", which usually indicates an absolute existence beyond the exigencies of time. And even if "hell" were taken as meaning a state of vicissitude and anguish on earth, we are still faced with the idea that it is bestowed by an indignant and justly punishing God.

It seems, in this poem, as if Emily wanted to have things both ways—for rhetorical purposes. She needed to inveigh against the abstract idea of eternal punishment, but she also needed to retain the thought of an avenging and rectifying deity such as we come across in the Psalms. Because the poem is disordered and melodramatic, she does not succeed in reconciling these two quite reconciliable ideas. Perhaps we do not need to take this piece too seriously.

But, in truth, Emily's attitude towards predestination is of a very muddled and curious nature. It is almost as if she had denied the idea of predestination as a specific Christian doctrine in order to reinstate it in another field. It is just possible that this rejection of it by Emily's consciousness was concurrent with its unconscious repression; and that it worked out through the subconscious taking, a different and half-disguised form.

In making these remarks I am chiefly thinking of the poem *Stanzas to—* which is one of the best of Emily's lesser poems:

Well, some may hate, and some may scorn,
And some may quite forget thy name,
But my sad heart must ever mourn
Thy ruined hopes, thy blighted fame."

'Twas thus I thought, an hour ago,
Even weeping o'er that wretch's woe.
One word turned back my gushing tears,
And lit my altered eye with sneers.

"Then bless the friendly dust," I said,
"That hides thy unlamented head.
Vain as thou wert, and weak as vain,
The slave of falsehood, pride and pain,
My heart has nought akin to thine—
Thy soul is powerless over mine."

By these were thoughts that vanished too—
Unwise, unholy, and untrue—
Do I despise the timid deer
Because his limbs are fleet with fear?
Or would I mock the wolf's death-howl
Because his form is gaunt and foul?
Or hear with joy the leveret's cry
Because it cannot bravely die?

No! Then above his memory
Let pity's heart as tender be:
Say, "Earth lie lightly on that breast,
And, kind Heaven, grant that spirit rest!

Of this poem Phyllis Bentley has written:

"This vision, which views the sin and defect clear-eyed, without illusion or palliation, but deeply compassionates the sinner for the nature which fate has given him, is entirely Emily's own."

In fact, it is only when she considers man as a creature quite separate from his natural background that she denies predestination. Her arguments, here, from the animal world substantiate the sense of inevitability which she very deeply possessed, and which informs her novel from beginning to end. As we shall observe, when we come to consider *Wuthering Heights*, there is every reason to believe that she saw predestination as the chief principle working in nature, the supreme law which creates opposite modes of life, and out of their conflict breeds development and change.

To return to Emily's treatment of Christian themes of thought, it is very doubtful whether she retained anything specifically Christian in her own imaginative faith at all.

One of the few poems which contains a typical assembly of Christian sentiments—the sense of sin, repentance, and grace beyond our strength to attain for ourselves—is *Sleep not, dream not; this bright day*, whose final stanzas contain the lines:

> 'Tis thus that human minds will turn,
> All doomed alike to sin and mourn
> Yet all with long gaze fixed afar,
> Adoring virtue's distant star.

But it would probably be wrong to translate this body of ideas into exact Christian notions. The idea of mourning here may well suggest misery and lamentation rather than conscious repentance, and the image of "virtue's distant star" is one of the magnets of aspiration which other systems of thought besides the Christian held to.[6]

[6] The stoic schools, particularly in their later manifestation, accepted as the goal of their aspiration some far-removed ideal of grace, akin to Emily's "virtue's distant star". In his *History of Ethics* (1902), Henry Sidgwick writes as follows of them: "In Seneca . . . this aspect of later Stoicism is strongly marked; he does not claim to be a sage, but only in progress towards Wisdom: and though the way to virtue is easy to find, the life of one who treads it is a continual struggle with lust and faults, a campaign in which there is no repose; in preparation for which a man needs such ascetic practice as is given by days of meagre diet and rough raiment deliberately chosen. Similarly Epictetus lays stress on the impossibility of finding the Stoic sage in actual experience: rare, indeed, are those who like himself are even in earnest progress towards Wisdom, who duly take to heart the momentous words "Endure" and "Refrain". Thus philosophy, in the view of Seneca and Epictetus, comes to present itself as the healer whom men seek from a sense of their weakness and disease—whose business is "with the sick, not with the whole"; the wisdom by which she heals is a quality that needs not long dissertations or dialectical subtleties, but rather continual practice, self-discipline, self-examination. The same sense of the gap between theory and fact gives to the religious side of Stoicism a new force and meaning in these later utterances of the school: the soul, conscious of its weakness, leans more on the thought of its kinship with God, whose prophet and messenger the Stoic feels himself to be; and in his ideal attitude towards external events self-poised indifference is now less prominent than pious resignation. The old self-reliance of the reason, looking down on man's natural life as a mere field for its exercise, seems to have shrunk and dwindled, making room for a positive aversion to the flesh as an alien element imprisoning and hampering the spirit; the body has come to be a "corpse which the soul sustains,"* and life a "sojourn in a strange land"† or a voyage on a stormy sea, where the only haven is death."‡ * Epictetus. † Marcus Aurelius. ‡ Seneca.

On the whole, it would probably be true to say that the mark of Christianity is not to be located in any definite statement; either in Emily's prose or verse, but rather in passages of gentler colouring than we are apt to associate with her. What, I think, its influence did effect was a certain melioration of an otherwise primitive instinctive nature. It fastened, for example, upon her sense of tenderness and elevated it into a principle of mercy and compassion, such as we find in the poem just quoted, *Well, some may hate, and some may scorn*. But, as we have seen in this poem, the compassion is not associated with any Christian notion of ethics and redemption. It is Christian in sentiment, but not in idea; for, as Phyllis Bentley has pointed out:

> "Courage, compassion and what some call mysticism, but I myself prefer to analyse as an awareness of the workings of the cosmos, are the most frequent[7] subjects of her poems."[8]

Christian in sentiment, then, as this compassion, it derives not from any Gospel doctrine as from some intuited notion of "the workings of the cosmos". Christianity, we can say, is not responsible for its presence: what it *is* answerable for seems to have been the development of an otherwise indigenous rudimentary feeling which has been elevated by it to the status and consciousness of a principle that, in turn, becomes connected or attached to a different train of thought.

A further point to make here also—and one we shall examine when we come to *Wuthering Heights*—is that Emily showed no interest in portraying a Christian type of character.[9] The rout of half-barbarian aristocratic figures[10] that throng the drama of the Gondals are curious combinations of Rousseau's 'noble savage' and de Laclos' unprincipled and intriguing Valmont; and, on the female side, of Iseult and

7 'significant' might have been a fitter word here than 'most frequent.'

8 *The Brontë Sisters*.

9 Edgar Linton, a true Christian character who features in *Wuthering Heights*, is either played down or patronised by Emily.

10 we recall how Matthew Arnold specially designated the nineteenth-century English aristocratic class as "the barbarians"

the Marquise de Merteuil. Whatever their virtues (and they are few), they are by no means Christian; and in whatever way they regard their vices (which they seldom do in any self-critical manner), it is not in the Christian fashion they regard them.

Pantheism, in Emily's verse, which I shall next examine, is the quality she shares in common with most of the best nineteenth-century English poets. In fact, it is the only quality; for stoicism is seldom encountered in their verse, and Emily's brand of mystic quietism is undeniably her own. But, in some measure, a streak of nature-worship runs through all the chief Victorian poets. Sometimes, as with Tennyson and Browning, it is a secondary characteristic; but more often, as with Clare, Beddoes, Swinburne, Meredith, and Hardy, it is the main-stream of feeling in their work. But just as the pantheism of these poets differed in each case, so it differed with Emily, in whom it terminated in a type of mysticism of a peculiarly personal order.

To hazard a generalisation that might prove helpful, we can say that after the Battle of Waterloo the revolutionary hopes of the romantic poets turned for consolation to the sphere of nature,[11] which seemed to offer more in the way of redemption than a reactionary political field. With the death of Shelley in 1822, and what is loosely spoken of as the apostasy of Wordsworth, this new switch-over became more and more the fashion.

Just as disappointed social-political aspirations caused many of these poets to seek an imaginative sanctuary in nature, so with Emily some personal or domestic dissatisfaction would seem to have been the reason for her turning in that direction also.

One thing we notice when reading the bulk of her 'nature' poems is that her note is more affirmative than in many of her

[11] Of course, there were exceptions to it. The Chartist poets, Ebenezer Elliott and Ebenezer Jones, are citable as examples here. But such poets did not produce verse on the level of Clare and Beddoes; and it is significant that for all the latter's participation in continental movements of reform and revolt, his political verse is extremely slight, both in quality and in quantity compared with his body of 'nature' poetry.

stoical stone-walling pieces. "Refrain" and "Endure", as Henry Sidgwick pointed out, are the two main commandments of the stoic creed; and to make a song and dance about such severe exhortations is not perhaps too easy a matter. At least, we have the feeling in Emily's 'nature' poems, that the thoughts which her subject have suggested have put her in a more rejoicing mood. In this part of her poetry she enters into the first phase of what we can call her "Yea-saying" utterance.

We have seen in poems previously quoted how riches, fame, love and ambition were held suspect by her, and imaginatively dismissed as so many snares and illusions. But over the plain physical fact of the bare life of the earth she had always exalted. Nature (as a body of laws and processes working themselves out through material phenomena) had always been the sole physical tie holding her to a mortal existence which she might otherwise have wished to quit.

> The loving spirit lingers long
> And would not pass away.

she had written concerning this elemental attachment, in which she disclaimed any longing for "ways divine".

As Emily felt the life of earth to be the only source of redeeming attraction during man's mortal existence, so she feels that the life of earth, even after the individual's death, is still man's final consolation. The poem in which this notion is worked-out (*"I see around me tombstones grey"*), I shall quote at length, as it is little known, and because the ideas which it expresses manifest the almost obsessive pull which nature exerted upon her:

> I see around me tombstones grey
> Stretching their shadows far away.
> Beneath the turf my footsteps tread
> Lie low and lone the silent dead;
> Beneath the turf, beneath the mould—
> Forever dark, forever cold,
> And my eyes cannot hold the tears
> That memory hoards from vanished years;

For Time and Death and Mortal pain
Give wound that will not heal again.
Let me remember half the woe
I've seen and heard and felt below,
And Heaven itself, so pure and blest,
Could never give my spirit rest.
Sweet land of light; thy children fair
Know nought akin to our despair;
Nor have they felt, nor can they tell
What tenants haunt each mortal cell,
What gloomy guests we hold within—
Torments and madness, tears and sin!
Well, may they live in extasy
Their long eternity of joy!
At least we would not bring them down
With us to weep, with us to groan.
No—Earth would wish no other sphere
To taste her cup of suffering drear;
She turns from Heaven a careless eye
And only mourns that *we* must die!
Ah mother, what shall comfort thee
In all this boundless misery?
To cheer our eager eyes a while
We see thee smile; how fondly smile!
But who reads not through that tender glow
Thy deep, unutterable woe?
Indeed, no dazzling land above
Can cheat thee of thy children's love.
We all, in life's departing shine,
Our last dear longings blend with thine;
And struggle still and strive to trace
With clouded gaze, thy darling face.
We would not leave our native home
For *any* world beyond the Tomb.
No—rather on thy kindly breast
Let us be laid in lasting rest;
Or waken but to share with thee
A mutual immortality.

Earth appears as a mourner for mankind, since men must die; but even so, says Emily, their death does not deprive the earth of men's affection, since their last wish is for an *earthy hereafter,* a prolongation of spatial existence beyond the state of temporal impermanence. Unlike the Christian creed which tells us that "Heaven (the firmament) and earth shall pass away", leaving only the realm of spirit, this poem looks to a resurrected nature, both inanimate and human. But if, Emily tells us, this "mutual immortality" is not to be had, then rather than "leave our native home/For *any* world beyond the Tomb", man would much prefer to be laid to "lasting rest" in the earth.

When Matthew Arnold came to write his splendid verse tribute to the Brontes,[12] he could not have known this poem, as it had not as yet been published. But it is surprising how he anticipated the full course of Emily's thought on the issues of nature, immortality, and death.

> Sleep, O cluster of friends,
> Sleep!—or only when May,
> Brought by the west-wind, returns
> Back to your native heaths,
> And the plover is heard on the moors,
> Yearly awake to behold
> The opening summer, the sky,
> The shining moorland—to hear
> The drowsy bee, as of old,
> Hum o'er the thyme, the grouse
> Call from the heather in bloom!
> Sleep, or only for this
> Break your united repose!

he writes, asking, for them, the same alternatives as Emily had elected for in her poem. Possibly, beyond the evidence of Emily's other poems, Arnold had been struck by the last chapter of *Wuthering Heights* in which the same ideas, the same alternatives, seem to find expression as in the poem. The last two paragraphs are well-known and justly famed for their delicate rhythm:

> "I sought and soon discovered the three headstones on the slope next the moor—the middle one gray, and half buried in heath; Edgar Linton's only harmonized by the turf and moss creeping up its foot; Heathcliffe's still bare.
>
> "I lingered round them under that benign sky, watched the moths fluttering among the heath and harebells, listened to the soft wind breathing through the grass, and wondered how any one could ever imagine unquiet slumbers for the sleepers in that quiet earth."

12 *Haworth Churchyard, April 1855.*

The narrator here tells us that "he wondered how anyone could ever imagine unquiet slumbers for the sleepers in that quiet earth"; but a page before this he recounts how he has met a shepherd-boy afraid of the ghosts of Heathcliffe and Catherine, whom he thinks he has encountered in their old walks:

> "I was going to the Grange one evening—a dark evening, threatening thunder; and just at the turn of the Heights I encountered a little boy with a sheep and two lambs before him. He was crying terribly, and I supposed the lambs were skittish and would not be guided.
>
> " 'What is the matter, my little man?' I asked.
>
> " 'There's Heathcliff and a woman yonder, under t' nab', he blubbered, 'un I darnut pass 'em.'
>
> "I saw nothing; but neither the sheep nor he would go on, so I bade him take the road lower down. He probably raised the phantoms from thinking, as he traversed the moors alone, on the nonsense he had heard his parents and companions repeat. Yet, still I don't like being out in the dark now, and I don't like being left by myself in this grim house. I cannot help it. I shall be glad when they leave it and shift to the Grange."

Man, then, Emily seems to be saying, belongs to the earth both in life and in death; and one of the most harmonious moments which he can know are those wherein his own personality is suspended (so that he is dead to himself, or to his own narrow identity) by immersion in the greater life of nature. Emily has many poems in which the death-wish (a feature of all the nineteenth-century romantics) assumes a positive and constructive tone. *I'm happiest when most away,* she writes in one poem:

> I'm happiest when most away
> I can bear my soul from its home of clay
> On a windy night when the moon is bright
> And the eye can wonder through worlds of light—

When I am not and none beside—
Nor earth nor sea nor cloudless sky—
But only spirit wandering wide
Through infinite immensity.

It is true that it could be objected of this poem that the real subject is not immersion in nature but total transcendence of all phenomena of the natural world as well as of the self:

When I am not and none beside—
Nor earth nor sea nor cloudless sky—

Such an objection would have much to support it; and, in fact, nature-worship is not the last stage of Emily's intensely private religion. Of what that last passage of faith consisted, we shall be inquiring into shortly. For the moment, I believe it true to say that just as stoicism was the means by which Emily overcame the immediate frustrations and griefs of life, and pantheism the means by which she escaped into a freer and more lyrical atmosphere than that which stoicism provided; so pantheism, in turn, went by the board when it had made possible the release into an even less confined sense of being. Another way of putting this would be to say that Emily's imaginative development might be envisaged as a ladder with three rungs: the bottom one being stoicism, the middle pantheism, and the top quietism.

However, returning to the poem in hand, we note that the transcendence of the self occurs

On a windy night when the moon is bright
And the eye can wonder through worlds of light.

Nature is to be conceived as providing the favourable environment for Emily's spiritual ascensions. And these undeliberated flights of the spirit are seen to coincide with certain felicitous[13] moods of nature, just as the record flight of a plane demands favourable meteorological conditions.

Another poem which develops this non-Wordswortian brand of pantheism,[14] in which Emily seeks in nature for some force

13 'Felicitous' must not be thought of as synonymous with 'fine weather'. Felicitous weather, for Emily, was that which harmonised with her moods; and, as we see, these were often stormy.

14 Excepting such famous passages as that from *Tintern Abbey* (. . . "that blessed mood/In which the burthen of the mystery", etc) Wordsworth's pantheism, for the main part, is more meditative and didactic than mystical.

that shall catapult her beyond an awareness of a pluralistic universe, is *Aye, there it is! It wakes to-night:*

Aye, there it is! It wakes to-night
Sweet thoughts that will not die
And feeling's fires flash all as bright
As in the years gone by!

And I can tell by thy altered cheek
And by thy kindled gaze
And by the words thou scarce dost speak
How wildly fancy plays.

Yes, I could swear that glorious wind
Has swept the world aside,
Has dashed its memory from thy mind
Like foam-bells from the tide—

And thou art now a spirit pouring
Thy presence into all—
The essence of the Tempest's roaring
And of the Tempest's fall—

A universal influence
From Thine own influence free;
A principle of life, intense,
Lost to mortality.

Thus truly when the breast is cold
Thy prisoned soul shall rise,
The dungeon mingled with the mould—
The captive with the skies.

Here, as in *I'm happiest when most away,* we have the suspension of the poet's self and of her disparate consciousness in a sense of new-found unity:

A universal influence
From Thine[15] own influence free;
A principle of life, intense,
Lost to mortality.

15 The use of the capital in "Thine" is puzzling. If we read it in the customary conventional sense as standing for deity, the meaning of the stanza would appear to be that in her pantheistic trance the poet feels herself free from the power and authority of God. Knowing as we do the constrictive Calvinistic teaching of Emily's aunt, it is just possible that the line represents a feeling of revolt. It is also possible to read it in a slightly less reactive sense, as implying that the state of self-suspension (which is one of the most exalted humankind can know) is a state in which the medium feels free: not only from her own personal identity and the identity of nature, but also from the identity of God.

But the fact that Emily also uses a capital T for "Tempest" in the previous stanza inclines me to believe that the T in "Thine" might be one of those arbitrary gestures which poets are occasionally known to indulge. Or it might even be an error in transcription.

And, again, just as in the last poem, this state of transcended self-identity has been arrived at by a natural agent—by "that glorious wind" which seems to have "swept the world aside", and along with the world all personal memory with its cribbed and confining effects.

But, in addition to these two statements concerning the condition of self-suspension, we observe that the state of transcended consciousness is spoken of in natural terms:

> And thou art now a spirit pouring
> Thy presence into all—
> The essence of the Tempest's roaring
> And of the Tempest's fall—

The state of self-transcendence is the same as the state of transcended nature. When, by an inward levitation of the mind, the daily sense of self is transcended, we perceive and live by the essence of our being. And this essence is the same as the one we share with nature when we obtain an intense vision of its workings. Perhaps one may paraphrase Emily's poem thus:

A third poem in which the appearances of nature are perceived as transformed into essences is entitled *A Day Dream*. The poet is lying on "a sunny brae" in early summer-time, inwardly dejected in spite of the bright scene. She converses with herself, and her thoughts run in this fashion:

> So, resting on a heathy bank,
> I took my heart to me;
> And we together sadly sank
> Into a reverie.
>
> We thought, "When winter comes again,
> Where will these bright things be?
> All vanished, like a vision vain,
> An unreal mockery!
>
> "The birds that now so blithely sing,
> Through deserts frozen dry,
> Poor spectres of the perished Spring,
> In famished troops will fly.
>
> "And why should we be glad at all?
> The leaf is hardly green,
> Before a token of the fall
> Is on its surface seen.

In other words, a case of *vanitas vanitatem;* whether one looks at the life of man or of the lower creations of existence.

The answer to this reducing argument comes to the spirit through a kind of vision in which she see "A thousand, thousand glancing fires", and hears "A thousand, thousand silvery lyres". To the music of these aerial instruments a host of "Glittering spirits" sing, the words of their song being as follows:

O mortal, mortal, let them die;
Let Time and Tears destroy,
That we may overflow the sky
With universal joy.

Let Grief distract the sufferer's breast,
And Night obscure his way;
They hasten him to endless rest,
And everlasting day.

To Thee[16] the world is like a tomb.
A desert's naked shore;
To us, in unimagined bloom,
It brightens more and more.

And could we lift the veil and give
One brief glimpse to thine eye
Thou would'st rejoice for those that live,
Because they live to die.

The 'lifting of the veil' introduces a Platonic idea that is seldom met with in Emily's writing. The world of appearances is usually felt to be enough (so far as it is the appearance of nature and not the appearance of man). There are, too, besides certain touches of 'fancy' ('whimsy' almost, one might say, with the picture of these spirits and their lyres in mind), one or two bad poetic lapses, as in the following stanza with its weak conjectural beginning.

Now whether it was really so
I never could be sure;
But as, in fit of peevish woe,
I stretched me on the moor,

A thousand thousand glancing fires . . .

16 I note here again the capital T, and assume it to be an error in the manuscript, unless it is Emily's strange notion of the courtesy of the "glittering spirits" towards the "mortal" whom they are addressing.

or the lame 'give away' in the final stanza:

The music ceased—the noonday Dream
Like dream of night withdrew
But Fancy still will sometimes deem
Her fond creation true.

Perhaps the unsustained integrity of style should make us chary of taking the thought of this poem too seriously, or of trying to show its consistence with other elements of Emily's poetic faith.

So far, I have concentrated rather on what Emily made out of her relationship with nature; namely, the preparatory drafts of a quite unique mysticism. Before going on, to consider this quality, I would like to furnish two examples of her pure appreciation of natural forces; two testimonies to nature-in-itself, so to speak.

In Charlotte's edition of the posthumous works of her sisters, the following poem (*Shall earth no more inspire thee*) is prefaced by a comment.

> "The following little piece", writes Charlotte, "has no title, but in it the genius of a solitary region seems to address his wandering and wayward votary, and to recall within his influence the proud mind which rebelled at times even against what it most loved."

Shall Earth no more inspire thee,
Thou lonely dreamer now?
Since passion may not fire thee
Shall Nature cease to bow?

Thy mind is ever moving
In regions dark to thee;
Recall its useless roving—
Come back and dwell with me.

The second stanza might well be a reference to a possible debate in Emily's mind between the claims of a comparatively straight-forward 'nature-worship' and the private cult she was evolving for herself.

The voice of the "genius" continues:

I've watched thee every hour;
I know my mighty sway,
I know my magic power
To drive thy griefs away.

Few hearts to mortals given
On earth so wildly pine;
Yet none would ask a Heaven
More like this Earth than thine.

Here we have, perhaps, the whole contradiction or paradox in Emily's make-up, which made her excursion into mysticism imperative. To demonstrate this, one has only to reverse the order of Emily's statements:

[Though] none would ask a Heaven
More like this Earth than thine;
Few hearts to mortals given
On earth so wildly pine.

In other words, although she *conceives* of the earth as her only possible home, she *feels* the need of something beyond—some supra-terrestrial goal or consolation. This quality—for one reason or another, probably as a result of her narrow religious upbringing for which her aunt was more responsible than her father—she was unable to find in orthodox Anglicanism or any of its Non-conformist off-shoots. At the same time as she was seeking for this final satisfaction of thought and feeling, she probably experienced a sense of compunction, of treason even, towards her old love of nature. The present poem ends with a plea voiced by the "genius" of nature—an affectionate recall to her simple source of worship:

Then let my winds caress thee;
Thy comrade let me be—
Since nought beside can bless thee,
Return and dwell with me.

A second poem (*In summer's mellow midnight*) takes up again this debate between the appeal of nature and some essential privacy that wishes and does not wish to respond. Charlotte's brief preface to the poem read thus:

"Here again", she writes, "is the same mind in converse with a like abstraction. "The Night-Wind", breathing through an open window, has visited an ear which discerned language in its whispers".

The speaker attempts to repudiate this voice:

I said, "Go, gentle singer,
Thy wooing voice is kind,
But do not think its music
Has power to reach my mind.

"Play with the scented flowers,
The young tree's supple bough,
And leave my human feelings
In their own course to flow."

But the natural emissary will not be gainsaid, and takes up the argument for their old affinity with a greater show of eloquence than before:

The wanderer would not leave me;
Its kiss grew warmer still—
"O come," it sighed so sweetly,
"I'll win thee 'gainst thy will.

"Have we not been from childhood friends?
Have I not loved thee long?
As long as thou hast loved the night
Whose silence wakes my song.

"And when thy heart is laid at rest
Beneath the churchyard stone
I shall have time enough to mourn
And thou to be alone."

The last stanza seems to clinch the matter. "The meaning of life", as Adler says, "is co-operation." While we live on earth, we ought to accept the earth, pay our dues and participate in its rites; we ought to love the earth and cherish it, instead of trying to deny its claim upon us and turning from us, till death denies *us*.

The kinship from infant days, which nature in this poem declares to have existed, between itself and the poet may remind us of Wordsworth's famous lines on the rainbow; though in his poem the statement of faith is inversely expressed

—the poet being the one, in this case, who claims relationship with nature:

> My heart leaps up when I behold
>   A rainbow in the sky:
> So was it when my life began;
> So is it now I am a man;
> So be it when I shall grow old,
>   Or let me die!
> The Child is father of the Man;
> And I could wish my days to be
> Bound each to each by natural piety.

In his fine essay on Emily, Charles Morgan suggests that the best of her poetry was "probably about one of three things":

> "the complete mystical experience that Emily appears to have enjoyed at some time in her early youth; her abiding desire, which made all other desires relatively unimportant to her, for repetition of it; or a partial re-experience—one of many, as I interpret her—from which, in an agony of spiritual disappointment, she had been dragged back."

And later, in the same essay, he writes:

> "She was tired of being enclosed. She was weary to escape to "that glorious world" of which, I believe, she had once enjoyed immediate apprehension. All her life, all her poems, all those parts of *Wuthering Heights* that bear the stamp of vision were dedicated to her desire that this direct experience might be repeated, that she might be again 'really with it and in it—not seeing it dimly through tears and yearning for it through the walls of an aching heart.' "

What was this experience to which she always harked back? It would seem that there can be no conclusive knowing; but it is just possible that it was some complete identification with nature which the self of the child would sometimes seem to enjoy.[17] It is possible it was such an experience, from the

[17] Evidence for this assumption might be found in the poem *I Saw thee, Child, one summer day,* which speaks of the fading of our sense of glory. In the Introduction to his edition of Emily's selected poems, Philip Henderson quotes this piece, upon which he remarks: "Evidently Emily had read Wordsworth's *Ode on Intimations of Immortality* with some attention and felt intensely how the shades of the mortal prison begin to close upon radiant childhood."

Penistone Crags (Trysting place of Heathcliff and Cathy).
(By courtesy of Walter Scott, Bradford)

Ponden Hall, "Thrushcross Grange" in *Wuthering Heights*.
(By courtesy of Walter Scott, Bradford)

memory of which the great German poet Hölderlin wrote his poem *Youth*:

Once when I was a boy
A saviour spared me
From the clamour and violence of men:
And safe and serene I
Played in the flowering grove,
The airs of the heavens

Played over me.
And, just as you gladden
The hearts of the flowers
As they sunward spread their
Delicate arms to you,
So you have gladdened my heart,
Father Helios! And like Endymion
I was your darling,
Heavenly Luna!

O all you faithful
And friendly deities!
If you could only
Know how my spirit adored you!

True, not yet did I call
You by name, nor did you give
Me a name, in the manner that men give
Names, as though they knew one another.
Yet I knew you far better
Than I ever knew men;
Stillness of ether I understood,
But the words of men never.

I was raised by the gentle
Murmur of woods
And I learned to love
Among blossoms.[18]
And I grew in the arms of the gods."

But, as Hölderlin in his poem *To Nature* recounts how he lost this sense of proximity which was once intense enough to be a vision—

That which moulded me mature and even,
All the world of youth, is dead and gone,
And this heart, which once was filled with heaven,
Now lies sterile as a field of stone;

18 Translated by Frederic Prokosch.

> Ah, the spring now sings to me of sorrow,
> Songs which once delighted, comforted,
> Vanished in the day and is the morrow,
> Spring lies barren in my heart and dead.[19]

—so Emily, too, may have lost this early sense; and, feeling that the dream of it is not sufficient, set out to rediscover the original experience or provide herself with a substitute for it by more esoteric means.

Up to this moment, I have used the terms 'mysticism' and 'quietism' in speaking of Emily's private cult, with a notion of their interchangeability which is hardly to be justified beyond the case in point. My choice of words has been dictated by my need to stress either one or another aspect of Emily's 'religion'. When I have wanted to focus attention on the *relationship* which her mind established with something beyond it, I have used the term 'mysticism'; but when I have desired to emphasise the sufficiency of faith and *privacy of belief or grace* which Emily sometimes felt she possessed then 'quietism' has been the word I have chosen.

Again, I have sensed the dilemma inherent in my choice; for mysticism generally carries with it some system of spiritual exercises by which the mind of the devotee is helped to attain unity with God. Now this seems singularly lacking in so far as it might have been expected to find expression in Emily's poetry. But if the idea of spiritual discipline appears absent in her poems, the sense of visitation (which we also associate with mysticism) is powerfully and prevalently present. So I shall continue to use both these terms, as the sense seems to require, until we come to an attempted definition of Emily's thought in a later chapter.

The notion of visitation, in these poems of Emily which deal with her 'interior' religion, is connected with what I shall describe as a gnostic cult of night. All religions—however 'interior', however private—need ritual and sacrament; and if one sets about, instinctively or consciously, inventing one's own religion, one needs to invent a ritual as

[19] Translated by F.P.

well. In Emily's thought we find that night is one of those ceremonial conditions which herald the approach of the 'holy of holies'; and in romantic metaphysical poetry this idea of Emily's is not without precedent. George Chapman, the Elizabethan dramatist, who was rumoured to have written his plays with the assistance of familiar spirits, devised an argument for night as the most propitious time for composition:

> Since day or light, in any quality,
> For earthly uses do but serve the eye;
> And since the eye's most quick and dangerous use
> Enflames the heart, and learns the soul abuse . . .
> Since night brings terror to our frailty still
> And shameless day doth marble us in ill, . . .
> Come consecrate with me to sacred Night
> Your whole endeavours, and detest the light.
> No pen can anything eternal write
> That is not steep'd of humour of the Night.

With the German poet Novalis, the imaginative and æsthetic aid which Chapman found the night to offer is elevated to a spiritual condition:

> "Aside I turn to the holy, unspeakable, mysterious Night. Afar lies the world, sunk in a deep grave; waste and lonely is its place. In the chords of the bosom blows a deep sadness. I am ready to sink away in drops of dew, and mingle with the ashes.—The distances of memory, the wishes of youth, the dreams of childhood, the brief joys and vain hopes of a whole long life, arise in gray garments, like an evening vapour after the sunset."[20]

But 'Night', as Novalis envisages it, is not an objective atmospheric state which merely envelopes us as subjects. We are penetrated by its own nature; and, by it, know not only itself but ourselves:

> "More heavenly than those glittering stars we hold the eternal eyes which the Night hath opened within us. Farther they see than the palest of those countless hosts. Needing no aid from the light, they penetrate the depths of a loving soul that fills a loftier region with bliss ineffable. Glory to

20 Translated by George MacDonald in his book *Rampolli* (1897).

the queen of the world, to the great prophetess of holier worlds, to the foster-mother of blissful love! she sends thee to me, thou tenderly beloved, the gracious sun of the Night. Now am I awake, for now am I thine and mine. Thou hast made me know the Night, and brought her to me to be of my life; thou hast made of me a man. Consume my body with the ardour of my soul, that I, turned to finer air, may mingle more closely with thee, and then our bridal night endure for ever."[21]

In the second of his *Hymns,* Novalis poetically rails against the coming of the morning in the same way as we shall find Emily doing:

"Must the morning always return? Will the despotism of the earthly never cease? Unholy activity consumes the angel-visit of the Night."[22]

For both of these romantic metaphysical poets, night stands as the harbinger of the spiritual world and day as the champion of a material universe;[23] and here it becomes important to suggest that the particular quality of a receptive nocturnal consciousness, which Emily shared with them, was neither a coincidence nor a matter of imitation (for it is almost certain Emily had not read them), but a case of common imaginative configuration, which the psychological likeness of their separate quests provided. In other words, it is possible that just as public religions symbolise the arch-types by some over-all image, so private religions—instinctively—are led to uncover certain symbols of the arche-types which resemble one another.

Some sort of physical explanation could probably be offered for such workings of the mind. Day, we could say, illuminates the world, so that all the multiplicity and distinction of its objects become apparent—creating, thereby, a pluralistic universe. Night, on the other hand, so darkens the world that all disparity and difference seem to be cancelled out; and from

21 and 22 Translated by George MacDonald.
23 note the Catharist-like dichotomy of this.

this removal of distinctions a new unity appears to be born. Now, as the mystical mind seeks always for some recognition of unity (which it takes to be a foremost attribute of God), its preference for the reign of night can be established.

Such an argument may help us to understand the mental processes of the poets in question, but has, of course, no more than imaginative applicability. Its reasoning is symbolic, not general.

But whatever the reason for Emily's choice, night certainly was her favoured period. Here is the poem which Charlotte printed under the title of *Stars,* in which we find the fullest expression of Emily's gnostic apostrophe to night:

Ah! why, because the dazzling sun
Restored my earth to joy
Have you departed, every one,
And left a desert sky?

All through the night, your glorious eyes
Were gazing down in mine,
And with a full heart's thankful sighs
I blessed that watch divine!

I was at peace, and drank your beams
As they were life to me
And revelled in my changeful dreams
Like petrel on the sea.

Thought followed thought—star followed star
Through boundless regions on,
While one sweet influence, near and far,
Thrilled through and proved us one.

Why did the morning rise to break
So great, so pure a spell,
And scorch with fire the tranquil cheek
Where your cool radiance fell?

Blood-red he rose, and arrow-straight
His fierce beams struck my brow:
The soul of Nature sprang elate,
But mine sank sad and low!

My lids closed down—yet through their veil
I saw him blazing still;
And bathe in gold the misty dale,
And flash upon the hill.

I turned me to the pillow then
To call back Night, and see
Your worlds of solemn light, again
Throb with my heart and me!

It would not do—the pillow glowed
And glowed both roof and floor,
And birds sang loudly in the wood,
And fresh winds shook the door.

The curtains waved, the wakened flies
Were murmuring round my room,
Imprisoned there, till I should rise
And give them leave to roam.

O Stars and Dreams and Gentle Night;
O Night and Stars return!
And hide me from the hostile light
That does not warm, but burn—

That drains the blood of suffering men;
Drinks tears instead of dew:
Let me sleep through his blinding reign,
And only wake with you!

We note, in this poem, how the needs of nature and the poet are not equated—for the sun which awakes and nourishes the former appears to the poet as an intolerable burden.

Many other poems by Emily echo this longing for the night and this oppressive dislike of the day. The last stanza of the piece *Wind, sink to rest in the heather* carries this refrain:

Sun, set from that evening heaven,
Thy glad smile wins not mine;
If light at all is given,
O give me Cynthia's shine.

How clear she shines asserts the same preference:

How clear she shines! How quietly
I lie beneath her silver light
While Heaven and Earth are whispering me,
"To-morrow wake, but dream to-night.

An otherwise feeble Gondal poem, *Written in Aspin Castle,* also takes up the familiar theme:

How do I love on summer nights
To sit within this Norman door,
Whose sombre portal hides the lights
Thickening above me evermore!

The best two stanzas bear further witness:

> "To-night, there is no wind to wake
> One ripple on the lonely lake;
> To-night, the clouds subdued and grey
> Starlight and moonlight shut away.
>
> 'Tis calm and still and almost drear,
> So utter is the solitude;
> But still I love to linger here
> And form my mood to nature's mood."

It is true that there *are* poems which do not insist upon this 'cult of night' which I have spoken of. One of them, dated August 12th, 1837, which Miss Ratchford does not identify as a Gondal piece, carries with it a tribute to the morning and its glad recuperative powers. Written in the form of a dialogue, the poem—through the lips of one of the speakers—recommends the healing properties of day to one, who in the evening, keeps sorrowful vigil. The tonic scene is vividly forecast with

> The dome of heaven expanding bright and blue,
> The leaves, the green grass, sprinkled thick with dew,
> And wet mists rising on the river's breast,
> And wild birds bursting from their songless nest.

but the other speaker asks only to be left in reverie, to be left with

> My blissful dream, that never comes with day;
> A vision dear, though false, for well my mind
> Knows what a bitter waking waits behind?

Emily appears to have recognised day as the period of nature's cosmic benevolence, as that division of the twenty-four hours, beneficent to men in their generality. From this generality, however, she seems to have excluded herself. For Emily's purpose, night provided an ideal atmospheric theatre for the visitation of that spirit which confessed itself *to her alone;* a solitary, private, and gnostic communicant.

But, as far as Emily herself was concerned, though the day might be a time beneficial to others, it was spiritually hostile to her higher intentions. This sense of antinomy is expressed in many of her poems: in the lines *Written in the Gaaldine Prison Caves*:

> Thy sun is near meridian height,
> And my sun sinks in endless night

but especially in *To A.G.A. (Thou standest in the greenwood now)*, where it takes on a rather curious form. In this piece, the opposition between the forces of night and day is of a more ambiguous order, suggestive of a state of *odi et amo*:

> I gazed upon the cloudless moon
> And loved her all the night
> Till morning came and ardent noon,
> Then I forgot her light—
>
> No—not forgot—eternally
> Remains its memory dear;
> But could the day seem dark to me
> Because the night was fair?
>
> I well may mourn that only one
> Can light my future sky
> Even though by such a radiant sun
> My moon of life must die."

Here, the moon-sun dialectic may make us think of the Linton-Heathcliff conflict in *Wuthering Heights;* but the fierceness of the sun's power, in this poem, though it be shown as destructive to the gentle "moon of life", is clearly not altogether undesired. The state is one of repulsion-attraction; and this constant warring between two principles is part of a dichotomised vision of the universe which I have hinted that Emily shared with the Catharist Christians.

With Emily's mystic-quietist poems, we get an example of what I shall call a sense of *communion within communion.* The initial stage, of which I have been speaking, is provided by a communion with night; but this, in turn, serves to usher in a deeper phase of sacramental knowing. But as soon as we begin to ask what this knowledge consists of, we find ourselves curiously baffled; and it is this bafflement we experience which helps to make of Emily both the fascinating enigma and the partly unsatisfactory poet that she was.

Aye, there it is! It wakes to-night
Sweet thoughts that will not die

she exclaims ecstatically in a poem which we have already quoted. But what is this *it* that works so strangely and so powerfully within her? Just precisely this, the poem does not tell us; for it goes on to speak of the subjective feelings which this unnamed agent has roused in the poet:

And thou art now a spirit pouring
Thy presence into all—
The essence of the Tempest's roaring
And of the Tempest's fall.

But immediately we begin to examine the lines closely, at least three ambiguities present themselves. Can we be sure that this "thou" (mysteriously to be distinguished from "Thine" with a capital in the next stanza) refers to the poet? Or does it refer to "that glorious wind" (which seems to be the natural operative agent), or to that even more inscrutable "it"?

In truth, there can be no final knowing. Emily *was* indeed a metaphysical poet (which means she was concerned with the expression of something more than idiosyncrasy); but the metaphysical knowledge which she possessed was not expressed by discursive means, by direct clear statement or definitive phrases. It was expressed, for the main part, suggestively, as with the symbolist poets. But, here, we encounter further difficulties; for this power of suggestion seldom found an adequate symbol that should both *hint at* and *stand for* the mystery she dealt in. To employ the words of T. S. Eliot, her poetry lacked "an objective correlative" language.[24] *She was talking to herself* nearly all the time; talking of things that were intimate to her but jealously guarded from the whole world. And the privacy of her speech was the more heightened in that her self-communication was not of a cool and rational order. It was passionate utterance;

24 A near-exception to this is her poem *The Philosopher's Conclusion* in which, in a rather Dantean manner, or—as Muriel Spark has pointed out—in the manner of the *Book of Genesis*, a triple river stands for three great cardinal forces or virtues (faith, hope and charity perhaps). But the device is most obscurely worked out.

passionate confession; but confession to nobody save her own self. How impossible it would be to imagine Emily resorting to the Roman confession as Charlotte had done in her torment in Brussels. Emily would scarcely confess to God, let alone to any priest or pastor. Not only did she not confess; but, poetically speaking, she did not *pray*:

> And if I pray, the only prayer
> That moves my lips for me
> Is—"Leave the heart that now I bear
> And give me liberty."

But it is the measure of her greatness, that in her six major poems (which we shall be dealing with in a coming chapter), the obstacles set up by her reticence are entirely *æsthetically* overcome, and in more than half of them *metaphysically* also. For the poems that remain—the poems we are at present treating—this cannot be said. With their passionate and emphatic rhythms, their lyrical insistence and intensity of feeling, they do not succeed in conveying a clear knowledge. They make their effect on us by a system of intermittent flashes rather than by some increasing illumination.

Once past the description of Emily's initial communion (which is that with nature or night), we find ourselves largely at sea. We are certain that there is a further one—*a communion within a communion*—but its nature seems to elude us, or to alter from poem to poem. In *My Comforter* it appears as a kind of gnostic awareness of her own being—a faith and trust in the individuality of her own undeterministic spirit:

> Deep down—concealed within my soul,
> That light lies hid from men,
> Yet glows unquenched—though shadows roll,
> Its gentle ray cannot control—
> About the sullen den.

And in another stanza of this poem, which speaks of the dichotomy we have remarked in Emily's thought, she speaks again of this inviolable identity: "What my soul bore my soul alone/Within itself may tell."

So stood I, in Heaven's glorious sun
And in the glare of Hell
My spirit drank a mingled tone
Of seraph's song and demon's moan—
What my soul bore my soul alone
Within itself may tell.

In another poem *How beautiful the Earth is still,* she renounces the pleasures and profits of the world, in order to

. . . cast my anchor of Desire
Deep in unknown Eternity;
Nor ever let my Spirit tire
With looking for *What is to be.*

In this poem, as in the last, there is the same obscure reference to a "Glad comforter", whose nature or function we cannot quite determine:

Glad comforter, will I not brave
Unawed the darkness of the grave?
Nay, smile to hear Death's billows rave,
My Guide, sustained by thee?
The more unjust seems present fate
The more my Spirit springs elate
Strong in thy strength, to anticipate
Rewarding Destiny!"

But what we can say of this stanza is that it illustrates—as Emily was only once more to illustrate—the rare exception of stoicism raised to an exultant lyrical pitch. In it the sense of *amor fati* becomes a song, as it did with Nietzsche when he wrote his *Dionysus Dithyrambs*:

O Shield of Destiny,
O carven tablets of Eternity:
Yea verily, thou knowest—what mankind doth hate,
What I alone do love. Thou art inviolate.
'Tis only Thou, O dire Necessity,
Canst kindle everlasting love in me.

"I have often asked myself", wrote the philosopher, "if I am not under deeper obligation to the hardest years of my life than to any other. As my innermost nature teaches me, all that is necessary, when viewed from an elevation and in the sense of a *great* economy, is also the useful in itself—

> one should not only bear it, one should *love* it. . . . *Amor fati*: that is my innermost nature."[25]

And again:

> It is great affliction only that is the ultimate emancipator of the mind.[26]

That, I think, is the fittest commentary one could possibly find for this poem.

But the only one of Emily's lesser compositions which is clear about the nature of her 'second' communion is the piece *To Imagination*:

> When weary with the long day's care,
> And earthly change from pain to pain,
> And lost, and ready to despair,
> Thy kind voice calls me back again—
> O my true friend, I am not lone
> Whilst thou canst speak with such a tone!
>
> . . . .
>
> Reason indeed may oft complain
> For Nature's sad reality,
> And tell the suffering heart how vain
> Its cherished dreams must always be!
> And Truth may rudely trample down
> The flowers of Fancy newly blown.
>
> But thou art ever there to bring
> The hovering visions back and breathe
> New glories o'er the blighted spring
> And call a lovelier life from death,
> And whisper with a voice divine
> Of real worlds as bright as thine.
>
> I trust not to thy phantom bliss,
> Yet still in evening's quiet hour
> With never-failing thankfulness
> I welcome thee, benignant power,
> Sure solacer of human cares
> And brighter hope when hope despairs."

Even here we notice certain reservations of acceptance. "Nature's sad reality" (so much less than what our sense of the ideal would have it) is frankly noted; and imagination itself does not escape scot-free from Emily's powerful critical regard. It is something to be thankful for, but its "phantom bliss" is not to be trusted.

[25] and [26] *Nietzsche contra Wagner.*

But of all Emily's lesser poems, the greatest—in its power to suggest this final communion and consummation—is the following one:

O thy bright eyes must answer now,
When Reason, with a scornful brow,
Is mocking at my overthrow;
O thy sweet tongue must plead for me
And tell why I have chosen thee!

Stern Reason is to judgment come
Arrayed in all her forms of gloom:
Wilt thou my advocate be dumb?
No, radiant angel, speak and say
Why I did cast the world away;

Why I have persevered to shun
The common paths that others run;
And on a strange road journeyed on
Heedless alike of Wealth and Power—
Of Glory's wreath and Pleasure's flower.

These once indeed seemed beings divine,
And they perchance heard vows of mine
And saw my offerings on their shrine—
But careless gifts are seldom prized,
And mine were worthily despised;

So with a ready heart I swore
To seek their altar-stone no more,
And give my spirit to adore
Thee, ever present, phantom thing—
My slave, my comrade, and my King!

A slave because I rule thee still;
Incline thee to my changeful will
And make thy influence good or ill—
A comrade, for by day and night
Thou art my intimate delight—

My Darling Pain that wounds and sears
And wrings a blessing out from tears
By deadening me to real cares;
And yet, a king—though prudence well
Have taught thy subject to rebel.

And am I wrong to worship where
Faith cannot doubt nor Hope despair
Since my own soul can grant my prayer?
Speak, God of Visions, plead for me
And tell why I have chosen thee!

All Emily's poetic personality—her imaginative, secretive, and self-denying nature—is set forth in these lines; yet, even so, we cannot tell whom this "God of Visions" is. Is it, as Muriel Spark thinks, "the nature-image that welded her being into unity"? is it the genius of artistic creation? or is it the chamelon spirit of wishful-thinking?

For all the force and *impasto* of the poem, we must admit that we cannot quite say. This address of Emily to her comprehensive *daimon* intrigues our intelligence and our imagination, but cannot truly satisfy either of them. For such satisfaction we must turn to her six major pieces.

THE POEMS

The Means

The two most salient characteristics of Emily's poetic style are: her flexible and various rhythms and her repetitive limited diction. In her minor poems, which we have been considering, this gives the impression of permutation within a given and narrow field: her 'turns' are many, but her range is small.

But there is something else about the style of these lesser poems which we must accept, and that is that they do not consistently register. In fact, it would probably be correct to say that the majority of them do not; for when we have subtracted the greater number of the bad Byronic 'cases' from the Gondal cycle, we find ourselves left with a body of poems which, for all their passages of power and lyricism, generally contain some flatness or flaw.

By flatness, here, I clearly do not mean any deadness or woodenness of rhythm, for in Emily's poems this last is a quality which we can almost always rely on. By flatness, then, I refer rather to her none-too-occasional proneness to lapse into cliches of over-heightened language—the banalities of the second-rate stock romantic manner:

> Farewell, unblessed, unfriended child,
> I cannot bare to watch thee die.

she writes in *A Farewell to Alexandria* (a poem which contains many excellent lines, but which *The Cornhill Magazine* printed —how appropriately!—under the title of *The Outcast Mother*).

There is also another kind of flatness in these poems; and that is the flatness of the common-place. Indeed, her diction is often flat from either of two antithetical causes: from straining too much after effect (and resorting to the melodramatic to achieve it), or from not searching hard enough for words (and so lapsing into the jejune).

Just as it is generally emotional moments which lead Emily astray in the first manner, so it is descriptive passages which lead her to a lowering of language in the second. This can be illustrated from the same poem from which we have already quoted: "the sun's departing ray", "the evening's golden beam", are just two examples of epithets with a certain descriptive slackness about them. Other poems can furnish a host of such examples: "shores" are "distant", "waves" are "rolling", "leaves" are "fresh" or "green", and "the heavens" "cloudless" or "blue".

Bluntness, weakness, or restrictedness of diction go hand in hand with felicity of movement, with strength of stress, and naturalness of cadence. What is the reason for this strange combination?

The answer I make to this question will necessitate a brief detour.

According to the thought of Schelling—exponent of the German 'nature-philosophy'—art should not imitate the forms of nature but the essence or spirit of the objects it depicts. This "creative energy", "the energy that inhabits" an object—this "creative life" which is "each thing's perfection" —can be intuited by the artist and released, as it were, in his own work. Without such inward apprehension, all works of art will wear a dead look, however harmonious their outward parts. But even granted this apprehension (which is something the subconscious mind undertakes) a further faculty must be called into play before the work is successfully completed. This is the faculty of intelligence, which gives to the movement of creative energy a lucid, self-descriptive and transparent regard. Without this conversion of the indwelling life into clear, objective, and conscious terms, the work—for all its motion or vigour—will be muddy like the face of a disturbed fast-flowing stream.

My point, then—to return to Emily—is that in her lesser

poems the rhythm results from a true intuition of "creative energy" by her subconscious mind. The effect of this—as we shall see—is that it manifests all those peculiar attributes of organic life: it is flexible, tensile, emphatic, yet delicate. We feel it possesses some inward sense of balance, which gives it both strength and grace of carriage. Hardly anywhere in Emily's verse is the ear offended by the mechanical 'tumpty-tumpty' beat of a super-imposed metre. Her rhythms appear to contain their own supply of change and repetition. We feel them to be self-generating forms.

Now rhythm is one of man's earliest possessions; and in primitive art and society, we find it to a much greater degree than in civilised communities. In fact, there is every cause to believe that a gain in man's reasoning faculty implies a loss to his sense of rhythm. It is as if the tempo of the two were opposed.

When we apply these reflections to Emily, they do indeed seem to explain her verse.

A primitive type, as we know her to have been—almost atavistic in certain aspects—her sense of rhythm was sensitive and developed, as if she imitated in her verse the spontaneous rhythms of natural creation—of animals, birds, and foliage, the moving patterns of winds and waters.

But just as we know her intelligence to have been powerful, we know from M. Héger, her teacher, how utterly intractable it was:

> I'll walk where my own nature would be leading:
> It vexes me to choose another guide.

she had written in the defiant poem *Often rebuked, yet always back returning*. No further evidence could be more forthright!

Of course, the intelligence must not be equated with the ratiocinative faculty exactly, but both of them are functions of the conscious mind, which we can hazard was less developed in Emily than her pristine subconscious.

Now if a poet's sense of rhythm is dependent upon his

primitive finesse—the responsive inner ear of his subconscious mind—then his choice of diction can be shown to depend on the critical assessment of his conscious powers of thought. Emily's rhythm, as we should expect, is superior in all her lesser poems to her rightness and breadth of diction; and if we believe that this question of diction is something determined by the conscious mind, then a further aspect of her vocabulary can also be explained by our knowledge of her.

That her narrowness and repetitiveness here, as well as her occasional excessive use of one word ("drear" and "dreary", for example) can be interpreted as the workings of a powerful, yet intractable, self-centred intelligence, is, I hope, not too high-flown a conjecture. With her own thoughts returning, obsessionally, to a few intense and intimate themes, what is more likely than that her language should show the same stiff narrow range. And when we remember that she was unwilling to share her confidence with any; and that, in addition, she was not quite clear in her own conscious mind about the nature of some of her thoughts, the inaccessibility or ambiguity or her language[1] and diction[2] becomes expected and explained.

This division between the fine free functioning of her instinctive rhythmic sense, and the often inadequate selection of words which her less developed consciousness gave rise to, accounts for the fact that in her lesser poems we can sometimes speak of her 'form' as distinct from her thought. By 'form', here, I mean the rhythmic planes and shape of her poems, which is all too often palpably superior to the meaning that it conveys.

Now this state of awareness in which we can distinguish between the form and substance of a poem is something that we do not experience when dealing with major poetry.

As Schelling wrote, in his lecture *Concerning the Relation of the Plastic Arts to Nature,* "Only by the consummation of

[1] and [2] I use the two terms in the following manner: 'diction' to signify the separate choice in individual epithets and words; and 'language' to signify the sum of such choices.

form can form be destroyed.'' Schelling's idea of a 'form' to be destroyed, here, is the notion we obtain of 'form' in a poem when we are able to distinguish it from the thought. The two, as he urged, should be indistinguishable, save to the most reflective analysis: that is, we should not become aware of one before, or distinct from, the other. We should not be able to say: 'I don't think the poet is saying anything interesting, but I do like his way of saying it'.

With Emily's lesser poems we can sometimes say this, because what we are getting is unmatched form—form to be destroyed—and not its consummation. But when we turn to her major poems, this distinction has disappeared. We are conscious of the poem as an immediate and indivisible utterance. We assent to it *in toto;* or not at all. Form's consummation has cancelled form's division.

And if we ask how this has been attained, by what mental processes the author has achieved it, the answer is written in the poems themselves: in the fact that, though more profound in thought and fervent in feeling than her previous poems, they are, at the same time, the more lucid. And this clarity which illuminates them is not the cool light of detachment: it is, instead, an incandescent glow in which the spirit voices its own self-knowledge.

So Emily's great poems represent those moments in which she achieved the goal of the sage who commanded us to know ourselves. When such inner vision of the self was effected, its outward expression was achieved by her also. With her subconscious mind she apprehended the currents of her life, whose direction her conscious mind made clear to her. In Croce's formula, such knowledge was expression: her consciousness became as fluent as a song.

All that remains for me to show in this chapter, is that the primitive rhythmic energy was ready, waiting in the lesser poems, for consciousness to bring it to full evolution, to bring it to the point of verbalisation, which is reached in Emily's six great pieces.

Consider, for example, her poem *D.G.C. to J.A.*:

> Come, the wind may never again
> Blow as now it blows for us;
> And the stars may never again shine as now they shine;
> Long before October returns,
> Seas of blood will have parted us;
> And you must crush the love in your heart, and I the love in mine!

The first stanza of this poem is entirely successful. Its rhythm is possessed of an individual movement which finely corresponds with the sense of the propitious moment that the poet speaks of. We note how effortlessly this effect is conveyed: how the rhyming-system of this stanza is not a closed, 'all-over' pattern ("again" does not rhyme but chimes with "return"; "us" rhymes with "us" not two but three lines later; and "shine" is a third-line rhyme for "mine"); but how internal and 'line-end' repetition make up for this lack, and produce an effect more rich than rhyme since more unexpected. "Never again", "blow", and "shine" are all repeated within the first three lines. Then comes a rest from repetition, till the sixth line, which runs beyond its anticipated length, and brings it back again by repeating "love" and "love".

But unlike the effect of a villanelle (where we often feel the repeated rhymes have only the charm of artifice), the repetition in this stanza seems to follow the contours of an excited voice. Along with the naturalness of the language, there goes a quality which is seldom to be found in a passage of spoken speech—that is, the sense of inevitability, of finally correct and measured words speaking about something which in itself is final. When we get instances of right words and rhythm remarking upon some situation in which a sense of destiny is felt to reside, we recognise their presence by a slight shiver. The nature of mortality haunts the utterance, and we hear the chill wind of fate in the poem.

But no sooner do we come to the second stanza of this piece than we find the magic ended. An elemental situation (which

Emily has imaginatively experienced) is changed for one of those melodramatic circumstances in which the Gondal cycle too prolifically abounds. This time it is a family vendetta; and we note that diction, thought, and rhythm immediately become a little blunted upon the introduction of this theme:

> For face to face will our kindred stand,
> And as they are so shall we be;
> Forgetting how the same sweet earth has borne and nourished all—
> One must fight for the people's power,
> And one for the Rights of Royalty;
> And each be ready to give his life to work the other's fall.

The last three lines present us with thought and language as crass and dull as a party-poster. We feel that the "rights of Royalty" and "the people's power" so badly define any such causes, for which they are slogans, that only fools would be convinced by them (political philosophy was not Emily's *forte*).

The next stanza sinks even deeper into the morass of muddle, for here we learn that it is not so much the "rights of Royalty" or the "people's power" that must be respected above individual interest, as "Ambition" (a new catch-phrase even less defensible than the last:

> The chance of war we cannot shun,
> Nor would we shrink from our father's cause,
> Nor dread Death more because the hand that gives it may be dear;
> We must bear to see Ambition rule
> Over Love, with his iron laws;
> Must yield our blood for a stranger's sake, and refuse ourselves a
> tear!

(If it is their fathers' cause that each have pledged themselves not to shun, how does it come about that they can talk of having to yield their blood for "a stranger's sake".)

The whole situation represents a case of trumped-up necessity. The thought is poor, and the feeling insincere, and the rhythm and language consequently suffer. No wonder, after two such stanzas, that Emily felt impelled to return to the pure music of the poem's beginning:

So, the wind may never again
Blow as now it blows for us,
And the stars may never again shine as now they shine;
Next October, the cannon's roar
From hostile ranks may be urging us—
Me to strike for your life's blood, and you to strike for mine.

But the motion of the words, in the varied lines, have lost something of their original lilt and spring.

Next October, the cannon's roar
From hostile ranks may be urging us—

compares unfavourably with the earlier lines:

Long before October returns,
Seas of blood will have parted us;

"Next October" is a prosy reference, and has none of the evocative suggestiveness of time running out which we get in "Long before October returns". We notice, too, that it seems to contradict the first and better reference, which presumably set the date for the recommencing of hostilities at some unspecified but earlier time. The factual muddle has perhaps resulted from the general blunting of language and thought.

A second comparison of lines in these two stanzas re-demonstrates the lowering of choice in the diction. "Hostile ranks" is a very abstract and regimental term of reference when contrasted with the estranging "Seas of blood". It is almost as if the immersion of Emily's thought (in the middle stanzas) in the fake world of Gondal heroics, has taken the edge off her discrimination.

But numberless examples could be cited of poems in which a virile and sensitive rhythm is let-down or flawed by false diction, or poems in which the rhythm just gives out, so that the poems come to an end, abruptly and prematurely, as it were. Such is the following fragment:

All hushed and still within the house;
Without—all wind and driving rain;
But something whispers to my mind,
Through rain and through the wailing wind,
    Never again.
Never again? Why not again?
Memory has power as real as thine.

What has happened here we cannot say. The note of plangency ceases to sound after the fifth line of the poem, as if Emily had stopped to reflect upon the experience she had been re-living.

Other pieces, such as *For him who struck thy foreign string* or *If grief for grief can touch thee,* exhibit a sureness and delicacy of rhythm which still fails to make the poem interesting in the manner of major poetry, because the thought and emotion of the poem follows a certain conventional line.

For all her fine auditory sense, Emily's power in poetry was demonstrated only when she was most original. This is not to say that she was unread, or that she did not *assimilate* a very great deal from the poetry of the past. But what she did assimilate was not a manner of thinking, so much as certain hints as to the use of language and rhythm. When she *did* reproduce another poet's manner of thinking (as in many of the Byronic Gondal pieces) the effect is generally farcical. She was too much herself to speak another's thoughts; and in the chapter that follows we shall study her thoughts and language when she was most herself.

THE POEMS

The End Attained

Emily's major poems are six in number. Here is their chronology. *There let thy bleeding branch atone* was composed in 1841, when Emily was twenty-two; *Cold in the earth, and the deep snow piled above thee* and *Death that struck when I was most confiding* in 1845, when she was twenty-six; *Julian M. and A. G. Rochelle* later in 1845, when she was twenty-seven; *No coward soul is mine* at the beginning of 1846, when she was in her twenty-seventh year; and *Often rebuked yet always back returning* whose date of composition is uncertain.

There let thy bleeding branch atone is dim in meaning when compared with the others. If we contrast the illumination (in terms of intelligible statements) present in this poem with the fierce brilliance of *No coward soul is mine* or the serene noon-light of *Often rebuked yet always back returning*, then its substance is indeed dark. But that which is not open to clear interpretation, may yet have power to work upon us.

There let thy bleeding branch atone
For every torturing tear:
Shall my young sins, my sins alone,
Be everlasting here?

Who bade thee keep that cursed name
A pledge for memory?
As if Oblivion ever came
To breathe its bliss on me;

As if, through all the 'wildering maze
Of mad hours left behind,
I once forgot the early days
That thou wouldst call to mind.

Of course, we can say, in a general fashion, that the poem has a prose meaning, and—for what it is worth—we can even précis it;[1] but what is more important here is its meaning for the sensibility, inherent in its images, and its word-music.

Of these, the first, in its repercussive power, is the image of "thy bleeding branch", with its strong evocation of a sense of mutilation, of self-amputation or sacrifice. It is difficult to say which of these three notions the image most powerfully seems to convey. We may think, as we register the physical impact of this horrific and potent figure, of the rough blood-stained cross of the Crucifixion, or of the Wood of Suicides in Dante's *Inferno,* where boughs that bleed[2] when they are broken are inhabited by those who took their own lives. We may also care to see in this image the first draft of "Time's withered branch" in the poem *Death, that struck when I was most confiding.* In this latter composition, the "withered branch" is sacrificed so "that other boughs may flourish"; and the same sort of expiation seems to be in mind in the present poem.

But whether we interpret the image as one of self-sacrifice or self-mutilation, the sense of loss remains the same; and it is this sense of loss, combined with a sense of self-pity and guilt, which fires the first stanza with its passion. This feeling comes out in a stark alliteration, in a word-music that does not flow smoothly and evenly throughout the stanzas, but rather in one that changes its key, so to speak, in each line. In the first verse we have two 'bs' ("bleeding branch"), in the second two 'ts' ("torturing tear"), and in the third two 'ss' ("young sins, my sins"). The pattern is varied by the fourth line, where the musical and imaginative stress comes on "everlasting", a four-syllabled word, after a run of nine one-syllabled ones. Its auditory length corresponds to the greater gravity of the question it poses—can there be no relief from sin and pain?

1 The poem appears to be 'about' memory, guilt, sacrifice or self-denial. "thy bleeding branch" makes one think of the Crucifixion, but there is no capital letter to "thy", so that the sacrifice suggested would seem to be not God's but that of some human person (it is possibly the poet addressing herself). But the sacrifice, whoever it is by, appears to be intended to purchase relief from tears of remorse and memory. At the same time, there is the hint, in the last two stanzas of the poem, that this persistence of memory will remain.

2 Dante had the idea from Vergil's *Aeniad.*

The second stanza employs a modified version of the same stark consonantal pattern as the first.

But of greater import and wider interest is the way in which the thought of this third stanza prefigures the obsession with memory which we get in the poem *Cold in the earth*. Whereas in this poem the speaker says that she cannot forget, in the latter poem what she asserts—with an even greater passion—is that she *dare* not remember:

And even yet, I dare not let it languish,
Dare not indulge in Memory's rapturous pain;
Once drinking deep of that divinest anguish,
How could I seek the empty world again?

Within the brief scope of its three stanzas, this poem appears to be the seed-bed for Emily's two great utterances upon the nature of earthly memory and passion.

Cold in the earth, of all Emily's poems, is probably the best known and the most anthologised.

Cold in the earth, and the deep snow piled above thee!
Far, far removed, cold in the dreary grave!
Have I forgot, my only Love, to love thee,
Severed at last by Time's all-wearing wave?

Now, when alone, do my thoughts no longer hover
Over the mountains on Angora's shore;
Resting their wings where heath and fern-leaves cover
That noble heart for ever, ever more?

Cold in the earth, and fifteen wild Decembers
From those brown hills have melted into spring—
Faithful indeed is the spirit that remembers
After such years of change and suffering!

Sweet Love of youth, forgive if I forget thee
While the World's tide is bearing me along:
Sterner desires and darker hopes beset me,
Hopes which obscure but cannot do thee wrong.

No other Sun has lightened up my heaven;
No other Star has ever shone for me:
All my life's bliss from thy dear life was given—
All my life's bliss is in the grave with thee.

But when the days of golden dreams had perished
And even Despair was powerless to destroy,
Then did I learn how existence could be cherished,
Strengthened and fed without the aid of joy;

Then did I check the tears of useless passion,
Weaned my young soul from yearning after thine;
Sternly denied its burning wish to hasten
Down to that tomb already more than mine!

And even then, I dare not let it languish,
Dare not indulge in Memory's rapturous pain;
Once drinking deep of that divinest anguish,
How could I seek the empty world again?

If we paraphrase this poem, we find how the statement of emotion develops by means of a paradox. The woman (Rosina of Alcona) recalls her early love—her "only Love", as she styles it—and questions herself upon her remembrance of this intense passion which death terminated. 'Have I forgotten to love you?' she asks, adding, that after fifteen years only the faithful would still remember, 'Ah, yes,' she answers, 'I have put you out of mind; since after your death I had somehow to learn how it was possible to live without joy. This, in some measure, I have achieved; but I could not have done it had I remembered you; and still, even now, I do not dare remember. To dwell upon you, would make me unfit to face a world in which I have no joy. I have forgotten you because I still love you, and to think upon that love would be death.'

The poem's most obvious merit is clearly the rhythm; and this is assisted by other devices which add to the uniqueness of its sound-effects. Perhaps the most important of these is the cæsura or division of the line in the first verse of each of the first four stanzas. This division is marked by a comma (in stanza 2 by the second comma). It is very difficult to analyse our exact reactions to this, but I suspect that it corresponds to the effect made upon us by the break of emotion in the voice of a singer or a speaker.

As we have noticed before, Emily is careful never to exhaust our response to some device of hers by unvarying repetition. In the next three stanzas, the cæsura is omitted, returning only in the final stanza. To take its place, she organises these next three stanzas to a rhetorical pattern. This she effects, in the first of these, by means of parallel statements: "*No* other Sun has lightened up my heaven/*No* other Star has ever shone for me: /*All* my life's bliss from thy dear life was given—/*All* my life's bliss is in the grave with thee." The two following stanzas are organised as couplets; not couplets as far as rhyme is concerned, but couplets in the sense that each pair of lines provides a separate unit of thought. The first two are concerned with the sense of loss and the desolation it brings to the spirit:

> But when the days of golden dreams had perished
> And even Despair was powerless to destroy,

After this, comes the break—the rehabilitation of the will trying to bring about an act of retrenchment:

> Then did I learn how existence could be cherished,
> Strengthened and fed without the aid of joy:

The next stanza observes the same organisation; but the break is less easy to recognise, because there is no preposition or adverb to indicate its occurrence. Nevertheless, the thought changes here, in the third line, as in the preceding stanza. This change constitutes an intensification of the death-wish spoken of in the first two lines, but therein held more firmly back:

> Then did I check the tears of useless passion,
> Weaned my young soul from yearning after thine;
> Sternly denied its burning wish to hasten
> Down to that tomb already more than mine!

We note, in the last two lines, how restraint is indicated by the initial words "Sternly denied", but how the language seems to slip the leash, showing us how the thought has done so, too: "burning wish to hasten/Down to that tomb already more than mine". "Already' 'and "mine" clinch the matter. They mark the end of a precipitate descent which the will has long been trying to contain. It is hints like this in her verbal texture, as much as her explicit statements, which tell us why stoicism was not enough for Emily. It could not, consistently or firmly enough, hold the memory of passion in place. If, then, her whole nature was not to grow cold, the only hope for her was to attempt a metamorphosis of this stock of inward passion. In *Death that struck when I was most confiding,* we see her following such a procedure.

Cold in the earth is a very masculine poem; by which I mean its structure shows all the stress, its rhythms and rhymes all the heavy definite beat, which we associate with masculine thinking. Exclamation (the first two lines have no verb), repetition of important key-words ("cold", "far", and "love" in the first stanza, to carry the analysis no further), rhymes of varying numbers of syllables ("Decembers"—"remembers", "spring"—"suffering", "more"—"shore", "languish"—"anguish"); these are but a few traits in the poem that serve to indicate its vigorous structure, its avoidance of a neat and light formal symmetry. In the next poem, we find them also, along with one or two new characteristics.

Death that struck when I was most confiding was written the same year as *Cold in the earth.* In a way, this latter can be described as an attempt to deal with memory in a relentless and ruthless fashion. But, as we have seen, this intention failed. The poem breathes such an intense current of nostalgia that the conscious effort to repress it leaves but little impression upon us.

In *Death that struck . . .* the effort is successful. Or rather we should say, nostalgia is not so much suppressed as transcended. The exaltation of *amor fati* suddenly seems to sweep over the poet; and, instead of attempting to drive underground the insidious memory of human passion, she appears to mount upwards, propelled by it. Her thoughts become not mundane but celestial. This is a metaphorical way of talking, but it is difficult to convey the vertiginous and vertical excitement that seems to give this poem wings, without resorting to figurative language. In part, I think, it can be explained by saying that the poem moves between two opposite poles—of negation and assertion. That which is negated is earthly life, with its prospects of hope and joy; and that which is asserted is "Eternity"—the state beyond time and human existence, and the reservoir out of which these come. And the same passion which formerly fed the aspirations of earthly life has now been turned, as a stream is turned, to feed and drive an 'eternal' mode of thinking:

DEATH

Death, that struck when I was most confiding
In my certain Faith of Joy to be,
Strike again, Time's withered branch dividing
From the fresh root of Eternity!

Leaves, upon Time's branch, were growing brightly
Full of sap and full of silver dew;
Birds, beneath its shelter, gathered nightly;
Daily, round its flowers, the wild bees flew.

Sorrow passed and plucked the golden blossom,
Guilt stripped off the foliage in its pride;
But within its parent's kindly bosom,
Flowed forever Life's restoring tide.

Little mourned I for the parted Gladness,
For the vacant nest and silent song;
Hope was there and laughed me out of sadness,
Whispering, "Winter will not linger long".

And behold, with tenfold increase blessing
Spring adorned the beauty-burdened spray;
Wind and rain and fervent heat caressing
Lavished glory on that second May.

High it rose; no winged grief could sweep it;
Sin was scared to distance with its shine:
Love and its own life had power to keep it
From all wrong, from every blight but thine!

Heartless Death, the young leaves droop and languish!
Evening's gentle air may yet restore—
No: the morning sunshine mocks my anguish—
Time for me must never blossom more!

Strike it down, that other boughs may flourish
Where that perished sapling used to be;
Thus, at least, its mouldering corpse will nourish
That from which it sprung—Eternity.

In this poem, as in certain modern novels, we are presented at the start with a *fait accompli*. The poet then goes back in time to recapitulate the thread of events which have led to this conclusion; and the last stanza reinforces the substance of the first.

But after the original chord, in which doom and exaltation are blended, we notice how the next five stanzas declare a faith in life and proclaim its beauty. And this instinctive persistence and praise is all the more to be remarked in that destructive forces have already made their inroads known. Time is envisaged as a tree, upon which sorrow and guilt work their havoc. Even after guilt has despoiled the plenitude provided by the foliage, the poet is consoled by thinking that, unseen but present, within the trunk "Flowed forever Life's restoring tide." And so the sense of fulness and fruition returns:

> And behold, with tenfold increase blessing
> Spring adorned the beauty-burdened spray;
> Wind and rain and fervent heat caressing
> Lavished glory on that second May.

It is possible, and perhaps necessary, to interpret this passage in the widest fashion; to say, that even after innocence is gone, and experience has confirmed a tragic view of life, existence still can offer abundant riches and nature appear as a granary of plenty.

Then comes the final knock of destiny. This time it is "Death", and upon its introduction the sense of possibility is utterly withered. But that which is no longer possible in time, may be so outside of it. Thus it is that the poet rejoices at death's appearance as eternity's herald. Since the "perished sapling" of time can never blossom gloriously again, she is glad to think that it will be felled, and that eternity will be the richer for its decaying wood.

Another element in her exaltation lies in the thought that the sacrifice of this dying branch will give other boughs a chance. (The whole poem furnishes a strangely prophetic and lyrical economy which might well, with certain reservations, have fitted in with Darwin's theory of the survival of the fittest—but perhaps these reservations are all important!)[3]

3 We have to remember that while Darwin was concerned with the physical economy of such matters, Emily was concerned with those most fittest to survive in a purely spiritual sense in this poem. *Wuthering Heights,* it is true, is another proposition; for there the economy, as with Darwin, is largely of a physical order.

In a sense, we can say that Emily was determined to live for joy (as Nietzsche was determined to stand up for life, and Rilke was determined to praise it). When she found, as in this poem, that joy could no longer be expected as a purely human condition for her, she turned her thoughts to eternity and death, as offering what the earth had ceased to offer.

However this may be, it is true that her next two great poems, in point of time, convey, the one—her deepest mystical experience, and the other—the noblest and highest statement of her metaphysical beliefs.

In the seven[4] fine stanzas of the poem *Julian M. and A. G. Rochelle,* we see how both the life-wish and the death-wish in Emily were working together to assert the reality of a mystical experience. All the power with which she was wont to praise and express the life of nature (and there is nature-imagery in this poem) is now at the service of what she calls "the Invisible" and "the Unseen". At the same time, she seems to recognise that such experience must take its toll of her, must exhaust the resources of her spirit by consuming them too rapidly. Such, at any rate, would appear to be the meaning of her words:

> A messenger of Hope comes every night to me,
> And offers, for short life, eternal liberty.

Not that she bewails such a situation. "If it but herald Death, the vision is divine", she proclaims. No longer an instinct for self-preservation, the life-wish in Emily was now urging her on in a direction where the death-wish beckoned.

> Yet, tell them, Julian, all, I am not doomed to wear
> Year after year in gloom and desolate despair;
> A messenger of Hope comes every night to me,
> And offers, for short life, eternal liberty.
>
> He comes with western winds, with evening's wandering airs,
> With that clear dusk of heaven that brings the thickest stars;
> Winds take a pensive tone, and stars a tender fire,
> And visions rise and change which kill me with desire—

4 the many other stanzas to this poem, as I have shown in Part I, *The Bogus Background,* are poetically insignificant.

Desire for nothing known in my maturer years
When joy grew mad with awe at counting future tears;
When, if my spirit's sky was full of flashes warm,
I knew not whence they came, from sun or thunder-storm;

But first a hush of peace, a soundless calm descends;
The struggle of distress and fierce impatience ends;
Mute music soothes my breast—unuttered harmony
That I could never dream till earth was lost to me.

Then dawns the Invisible, the Unseen its truth reveals;
My outward sense is gone, my inward essence feels—
Its wings are almost free, its home, its harbour found;
Measuring the gulf is stoops and dares the final bound!

Oh dreadful is the check—intense the agony
When the ear begins to hear and the eye begins to see;
When the pulse begins to throb, the brain to think again,
The soul to feel the flesh and the flesh to feel the chain!

Yet I would lose no sting, would wish no torture less;
The more that anguish racks the earlier it will bless;
And robed in fires of Hell, or bright with heavenly shine,
If it but herald Death, the vision is divine!

No other poem in the English language conveys *and* describes the mystical experience so consummately as this. But it is the experience of a mystic possessed of no communal religion, and therefore lacking any general speech of symbolism to account for the event. We cannot say who or what the power is that has visited Emily, but what we can do is to follow the workings of that spirit upon her from the time of its approach to its departure.

The "messenger of Hope", of which she speaks, produces within her a sense of timeless freedom. His approach is marked by certain natural symptoms, in which the life of the elements take on a greater vividness. It would be wrong to describe these symptoms (mentioned in stanza 2) as just so many pantheistic stirrings. There is no symbolism or personification, nor any hidden metaphysics, which would justify us in making such a statement. None the less—as we have observed in the chapter on Emily's "Foreground Thought"—the natural activities of wind, and sky, and light, often produced the initial working of some mystical train of thought within her.

Then, too, we have seen how night itself was a time that seemed specially propitious for Emily's transcendental moods.

What it is that comes to her can only be described, in stanza 3, in terms of what it is not—"Desire for nothing known in my maturer years". This corresponds to what the mystics of the school of St. John of the Cross referred to as the *via negativa*—the negative way to the absolute truth.

The next stanza is concerned with that making void of the contents of the spirit, so that it may receive the substance of the mystical visitation. Then, when "earth is lost", the mind receives the body of the experience. This is described in stanza 5, and can only be hinted at by the use of such terms as "the Invisible" and "the Unseen", and the idea of a purely spiritual faculty (opposed to the ordinary "outward sense") which perceives the otherwise imperceptible.

Stanza 6 speaks of the return to a state of normal consciousness, and how this consciousness strikes the late communicant almost as a kind of death. Stanza 7, which terminates the inspired portion of the poem, confesses that however bitter may be the average awareness of existence after such exalted perception, it is amply compensated by the vision granted. 'And perhaps', it suggests, 'this disappointment may hasten death, the supreme blessing.' The emotional core of Emily's religion suddenly becomes clear to us—hers is a mysticism of the death-wish.

So direct and lucid is this poem that stylistic comments are hardly called for. It exists in the clarity of its own beauty, with an obviousness that only great art can afford if it is to avoid the banal.

No coward soul is mine is Emily's crowning poetic peak. It is also the consummation of her thought—her highest and clearest statement of it. Just as the last poem was concerned with eternity apprehended through death, so this poem apprehends eternity in terms of a positive—immortal life. In the last poem, Emily's apprehension of her theme was mystical, and therefore not capable of direct formulation. In this poem, it is intellectual: her language is fervid, succinct, and classical. But besides the development of general ideas (which constitute metaphysical poetry), this poem resorts to abstracts and concepts; to words like "Faith", "Undying Life", "Existence", "Being", "Immortality". Terms of such grave and universal import are usually enough to sink any poem, especially if it be couched in lyrical form. Yet so great is the propulsion of thought and rhythm here, that the poem strikes us as being more direct than most short poems of sensuous diction. For all the generalising reference of its language, the poem is neither impersonal nor cold. It has Emily's signature stamped upon it—is private and subjective experience intellectualised to the highest degree, but still retaining the original colours of the mind which made it its own. After the seventeenth century, there is no religious poem in the English language which has the same intensity and integrity of expression comparable to it, until we come to Gerard Manley Hopkins.

NO COWARD SOUL IS MINE

No coward soul is mine
No trembler in the world's storm-troubled sphere
I see Heaven's glories shine
And Faith shines equal arming me from Fear.

O God within my breast,
Almighty ever-present Deity,
Life, that in me has rest
As I Undying Life, have power in thee.

Vain are the thousand creeds
That move men's hearts, unutterably vain,
Worthless as withered weeds
Or idlest froth amid the boundless main

To waken doubt in one
Holding so fast by thy infinity
So surely anchored on
The steadfast rock of immortality.

With wide-embracing love
Thy spirit animates eternal years,
Pervades and broods above,
Changes, sustains, dissolves, creates and rears.

Though Earth and moon were gone
And suns and universes ceased to be
And thou wert left alone
Every Existence would exist in thee.

There is no room for Death
Nor atom that his might could render void
Since thou art Being and Breath
And what thou art may never be destroyed.

The greatness of this poem consists in the presence of deep emotion and intellectual clarity. Compare, for example, the impassioned invocation of the second stanza with the formulation of the workings of deity in the fifth stanza. May Sinclair has objected to the latter stanza on the grounds that it "recalls almost painfully the frigid poets of Deism of the eighteenth century". With this censure, I cannot agree. The Augustan poets would never have strung out that fine fourth line of the stanza—"Changes, sustains, dissolves, creates, and rears" so suggestive, with its protean row of verbs of the motions of some perennial process. And it is the exact definitive value which the words of this poem possess—infused, as they are, with a compulsive emotion—that makes for its double appeal to the heart and to the head.

Yet with all the clarity present in this piece, it is surprising how often lines from it are quoted to prove points that Emily never held:

Vain are the thousand creeds
That move men's hearts, unutterably vain

is often cited, out of its context, as demonstrating Emily's complete scepticism. But what she actually said was not that these creeds are vain in themselves, but that the presence of many religions did not move her to a profession of doubt, since her own beliefs were

So surely anchored on
The steadfast rock of immortality.

Sceptical, one might still allow her statement to be; but it is the scepticism which some of the mystics have experienced when confronted with differing theological formulæ. It is not the scepticism of the agnostic, of the mind converted to doubt by a study of comparative religions.

Of *No coward soul is mine,* there is no need for me to speak further, in the way of exposition. It is one of those poems that perfectly defines itself. In it, Emily's currents of thought come together like various vapours and liquids pumped through the jet of a high-pressure lamp. They fuse and take light instantaneously; and the words that serve to express these thoughts become—like a pure and incandescent mantle—a lighted envelope through which the light pours through. Her deepest thoughts and most instinctive feelings burn in this poem with the total fusion that comes only seldom in a life-time; since the statements they combine to shape are both so personal and so comprehensive.

The final poem belonging to Emily's great set of six is *Often rebuked, yet always back returning*. In this context, we might choose to see the piece as a kind of postscript on Emily's poetics. It does not tell us much about her notions of mysticism and the metaphysical, but it serves to assert her utter independence—the means by which she guaranteed and guarded her powerfully personal perception of these. But apart from the place it occupies in the body of Emily's poems, it is of value through its fine expression of single-mindedness. No higher proclamation of the purposeful mind in lyrical poetry has ever been issued:

Often rebuked, yet always back returning
To those first feelings that were born with me,
And leaving busy chase of wealth and learning
For idle dreams of things that cannot be:

To-day, I will not seek the shadowy region;
Its unsustaining vastness waxes drear;
And visions rising, legion after legion,
Bring the unreal world too strangely near.

I'll walk, but not in old heroic traces,
And not in paths of high morality,
And not among the high-distinguished faces,
The clouded forms of long-past history.

I'll walk where my own nature would be leading:
It vexes me to choose another guide:
Where the gray flocks in ferny glens are feeding;
Where the wild wind blows on the mountain side.

What have those lonely mountains worth revealing?
More glory and more grief than I can tell:
The earth that wakes *one* human heart to feeling
Can centre both the worlds of Heaven and Hell.

Strangely enough, Mr. C. W. Hatfield inclines to the belief that Charlotte, not Emily, was the author of it; and in his edition of the Poems he writes:

> . . ."that it savours more strongly of Charlotte than Emily, seeming to express Charlotte's thoughts about her sister, rather than Emily's own thoughts. Since the purpose of Charlotte's publicity was to help bring the public to a better understanding of Emily's work, it would have been in keeping with the editorial liberties she took in other connections to offer such an interpretation of her sister in the guise of Emily's own words."

Charlotte, we know, was not past this sort of thing; but nothing proves that she had ever committed familiarities of quite so dark an order. The only evidence for Mr. Hatfield's belief is of a negative nature: namely, that of the eighteen poems of Emily, which Charlotte published in 1850, seventeen only have been found in manuscript; the eighteenth, and missing one, being the manuscript of this very poem.

But against this, there must be considered the internal evidence of the two poets as present in their work; and, for a sensitive treatment of poetry, evidence of this kind must be paramount.

Can we imagine Charlotte ever writing the first two lines of stanza 1, all of the superb stanza 5, and any but the second line (perhaps) of stanza 6? It is possible, I believe, that all of stanza 3 might have been Charlotte's writing. The inexpressive clutter of adjectives, and the very marked literary phrasing of a rather conventional order, are certainly different from Emily's style, both in her good and bad poetic moments.

They have neither the directness of the one, nor the strident bombast of the other.

Whether we must take this stanza to be saying, that she—Emily—will not indulge in her Gondal fantasy on this occasion; or that she is neither going to read nor write about the heroes of myths and history, but—instead—is going to soothe her mind with the objects of nature, there is no means of knowing.

If the first supposition is the right one, it seems a little inappropriate to refer to the chronicles of the machiavellian Gondals, and the drama of their blood-drenched politics, as "high morality"; but the way in which authors conceive of their own work should teach us to accommodate incongruities.

To me, it seems most likely that the poem is, substantially, Emily's, with one or two lines or phrases—and possibly the whole of stanza 3—by Charlotte. This hypothesis would account for the missing manuscript of the poem, as much as if it were all Charlotte's work; since, presumably, the latter would not wish for the original of a poem so much revised by her to come to light.

Many of the strands of Emily's thought I have striven to unravel in her poems, will be encountered again in *Wuthering Heights,* though in a less metaphysical content. Unlike Blake, who only succeeded in being metaphysical when he was most impersonal (that is, in his *Prophetic Books,* as distinct from his individual utterance in the *Songs of Innocence and Experience*); and unlike Shelley, who often confounded the metaphysical with the unsubstantial—ideas and notions with fancies and dreams—Emily was most metaphysical as a poet when she was being most herself. And when she was herself, her ideas were clear. Her personality imparted to her notions —however universal in import they might be—a keen particularity of language and rhythm; which gives, in its turn, to what Yeats once called "the fascination of what's difficult", the strong immediacy of the unreflecting.

"WUTHERING HEIGHTS"

Divided Witness

Too much and too little has been made of this novel — perhaps inevitably, through its very nature; for, as Rossetti wrote in 1854, "It is a fiend of a book. The action is laid in hell—only it seems places and people have English names there". Indeed, *Wuthering Heights* is charged with a voltage that precludes all temperate responses. The reader tends to think of it as either one of the greatest English novels, or as something that is hardly fiction at all—the strayed masterpiece of a mistaken genius.

As I do not hold either of these views, I shall first give a sample of opinions on this book; next, examine its plot and its characters, its style, and the values it seems to maintain; and then attempt to reformulate its type, achievement, merits and demerits, with some consideration of the place it holds in relation to fiction before and after Emily.

It is natural that we should begin by resorting to Charlotte for her impression.

> *"Wuthering Heights"*, she wrote in her Preface to the second edition of this novel, "was hewn in a wild workshop, with simple tools, out of homely materials. The statuary found a granite block on a solitary moor; gazing thereon, he saw how from the crag might be elicited a head, savage, swart, sinister; a form moulded with at least one element of grandeur—power. He wrought with a rude chisel, and from no model but the vision of his meditations."

Charlotte, we see, put her finger on all the principal traits of this work: its strange, 'home-grown', Homeric independence, the solitary nature of its performance, its unconcerned lack of reference to current literary theories of the nature of fiction, and the general uncivilised yet sublime spirit which infuses so many of its pages. Her judgment has proved the starting-off point for many other critics who have written on this novel. For example, Sir Herbert Read endorses it, when he writes:[1]

> "*Wuthering Heights* remains, the towering rock of Charlotte's metaphor, extremely definite, completely achieved, and of an amazing unity of tone".

But along with her positive statement of Emily's achievement in *Wuthering Heights,* it must not be forgotten that Charlotte felt bound to register her sense of uneasiness about it. Speaking of the folk and peasantry of Haworth, whom Emily used as the first drafts for her characters, Charlotte wrote:

> "what her mind had gathered of the real concerning them, was too exclusively confined to those tragic and terrible traits of which, in listening to the secret annals of every rude vicinage, the memory is sometimes compelled to receive the impress. Her imagination, which was a spirit more sombre than sunny, more powerful than sportive, found in such traits material whence it wrought creatures like Heathcliff, like Earnshaw, like Catherine. Having formed these beings she did not know what she had done." "Whether it is right or advisable", she continues, "to create beings like Heathcliff, I do not know: I scarcely think it is. But this I know: the writer who possesses the creative gift owns something of which he is not always master—something that, at times, strangely wills and works for itself."

In these last sentences, we see Charlotte's dilemma. Her plea for Emily's creation is that it was the work of necessity. This work she knew to be possessed of grandeur, but about its moral desirability, the wisdom of it, she was more than doubtful.

The majority of critics, writing after this statement, have

[1] see his essay *Charlotte and Emily Brontë* in his volume *Reason and Romanticism* (1926).

inclined to emphasise, in their own pronouncements, one or the other of its component parts: to plead necessity on Emily's behalf, and leave it at that; or to find in its lack of wisdom and balance a telling and sufficient condemnation. "There never was such a thunderstorm of a novel",[2] proclaimed Arthur Symons; whilst on another occasion[3] he wrote:

> "*Wuthering Heights*" is one long outcry. A soul on the rack seems to make itself heard at moments, when suffering has grown too acute for silence."

For Symons, the fact that the book was possessed of a powerful resonance was quite enough. With the moral and aesthetic implications of this, or the repercussion of its tone upon later fiction, he was not at all concerned.

For Swinburne, too, the upshot of the matter is very largely the same:

> "The book", he writes, "is what it is because the author was what she was; that is the central fact to be remembered."[4]

Like many of the free-lance English critics, writing in a time of social individualism, Swinburne and Symons were chiefly interested in the glorious isolation of the book before them. Questions of how the work affected — whether it strengthened or weakened—traditions: traditions of fiction and of conduct, were generally ignored by them. The academic critic, however, with his training in historical continuity, tends to assess a work within a perspective of past and future. So little of this prized continuity seemed to be discernable in Emily's work that Saintsbury concluded that:

> "*Wuthering Heights* is one of those isolated books which, whatever their merits, are rather ornaments than essential parts in novel history."[5]

Saintsbury, of course, we accept as a critic who had the courage of his prejudices; but, in a less cavalier fashion, we find

2 see his book *Dramatis Personæ* (1925).

3 *Emily Brontë* (1906), reprinted in *Figures of Several Centuries* (1916).

4 see his essay *Emily Brontë* in the volume of his work entitled *Miscellanies* (1911).

5 *The English Novel,* by George Saintsbury (1913).

his opinion corroborated by Hugh Walker,[6] who observed:

"*Wuthering Heights* is a novel of extraordinary power. . . . But it is a book not to be read with pleasure. The first picture of the Heights is revolting from its brutal inhumanity. To those who know only the softer southern life, the wild stories and the rugged characters of Yorkshire seem to be here exaggerated almost beyond the bounds of belief; and however these stories may explain, they do not in art justify such a picture. The book is spoilt because its author has not known how to humanise it. If Charlotte Brontë's work is impaired because she makes too deep the shadows and shows too little the lights of life, Emily sins in that way tenfold more grievously. And yet there is an irresistible attraction in all that remains of this austere and sombre genius. What might not such "passion, vehemence, grief, daring," have accomplished if years had brought a mellower wisdom to guide them? Emily Brontë was clearly the inferior of her sister in artistic sense; and what she has accomplished, with the exception of her noble poems, is far less valuable. Even in the hands of Time she might have proved an intractable pupil, and have marred other novels as she marred *Wuthering Heights* by the very excess of the qualities which made her great."

By nature more logical and formal than his English counterpart, the independent French critic will often be found to bear out what the academic critic over here has arrived at. So, in his book *The Brontë Sisters* (1927), Ernest Dimnet writes:

"One realises that it is wrong to *Wuthering Heights* to call it a novel. It is a sort of Homeric poem where all the details are true, but in which, however, there is perceived something unreal. The truth, but not of this world. That is the fault in the book, a lack of equilibrium and harmony, something troubling like a dream or, too often, a nightmare. But this is also its magic. Emily has had the unusual power to believe herself and to make us believe in characters and

6 *The Literature of the Victorian Era,* by Hugh Walker (1913).

events of which a fifteen-year-old boy could demonstrate the impossibility."

A somewhat analagous judgment to this is passed by F. R. Leavis—an academic critic with a more than usual dislike and suspicion of academic opinion—when he writes:[7]

"I have said nothing about *Wuthering Heights* because that astonishing work seems to me a kind of sport. It may, all the same, very well have had some influence of an essentially undetectable kind: she broke completely, and in the most challenging way, both with the Scott tradition that imposed on the novelist a romantic resolution of his themes, and with the tradition coming down from the eighteenth century that demanded a plane mirror reflection of the surface of 'real' life. Out of her a minor tradition comes, to which belongs, most notably, *The House with the Green Shutters*."

But perhaps this statement begs the question; for if *Wuthering Heights* is a great work, can it be situated in a minor tradition? And greatness, of some kind or another, either spasmodically or continuously present, seems, by a general consensus, allowed it.

In his splendid essay on *Wuthering Heights,* Lord David Cecil suggests a way out of the implicit dilemma which Charlotte was the first to sense.

"We take for granted", he writes, "that an author writing a novel in the Victorian age is trying to write an orthodox Victorian novel; and we estimate it accordingly. Now by any such criterion there is no doubt that Emily Brontë is a very imperfect novelist indeed. If *Wuthering Heights* was meant to be the same sort of novel as *Vanity Fair* or *David Copperfield,* it is a lamentable failure.

"But it was never meant to be anything of the kind. The first fact to be realised about Emily Brontë, if we are ever to appreciate her properly, is that her achievement is of

[7] in his book *The Great Tradition* (1948).

an intrinsically different kind from that of any of her contemporaries."

But this, continues Lord David, is not to say that Emily is an exotic—"hers is an English imagination". It is just that the national traits of this—violence, unself-consciousness, and spirituality—are expressing themselves in a different form from that which her contemporaries employed in their writing of fiction.

Is this, then, the real retort to those critics who find *Wuthering Heights* great in spite of itself; who feel that its greatness does not belong to the form which Emily appropriated for it, but somehow persists, notwithstanding the medium?

Before we can answer one way or another, it is necessary for us to examine the character, plot, and spirit of this novel.

"WUTHERING HEIGHTS"

Plot and Players

One of the controversies which critics have waged around *Wuthering Heights* concerns the nature of its plot, its construction, and—more particularly—method of narration. Briefly, one school is of the opinion that both of these are inadequate—it is obscure and involved; whilst the other maintains that its obscurity is due to our lack of attention and not to any defective treatment of the theme.

Both the plot and the narrative manner have been precised by Phyllis Bentley, whose excellent resumé of the book shows, at least, that the tale *can* be reduced to order. In her monograph, *The Brontë Sisters,* we find the following condensed account:

> "The story of *Wuthering Heights* is in essence simple, concerning two symmetrical families and an intruding stranger. The Earnshaw family—a bluff, prosperous Yorkshireman, his wife, his son Hindley, his daughter Catherine—live in their handsome old family farmhouse, Wuthering Heights, up in the folds of the moors. . . . The Linton family, richer and more genteel, landed gentry—Mr. Linton, his wife, his son Edgar, his daughter Isabella—live down in a neighbouring valley at Thrushcross Grange. One day Mr. Earnshaw brings home to the Heights a sallow, ragged little boy he has found wandering in the streets of a city which he has visited for business. To this waif he gives the name of Heathcliff. The children grow up together; Catherine loves Heathcliff, while Hindley hates him from jealousy of his father's fondness for the stranger. Mr. Earnshaw and his wife die, Hindley degrades Heathcliff in every way he can; the lad grows brutal and morose and Catherine turns from him to the mild Edgar Linton. Heathcliff decamps, to return later when Catherine is Edgar's wife, rich and

with the manners of a gentleman concealing his dark, fierce heart. Between Heathcliff and Edgar, Catherine becomes distracted; she gives birth to Edgar's daughter, Cathy, and dies. Heathcliffe then sets himself to ruin both families in revenge. He turns Hindley into a drunkard and gambler and wins all his possessions, so that his son Hareton Earnshaw is a pauper in Heathcliff's house. Heathcliff contrives to marry Edgar Linton's vain, silly sister Isabella, and after her death marries Linton's daughter Cathy to his own peevish, ailing son. But all his revenge is foiled by Cathy and Hareton, who love each other and redeem each other, and by his own affection for Hareton, his old enemy's son."

This is a cogent summary; but perhaps its last words are misleading, for—as it stands—it gives the impression that either, in their fondness for each other, Cathy and Hareton outwit Heathcliff; or that Heathcliff suffers a change of heart. Neither of these are, strictly speaking, correct. It is true that Heathcliff's attitude changes; that instead of his implacable persecution of Cathy and his grudging half-disguised affection for Hareton, he lapses into a state of leniency. But this new toleration he displays is not one of active kindness; there are no elements of remorse in it, no signs that he wishes to expiate his past. It is just that he is no longer concerned with those who were once his chosen victims. In the past, he had shown a positive interest in doing harm to the children of his enemies. Now, he shows no positive interest in adjusting the balance by doing them good. To his malevolence there succeeds, not goodwill but sheer indifference. His focus has shifted from the plane of revenge, and—in so doing—has shifted from this world.

"It is a poor conclusion, is it not?" he observes to the old housekeeper, Nelly Dean, in the last days of his life, "an absurd termination to my violent exertions? I get levers and mattocks to demolish the two houses, and train myself to be capable of working like Hercules, and when everything is ready and in my power, I find the will to lift a slate off either roof has vanished! My old enemies have not beaten me; now would be the precise time to revenge myself on their representatives: I could do it; and none could hinder me. But where is the use? I don't care for striking; I can't take the trouble to raise my hand! That sounds as if I had been labouring the whole time to exhibit a fine trait of magnanimity. It is far from being the case: I have lost the faculty of enjoying their destruction, and I am too idle to destroy for nothing."

And this is as far as his reputed change of nature goes. Neither is this indifference to those he once so passionately hated a result of the workings of time upon him. It is not that the early remembrances have lost their edge and poignancy, so that he can say 'Let the past be forgotten'. The reverse of this is actually the case; for time, instead of receding into forgetfulness, has caught up with him with increased intensity: twenty years after her death, Heathcliff becomes more and more aware of the presence of Catherine, his lost love, and finally sees her ghost.

After this, he pays no attention to any of the household with whom he lives, forgets to eat, and has even to remind himself to breathe. A man with an iron constitution, in the tough, late-middle prime of his existence, he literally starves himself to death. But this is only the negative aspect of his relinquishing the reins of power. What is more positive in his new condition is the formulation of a vague long-cherished desire.

"I have a single wish", he tells Nelly Dean, "and my whole being and faculties are yearning to attain it. They have yearned towards it so long, and so unwaveringly, that I'm convinced it *will* be reached—and *soon*—because it has devoured my existence: I am swallowed up in the anticipation of its fulfilment. My confessions have not relieved me; but they may account for some otherwise unaccountable phases of humour which I show. O God! It is a long fight, I wish it were over!"

This wish is the expression of his life-long instinct to be united with Catherine Earnshaw. But Catherine Earnshaw has been dead for twenty years. His wish is no other than the death-wish.

Again, it has sometimes been suggested that Heathcliff's new leniency to Cathy Linton is the effect of a sudden revelation in which he sees mother and daughter as one.

> "The present Catherine", observes Nelly Dean, "has no other likeness to her [mother] [apart from the question of eyes] except a breadth of forehead, and a certain arch of the nostril that makes her appear rather haughty, whether she will or not."

Heathcliff becomes aware of this powerful likeness when, on one occasion, he is about to beat her:

> ". . . he shifted his grasp from her head to her arm, and gazed intently in her face. Then he drew his hand over her eyes, stood a moment to collect himself apparently, and turning anew to Catherine, said with assumed calmness: 'You must learn to avoid putting me in a passion, or I shall really murder you some time!' "

But there is no birth of affection for Cathy, arising from his sense of her likeness to her mother. It is just that, once more, the past overcomes him and invalidates all his passion of anger for anyone living merely in the present. Hareton, also, has in common with Cathy the eyes of Catherine Earnshaw. This is interesting; for he is the child of her brother Hindley's marriage. But his resemblance to Catherine Earnshaw is closer than that of her own daughter. Heathcliff observes this, and it affects him strangely.

> "Five minutes ago", he tells Nelly Dean, "Hareton seemed a personification of my youth, not a human being: I felt to him in such a variety of ways, that it would have been impossible to have accosted him rationally. In the first place, his startling likeness to Catherine connected him fearfully with her. That, however, which you may suppose the most potent to arrest my imagination, is actually the least: for what is not connected with her to me?"

What Heathcliff is saying here is the very inverse of

Catherine's statement to the house-keeper earlier in the book:

> "Nelly! I *am* Heathcliff! He's always, always in my mind: not as a pleasure, any more than I am a pleasure to myself, but as my own being."

Now Heathcliff feels *himself* to be Catherine; because she is both in Hareton and Cathy. But in finding her likeness in the two young people, he is not won over openly to love them, or even to deal with them fairly. Cathy remains an "accursed witch" and an "insolent slut", as he has always styled her; and his reluctant feeling for Hareton does not lead him to make restitution for the way in which he has degraded Hindley's son.

Apart from the premonition that he is going to be reunited with Catherine in death, Heathcliff sees in Hareton and Cathy a duplication of his own passion. Hareton—degraded by Heathcliff—is in love with Cathy, the young lady of the house, in much the same way that Heathcliff himself—an outcast in Hindley's house—was aspiring to the hand of the young 'genteel' Catherine, who had originally been his playmate. Both in the world of spirit and flesh, time is catching up with him. In the world of the former, the sense of the past is obliterating his awareness of the present; whilst in the latter, with Hareton and Cathy, his past repeats itself through a younger generation.

It is this theme of repetition which adds a certain confusion to the book, unless we read it with careful attention. But the confusion is generally short-lived. It attends, perhaps, on our first reading; but as soon as we detect the curious parallels which the human relationships exhibit within it, our feeling of obscurity is dispersed. And the same name, or variations of it (for example, Catherine Earnshaw—Catherine Linton I—Catherine Linton II who, in turn, is to become Catherine Earnshaw II through her marriage to Hareton Earnshaw[1]) no

[1] This is the name, we remember, carved in stone above the threshold of *Wuthering Heights*. It carries with it the date "1500". In Hareton Earnshaw's repossession of the farm-house, after Heathcliff's death, and after his period of degrading dispossession, there is a proper poetic justice. At last he owns the house that bears his name, instead of merely living there in sufferance. The words carved in stone are like a prophecy.

longer appear to us as deliberate devices to make darkness darker, but as assurances of a careful plan and purpose. As May Sinclair writes, in her Introduction to the *Everyman* edition of *Wuthering Heights*:

> "The very light in it grows clearer and clearer with each reading, till you wonder how you could ever, even for a moment, have confused the two Catherines, or found the relations of these Earnshaws and Lintons and Heathcliffs obscure. I know of no tale that . . . unfolds with such cumulative simplification."

There are certain points of improbability in the plot of *Wuthering Heights* (and when we come to the characters, improbabilities become the greater); but, in general the novel can be shown to have a premeditated form, and a theme which is not haphazardly treated. Indeed, C. P. Sanger, in his lucid little monograph *The Structure of Wuthering Heights* (1926), has attempted to prove the perfect harmony of facts and details in the book. Questions of the age of its characters, issues relating to points of law—all such matters, he demonstrates, have been faithfully worked out by Emily in advance. But a plot is something more than a concord of facts. It is a sequence of incidents described in keeping with probability, or in keeping with some unity peculiarly its own. And one of the factors that can heighten or lessen the sense of probability is the method of narration chosen. In the case of *Wuthering Heights,* the method has come in for a good deal of censure. Phyllis Bentley, who analyses this, in her monograph *The Brontë Sisters,* admits that "the clear outlines of [the] story are often confused in the readers' minds" by the device which Emily employs, but thinks that it also "renders high dividends in excitement and suspense". The telling of the tale is effected by what Phyllis Bentley calls "a series of first person narrations which do not go straight forward in time". Here is her account of Emily's presentation:

> "She begins the book towards the end of the story, when Heathcliff is apparently triumphant. He owns both

Wuthering Heights and Thrushcross Grange, and the descendants of Lintons and Earnshaws are completely in his power. His tenant at Thrushcross Grange, Mr. Lockwood, coming to the Heights to call on his landlord, is first perplexed and then made madly curious by the strange behaviour and mysterious relationships of the people he finds living there. The reader, too, is made intensely curious and longs to hear the explanation of it all, which presently Lockwood, before he leaves the neighbourhood in disgust with the climate, hears from the Earnshaws' old nurse, Nelly Dean. Within her narrative come other first-person narratives, of young Cathy and of Isabella. Then, later, Lockwood comes back again, sees a completely changed situation at the Heights and again hears the explanation from Nelly Dean."

The tale, then, shifts, as May Sinclair points out,[2]

"from Lockwood to Nelly Dean, though Lockwood through four-fifths of it is telling what Nellie tells, though [a second house-keeper] Zillah's tale is taken up into Nelly Dean's."

Swinburne,[3] who agrees in theory with those who censure her narrative method, comes to the conclusion that "the attainment of the end justifies the employment of the means."

"The whole matter of report", he writes of *Wuthering Heights,* "however we get at it, is found when we do get at it to be vivid and life-like as an actual experience of living fact."

If Emily's indirect method can still communicate to us this sense of animation, then only a pedant would object to it.

"To judge", writes Swinburne, "by the vigour with which this objection [against Emily's method] is urged, it might be supposed that the rules of narrative observed by all great novelists were of an almost legal or logical strictness and exactitude with regard to probability of detail." This, he proves by illustration, is not so:

"Defoe still remain the one writer of narrative in the

2 Introduction to the *Everyman* edition of *Wuthering Heights.*

3 his essay *Emily Brontë* in his volume *Miscellanies.*

first person who has always kept the stringent law of possibilities before the eye of his invention."

Scott, Dickens, Thackeray, and Wilkie Collins have all employed the indirect method; have all ignored the sense of probability, not in what they told but in how they did the telling.

Swinburne notes too that each teller of the tale of *Wuthering Heights* "is invested for the nonce with the peculiar force and distinctive style of the author". But because that style is forceful and distinctive, he does not censure its ventriloquistic use. Largely true as his statement is, and truer still as are his conclusions, there does yet exist an appreciable difference between Nelly Dean's and Lockwood's narrations. The first—for all its appropriation of a more extensive vocabulary and syntax than the case of the speaker would seem to justify—is homely, unself-conscious, and didactic, with all the moral clichés of a nature honest in action but limited in thought. The second is youthfully self-conscious, a little affected and facetious, and with a vein of unreal cynicism in it. Emily, indeed, goes so far, in her effort to conform to the laws of probability, as to try to explain Nelly Dean's power of speech in terms of an unusual self-education:

> "I have read more than you would fancy, Mr. Lockwood", she confesses. "You could not open a book in this library that I have not looked into, and got something out of also: unless it be that range of Greek and Latin, and that of French; and those I know one from another: it is as much as you can expect of a poor man's daughter."

But this probability as to choice of language is a small matter in comparison with the probability of matters it serves to convey. And, here, it becomes important that all the descriptive force which Emily could muster should be placed at the disposal of what is to be told. As the substance of this is very often grim and fantastic to the point of being *outré,* it becomes all the more necessary that it be presented with all the resources of vigorous language. To limit the speech of these unusual happenings to a diction defined by the party who narrates them, would be to relinquish a force of utterance which these wild incidents stand in need of.

But in a manner, Emily does preserve some measure of the class and nature of the speaker, whilst still retaining her right to use such resources of language as her events demand. This she does by letting us feel the station and personality of the speakers when they first take up the tale, but allowing these to drop easily away as we become engrossed in the narration. Thus our sense of the presence of Lockwood—ineffectual, educated, amiable but youthfully misanthropic—recedes as we follow the facts he relates. So, likewise, with Nelly Dean. The patient, sententious, kindly busybody is forgotten in the details she recounts. The homely murmur of a village stream (which is how we may choose to regard her gossip) imperceptibly becomes the gathering spate of a vast and impetuous river (the tragic tide upon which the chief characters seem relentlessly borne forward).

Another aspect we may remark about these implausible alternative narrators is that their ultimate conformity of language serves yet another heightening purpose. By relinquishing the focus of attention upon themselves—the speech and manners of their individual natures—they become disinterested witnesses. In a way, they are both tragedic spectators and the voices of time itself (for tragedy is rooted in the nature of time).

Of the characters of *Wuthering Heights*, we may make the following provisional observation: namely, that while the minor characters are presented (to resort to E. M. Forster's distinction) one-dimensionally, "in the flat", the major figures are conceived "in the round", and as if engaged in movement. So we do not envisage Catherine or Cathy in terms of a recurrent gesture or phrase, as we do—say—Becky Sharp or Mr. Micawber. Emily's principal characters are—for the most part—too complex, too unresolved in purpose or direction, too much caught up in the process of a kind of fierce internal motion, for a surface cipher to stand duty for their make-up. What we think of as typical of these heroines are not the actions they repeat, but the actions they perform once only; as when Catherine, in her delirium, plucks the feathers from her pillow, imagining herself upon the moors, with the down of different birds floating through the air towards her; or, in the case of the young Cathy, her wilful break-away upon her pony, from the safe confines of Thrushcross Grange, to go adventuring up Penistone Crags.

These gestures of theirs are not *character-actions* (recurrent traits of a set personality), but—within the novel texture—dramatic actions: revelations, that is, not of the permanencies stably and solidly adhering to the person, but of the *forces* that move and shape the being. They are vivid, singular, and expressive enough to need no repetition; and it is of their nature that they cannot be repeated, since fate has moved forward with their single performance; and the freedom of action of the person who performs them is thus, by so much, unalterably reduced.

So Cathy's visit to Penistone Crags—the occasion on which she meets her cousin Hareton, who "opened the mysteries of the Fairy Cave, and twenty other queer places" to her—cannot, in any real sense, be repeated. Her adventure that day was decisive, and by their decisiveness she is a changed person. All of her future relations to Hareton, her hostility towards him and her final love, are prefigured in the incidents of their first encounter. Like the leaders of two rival houses, they come across each other at the entrance to Wuthering Heights. Both are accompanied by their dogs who, like two trains of myrmidons, engage in pitched battle with each other. But Cathy and Hareton have not met before, so—at the start—there is no enmity. Cathy does not know that Hareton is her cousin; and, although he is roughly dressed, takes him for the son of Heathcliff, master of Wuthering Heights. In this capacity, she is well pleased with him, and when Nelly Dean arrives to take her home, she finds the two young people good friends. But Cathy (as an over-indulged daughter) has a pride of blood like her mother Catherine, which led the latter to prefer the genteel Edgar to coarse-mannered Heathcliff. Thus, when Cathy discovers that she has been amiably conversing, not with the young heir to Wuthering Heights, but with a degraded labourer, she reacts by becoming insolent to him. He, in turn, with his own natural pride, does not submit to her arrogant words. And when Cathy learns that this disobedient menial is also her cousin, she feels the more insulted. But before they part, Hareton comes with the peace-offering of a new-born puppy for her. She rejects his gesture; but in his action the seeds of a future reconciliation lie.

In a similar way, Catherine's delirium marks a turning-point in her existence. Not only does it indicate the crisis of her illness—after which the currents of her life shift their direction and flow towards death—but it marks also a mental change. It serves as the symbol of a trauma, the experiencing of which has led her nature wholly to reject her husband's love. Until that moment, her affection for Edgar had been real though limited in scope. Physically, she had found him attractive; and if there had never been any question of her sharing with him that sympathy of soul which she had enjoyed with Heathcliff, Edgar's tenderness and kindness had given him no small claim upon her heart.

> "What you touch at present you may", she tells her husband, who comes to see her during her illness, after a quarrel, "but my soul will be on that hill-top before you lay hands on me again. I don't want you, Edgar: I'm past wanting you."

What has happened is that her love for Heathcliffe—buried for so long—has burst to the surface again, on his reappearance. But in the trauma which is expressed by her delirium, we find few references to the grown Heathcliff. It is to the Heathcliff of her youth that her wandering mind returns. Plucking the feathers from her pillow, she ruminates fancifully upon them:

"And here is a moor-cock's; and this—I should know it among a thousand—it's a lapwing's. Bonny bird; wheeling over our heads in the middle of the moor. It wanted to get to its nest, for the clouds had touched the swells, and it felt rain coming. This feather was picked up from the heath, the bird was not shot: we saw its nest in the winter, full of little skeletons. Heathcliff set a trap over it, and the old ones dare not come. I made him promise he'd never shoot a lapwing after that, and he didn't. Yes, here are more! Did he shoot my lapwings, Nelly? Are they red, any of them! Let me look."

But the course of her spirit is setting towards death, as much as to the object of her rekindled love; and Heathcliff the boy, and Heathcliff the man exist together in her mind when she looks from her bedroom at Thrushcross Grange, imagining that she can see the candle in her window at *Wuthering Heights* (some five miles away, and quite invisible):

"Look!" she cried eagerly, "that's my room with the candle in it, and the trees swaying before it: and the other candle is in Joseph's garret. Joseph sits up late, doesn't he? He's waiting till I come home that he may lock the gate. Well, he'll wait a little while yet. It's a rough journey, and a sad heart to travel it; and we must pass by Gimmerton Kirk, to go that journey! We've braved its ghosts often together, and dared each other to stand among the graves and ask them to come. But, Heathcliff, if I dare you now, will you venture? If you do, I'll keep you. I'll not lie there by myself: they may bury me twelve feet deep, and throw the church down over me, but I won't rest till you are with me. I never will!"

The full stream of her mind has turned back towards the past. The present—save as a dimension of pain—possesses no reality for her. The future holds only a sense of death.

Actions and incidents of this kind cannot be recurrent. They are mile-stones that lead the way towards the consummation of individual fate. They are typical of the person who enacts them, but their typicality does not belong to the constant attributes of the character. What they *are* typical of is the disposition of the personality towards some magnetic, and perhaps predestined, end. They symbolise the mobility of fate working within the individual.

In contrast to this dramatic portrayal of character, we have in the minor figures of *Wuthering Heights* a static presentation of personality. Joseph, the serving-man, and Nelly Dean, the house-keeper, do not change their words or ways one iota. They grow older, and in Nelly Dean's case the occasional play of nostalgia over memories of her youth is sometimes evoked. But she is "a canty dame"; a busy, kindly, practical body, seldom giving to thinking of herself. In her narrative of the chief characters, we have a mirror held up to the past, a mirror whose glass is sometimes dimmed with sadness for those whom it reflects, but hardly on its own behalf at all.

Joseph, the serving-man, is presented yet more simply. Apart from his attachment to Wuthering Heights, it is hard to imagine him possessed of a past. He is, pre-eminently, portrayed 'in the flat'. Both he and Nelly Dean are bound by ties of association to the environment of the drama, and this rootedness in the place gives them an added stability in the way that their image affects the imagination. "My mother had nursed Mr. Hindley Earnshaw that was Hareton's father", Nelly Dean tells Mr. Lockwood. While speaking of her early days she says "I ran errands, and helped to make hay, and hung about the farm ready for anything that anybody would set me to." Our sense of the permanence of these characters may have owed something to Emily's reading of Wordsworth, in whom the idea of the stabilising influence of one given place in the growth of character is often enough encountered.

But the sense of permanence which Nelly Dean and Joseph evoke is out of all proportion to the miscellany of moods and mannerisms which go to make up a character in life. They are largely functional figures (Nelly's activity being that of narrator, whilst Joseph's purpose appears to be that of creating a kind of humorous relief). This relief, it is true, is of a singularly unbuoyant order. It is a grim and narrow humour that we get from this Calvinistic servitor. "The wearisomest self-righteous Pharisee that ever ransacked a Bible to rate the promises to himself and fling the curses to his neighbours" is Nelly Dean's description of him. But for all the unpleasantness of his nature, and the canting sententiousness of his speech, we must admit that the language he uses shows Emily a master of dialect. Compared with Joseph's native invective, Heathcliff's talk is rhetorically Byronic. Joseph—the most undeveloped character in this novel—expresses himself more authentically than any of the other more complex figures. No doubt there is a touch of caricature in Joseph, through whose creation Emily was able to publish her scorn of Calvinism, and so get even with her aunt, who was always thrusting such doctrines down her throat. But, I think, there is more than satire in Joseph. Emily, though intellectually rebellious, was attracted by harshness and narrowness;[4] and when this went combined with the local vigour of an altogether unsophisticated speech, I suspect she found the material fascinating. In Joseph's remarks and monologues, she certainly achieved one of the most racy uses of rustic speech in English fiction.

Of the major characters in this book, I have no doubt that Catherine is the greatest—the fullest and most original in creation. Besides her uniqueness, Heathcliff appears as a tedious stock Byronic figure—his mouth filled with oaths and his fist raised to strike—a perversely idealised adolescent in a tantrum. How many lines of misanthropic rant by the author of *The Corsair, The Giaour,* and *Lara* might be applied to Heathcliff's condition!

> For I have buried one and all,
> Who loved me in a human shape;
> And the whole earth would henceforth be
> A wider prison unto me.

4 That Emily well understood the nature of such a repulsive sympathy can be shown from many passages in her works. "But no brutality disgusted her: I suspect she has an innate admiration of" says Heathcliff of his wife Isabella.

"I learned to love despair" says one of Byron's heroes; and despair and revenge make up the gamut of Heathcliff's emotions after Catherine's death. To recognise the 'note' of the Byronic type in Byron is to have recognised all one needs to know of the character of Heathcliff, who is Byron in prose dress.

Catherine, it is true, has a prototype in literature; though it is unlikely that Emily used the original figure as a base for her creation. Or if she did, she so developed the traits of character and their outcome in action, that there can be no suggestion of a copy. None the less, it is interesting to notice that Emily's heroine bears the same name as Shakespeare's Katharina, in *The Taming of the Shrew*. But Emily's shrew is a tragic one; and Cathy (her daughter, who—in some ways—completes her mother's emotional intention) is not overcome by ring-master tactics but by Hareton's independent nature, thawing out into co-operation and affection.

But if Catherine appears as the unbroken filly, the shrew who is not tamed by her husband Edgar (even though we are given to understand she loves him), this is only one aspect of her make-up and a merely symptomatic one at that. For Catherine, in fact, is a curious case of self-love carried to the extreme; the degree of her obsession giving an almost paranoic quality to what she observes. When she lies with a self-induced frenzy, weak from want of food, she seems at times to be near to arriving at the truth about herself:

> ". . . I begin to fancy you don't like me", she tells Nelly Dean during her illness. "How strange! I thought, though everybody hated and despised each other, they could not avoid loving me. And they have all turned to enemies in a few hours. *They* have, I'm positive—the people *here*."

The falsehood or illusion lies, of course, in imagining that nobody could avoid loving her. They had not suddenly changed to enemies merely because for a moment she was able to see that they were not infatuated. She had chosen to believe that everybody was under her spell, and when she sees that spell denied, she concludes that her faithful *devotées* have now become her adversaries. Her whole perspective is egoistic and unreal.

This ambiguous double-vision in which Catherine sees yet does not see herself—in which she recognises the truth and then straightaway distorts it—has its symbolic counter-part in the scene where she catches sight of her face in the mirror but does not identify it as her own. To her, it appears a strange and frightening countenance—*because she has willed not to recognise herself*. Catherine, indeed, represents the spirit of chaos in human affairs. Only in nature does she find that freedom which her will demands; only on the moors does she discover that liberty from personal responsibility which her unbridled egoism insists upon. And as she accepts no principle of inter-dependence during her life, so in death she wishes to avoid it. She wants to be buried "in the open air, with a headstone", and not in the Linton's chapel where her husband's family have been laid.

But unlike the lower creations of nature, she has gone against the deepest law of her being. This she has transgressed by her marriage to Edgar, when—all the time—she knew that her closest affinities were with Heathcliff. Her motives for this union were pride and social ambition, as well as a feeling of physical attraction. But compared with her basic sympathy with Heathcliff, these—as she admits to Nelly Dean—were insufficient. It is this violation of her integrity and of her self-knowledge which constitutes her tragedy.

I have said that Catherine represents the principle of excessive self-love, the only escape out of which lies through complete love of another. But this she does not find with Edgar; and the violation which she inflicts upon herself converts her self-love into a force of chaos. When, through her illness, this spirit of chaos and utter caprice are, in turn, constrained, there exists no remaining outlet for her energies save in a desire for death. With its total annihilating powers, death must always stand as the consummation of all chaotic forces, so that we see how, in her death-wish, Catherine turns the spirit of chaos (barred further egress) back upon herself.

Catherine's lover, Heathcliff, is a tiresome figure. Because he is all energy and movement, and gives the appearance of animated action, we incline to look upon him as real. Unlike Lockwood, the passive spectator, who is clearly no more than a mouth-piece for the story, Heathcliff is situated right in the centre of the drama. And yet he is, truly, less plausible than Lockwood. His reality is that of a lay-figure. He serves as a conduit for the passions which Emily unleashes in the novel. But these great passions he is meant to convey—love, revenge, and hate—fail to find in him convincing mortal dress. He is either the super-man or the sub-man: the broad middle register of the human, he misses.

This account of Heathcliff differs, I know, from the generality of opinion upon him. May Sinclair calls him a "magnificent gipsy", and finds his atavistic actions pregnant with intense spirituality. "Heathcliff's vengeance", she tells us, "like his passion for Catherine, is an immortal and immaterial thing."[5] This—especially the second epithet—I admit to finding all but meaningless. The revenge he takes on the house of Linton; the hatred he shows for his son by Isabella; his cruelty to her; his corruption of Hindley—all of these are expressed and executed in so many definite physical acts. There exists no reason for glamourising the violent brutalities of this 'ham' barbarian. Even May Sinclair—who is swept off her feet by the dizzy bedevilment of this character—has her moments of lucid assessment. In one of these she admits that

> "Judged by his bare deeds, Heathcliff seems a monster of evil, a devil without any fiery infernal splendour, a mean and sordid devil."

But her objective respite is brief. Very soon the satanic spell closes down on her; so that she is shortly telling us that

"... not for a moment can you judge Heathcliff by his

[5] *The Three Brontës*, by May Sinclair.

bare deeds. Properly speaking, there are no bare deeds to judge him by. Each deed comes wrapt in its own infernal glamour, trailing a cloud of supernatural splendour."

What this "infernal glamour" is, I should find it difficult to say, unless the critic is referring to the turgid rhetoric in which Heathcliff is usually made to talk.

"I have no pity! I have no pity!" Heathcliff assures Nelly Dean, after he has just man-handled his wife. "The more the worms writhe, the more I yearn to crush out their entrails! It is a moral teething; and I grind with greater energy in proportion to the increase of pain."

It is possible that certain minds, who prefer their poetry presented in bad prose (—and observe how stilted, as colloquial speech, is the last clause in the above quotation!—), enjoy and venerate this sort of thing. For myself, it seems so much melodramatic nonsense.

Deprived of the satanic nimbus which enthusiastic critics have conferred on him, Heathcliff is seen as a rough perfidious lout. For all the dedication of his love to Catherine, he is quite prepared to seduce Isabella, marry her, and then alienate her from him. To Catherine's daughter he shows no affection, but traps her into marriage with his dying son, and next holds her captive at Wuthering Heights. If he were more plausibly portrayed, he would probably be the most unpleasant hero in all classical fiction.

But my point is that he is entirely unreal. As with a first reading of Byron, we may very likely be carried away by the force with which his unreal heroes are conceived, so with a first reading of *Wuthering Heights*. There is so much energy poured into this novel, so many figures and incidents charged with compulsive and authentic power, that the character of Heathcliff rides with the tide. He is carried like a passenger on the wave of events. And this illusion is preserved the longer, because Heathcliff *seems* to be engaged in the same intense activity as the other figures. He appears to have a powerful inner life, just as Cathy, Hareton, and Catherine do; and it is only when we reconsider him that we feel a lack of flexibility, a sense of internal development missing. This becomes the more pronounced as the story progresses. There is nothing, for example, as convincing as Heathcliff's scene with Hindley over the horses which Mr. Earnshaw gives them, later in the book. Heathcliff as a boy is a genuine person: Heathcliffe as a man a melodramatic dummy. And the reason for this, I think, is quite simple. For a depiction of the early Heathcliff, Emily resorted to her knowledge of local life and to imagination. The later Heathcliff is the result of reading Byron and repeating his effects. May Sinclair—who admits to the Byronic colouring in Emily's poetry—has remarked how Zamorna, a *Gondal* hero, anticipates the creation of Heathcliff. The name Zamorna is itself a witness to the Byronism of this character; and when Zamorna is developed into Heathcliff, and takes on a more realistic appearance, the Byronic infection is the more insidious simply because it is less obvious. Whereas we can hardly be expected to believe in Zamorna with his operatic name and all his other specious attributes, we begin by taking Heathcliff seriously, because—on a first encounter—he at least looks like a human being. But what, in the *Gondal* poems (as far as human character is concerned), is nothing more than the wish-fulfilment images of an introverted adolescence, assembled from the spare parts of bad Byronic verse, becomes in *Wuthering Heights*, a dangerous illusion—something that bears some resemblance to real life, and asks to be taken seriously as such. It is a tribute to the credulity of many of Emily's commentators, that this has seldom been asked in vain.

As to the other characters in this novel, they are—barring Cathy—situated in what we may term the fictional middle-distance. They are not elaborated and brought into focus, save for a passing moment or two. Of Hareton, indeed, we have some knowledge, through his relations with Cathy and an early meeting with Nelly Dean. (His encounter with Lockwood in the first few pages really tells us very little.) But it is of Hareton, through Cathy's eyes, that we finally become aware. He is a Heathcliff whose youthful degradation does not lead to the former's tragic end; and perhaps his chief purpose in the novel is to redeem the pattern that precipitated Heathcliff into his villainies.

Isabella Linton, when she is courted by Heathcliff, leaves no deep impression; but in her hatred for him after their marriage, she conveys a more definite sense of her presence. Hindley remains in the middle-distance almost throughout the whole novel. His ruination at the hands of Heathcliff is (as so often with Emily) over-painted and devoid of pathos.

Cathy, like her mother before her, is excellently drawn. She is real—more earthy than Catherine—and yet splendidly spirited. But there is a gentleness and compassion hidden in her nature which her mother was without. Self-willed, like Catherine, and proud, she is not egoistical like the older woman. She knows how to sue for peace with Hareton; how to forgive, and how to foster love.

Lacking the complex inner life, which drives the older Catherine to her fate, Cathy—as I see it—is the proof that Emily could create other types of character besides the abnormal. Cathy I would rate, along with Joseph, as the substantial evidence that Emily possessed some of the more solid talents for novel-writing, as well as a great share of more unusual ones.

But one of the talents Emily did not possess was that of creating a moral character; for her figures—like Catherine, Heathcliff, and Hareton—are either a law unto themselves, or —like Nelly Dean and Joseph—simple adherants to convention. Only in Edgar Linton has Emily attempted to draw a character consciously aware of virtue, and all she has succeeded in making of him is a formal type whom she overtly despises.

Alone of all the characters in *Wuthering Heights*, Edgar knows how to conduct himself. His traditions of behaviour are not parochial, his sense of goodness not merely superstitious.

Through this wider reference informing his actions, Edgar can be said to live 'under the Law' in a positive and voluntary fashion. He stands for the social and domestic side of man, for the principle of co-operation. Neither is his goodness of a coldly rational order. His morality is not utilitarian.

To his capricious and temperamental wife, he is affectionate, attentive, and forgiving. To his daughter, he is devoted; undertaking her education; friendly, and yet providentially thoughtful for her present welfare and her future safety.

As his actions and his words come to us through Nelly Dean, we are given the house-keeper's comments upon them, and they are always approving and respectful. But all the time, we have the impression of Emily continually playing him down. We feel that she dislikes what she had to create; but through this inability of hers to overcome her prejudice, she fails to provide a strong enough foil for the over-boosted Heathcliff. This failure sufficiently to animate the character of Edgar means that there is only one important male figure properly realised. This is Hareton; but his whole role — compared with that of the two older men—is subsidiary. In Heathcliff I find it impossible to believe: in Edgar I am able to do so, but only with the sense of opportunities which the author, I feel, has deliberately thrown away.

The characters that count are Catherine and Cathy.

10

"WUTHERING HEIGHTS"

Spirit, Style and Values

"She is the most poetical of all our novelists", Lord David Cecil has written of Emily. What, quite, are the implications of this statement? Does it mean that we are to look in *Wuthering Heights* for a lush and ornate prose; that we are to expect a wealth of description, and possibly a surplus of scene-painting; or are its connotations other than this?

Of the kind of self-conscious and embroidered writing, which we sometimes refer to as poetical prose, there is certainly no trace in this novel. Emily's descriptive passages are sparse, and seldom extend for more than a few lines. Speaking of the land at Wuthering Heights, she writes:

> . . . "one may guess the power of the north wind blowing over the edge by the excessive slant of a few stunted firs at the end of the house; and by a range of gaunt thorns all stretching their limbs one way, as if craving alms of the sun."

There is no elaboration of details here, and absolutely no labouring of the point. The few images serve to create a background because of their highly indicative nature. The very bareness of the description evokes our sense of the bareness of the landscape. More closely and richly to work over the scene would be out of keeping with its own characteristics. Emily, in her descriptive passages, deals with her material in its own spirit.

In his *English Prose Style,* Sir Herbert Read discovers the appeal of Emily's prose to reside in its "emotional intensity" —an intensity which seeks to express itself in a "stricter realism" than her times employed. He compares a passage from Jane Austen's *Persuasion*—the one that recounts Louisa's accident—with the passage in *Wuthering Heights* which tells how Nelly Dean comes upon Heathcliff dead in his bed, by the open window:

> "The following evening was very wet, indeed it poured down till day-dawn; and, as I took my morning walk round the house, I observed the master's window swinging open, and the rain driving straight in. He cannot be in bed, I thought: those showers would drench him through. He must either be up or out. But I'll make no more ado, I'll go boldly and look.
>
> Having succeeded in obtaining entrance with another key, I ran to enclose the panels, for the chamber was vacant; quickly pushing them aside, I peeped in. Mr. Heathcliff was there—laid on his back. His eyes met mine so keen and fierce, I started; and then he seemed to smile. I could not think him dead: but his face and throat were washed with rain; the bedclothes dripped, and he was perfectly still. The lattice, flapping to and fro, had grazed one hand that rested on the sill; no blood trickled from the broken skin, and when I put my fingers to it, I could doubt no more: he was dead and stark!
>
> I hasped the window; I combed his long black hair from his forehead; I tried to close his eyes; to extinguish, if possible, that frightful, life-like gaze of exultation before anyone else beheld it. They would not shut: they seemed to sneer at my attempts, and his parted lips and sharp white teeth sneered too!"

With the "economy, directness and speed" of this description, he contrasts the stilted attempt at rapidity which we get in the passage from Jane Austen, and which merely succeeds in making pathos artificial.

> "With the Brontës", continues Sir Herbert, "a new vitality and stricter realism came into English fiction; it was a return to Swift and Defoe, or rather, to the fount of even these writers, for we know that the Bible was the most considerable influence in Emily Brontë's life."

This is excellently said; and I would go on to analyse the

poetic realism of Emily's style as residing in a combination of lyricism and reserve. These opposite traits are brought together in artistic conjunction most naturally by Emily; and it is the play of these characteristics that makes for the genuine tone of the novel. Without the lyrical element present, the note of dourness and reserve would leave *Wuthering Heights* a pedestrian chronicle of cruelties committed in a brutish district, and with little in it to redeem the story. Similarly, without the reserve, the lyricism would want conviction. Lockwood's nightmare, Heathcliff's obsession, Catherine's delirium and ghostly reappearance: these, by themselves, would be too much if *Wuthering Heights* was to have avoided the fate of being just another Gothic novel. Then, too, the environment is such that *Wuthering Heights* might have become a simple idyll of the soil, with the regional interest as the chief factor. The "unreclaimed" nature of this "remote region" is certainly one of the charms of the book. The wildness and remoteness is well suggested when we learn that, although the Earnshaws live on a farm, they lack even such rustic luxuries as apples and pears. In fact these fruits are looked upon as novelties, for when the elder Mr. Earnshaw sets out on his sixty-mile tramp to Liverpool, he promises Nelly Dean he will bring her a pocketful back with him.

But these are only incidental touches, for *Wuthering Heights* must not be looked on as a Yorkshire idyll in the manner of *Under the Greenwood Tree.*

In short, I would say that the note of reserve and dourness in the novel stem from Nelly Dean and Joseph; for although the former character does not play an important part in the tale, it is her narration of the incidents that sets much of the tone of the book. Then, too, she strikes us as 'an average type'. We see her as representing a norm, beside which the extremes and excesses of the other characters are measurable. When, therefore, I say that the note of reserve largely stems from Nelly Dean, I do not wish to suggest that her nature is aloof. The reserve of which I speak operates as a kind of counter-agent. It is something placed in the scales to balance the effect of the lyricism which stems from Catherine and her relations with Heathcliff.[1] We can call it, if we like, the voice of common-sense, or the weight of ordinary convention.

Of Joseph's dourness, little need be said. His uncouth cloddish utterance—which is just as regional as the natural beauty of the environment — holds in check the idyllic or pastoral note in the novel. With such a character as Joseph featured in the pages, there is no danger of our looking for "nymphs and shepherds" in *Wuthering Heights*.

In a way, we can say that the note of reserve derives from the lower-born, and the note of lyricism from the higher-born characters.[2] Catherine and, later, her daughter Cathy are the chief source of lyricism in this book. In part, it results from their spontaneous natures, and in part from the wildness of their behaviour. Cathy's escapade to Penistone Crags is an example of the latter, while in her scenes with Linton Heathcliff her spontaneous temperament is often revealed. We remember, particularly, her account of how she would prefer to spend a perfect summer day,

> ". . . rocking in a rustling green tree, with a west wind blowing, and bright white clouds flitting rapidly above; and not only larks, but throstles, and blackbirds, and linnets, and cuckoos pouring music on every side and the moors seen at a distance, broken into cool dusky dells; but close by great swells of long grass undulating in waves to the breeze; and woods and sounding water, and the whole world awake and wild with joy."

It will be seen that I have made much of the principle of balance in *Wuthering Heights*. I have spoken of the way in which the characters created 'in the round' are off-set by those created 'in the flat', and how the spirit of the novel is

[1] I say that the lyrical note in this novel stems from Catherine, and from her relationship with Heathcliff. I hope it is clear, after what I have written that I do not find Heathcliff himself a 'lyrical' or 'poetical' creation. Neither in character nor in speech, do I consider him to be possessed of any true individuality (without which poetry cannot exist). His monologues—and most of his dialogues—I write off as rant (and rant is not poetry). But he is—if not himself poetic—the occasion of poetry in Catherine.

[2] But Edgar Linton is an important exception.

achieved by a balance of the dour and lyrical tone. And where this balance is harmoniously maintained, I have held that the novel must be said to succeed; just as where the balance breaks down—as in the discrepancy of status between Edgar Linton and Heathcliff — the story appears to lose authenticity.

But the most eloquent defence of *Wuthering Heights* as a novel, constructed on the principle of balance, is that made by Lord David Cecil in his *Early Victorian Novelists*. Briefly, his thesis is that the setting of *Wuthering Heights* is "a microcosm of the universal scheme as Emily Brontë conceived it". The Earnshaws represent the principle of storm, the Lintons the principle of calm and peace. These two forces, which taken together explain the nature of the universe, must not be conceived in a moral fashion. Their dialectic is one which refers to some primordial state of things before the event of good and evil. Neither is their interplay to be given the sanction of necessitarian ethics. They are archetypal opposites, there from the very beginning of time; a sense of whose presence Emily possessed by her faculty of cosmic intuition. What we realise, after reading Lord David's analysis, is that *Wuthering Heights* has affinities, not with the early Victorian novel, but rather with the work of great Romantic poets, with Blake, Byron, Shelley, Rossetti.

Lord David contends that *Wuthering Heights* is not a character-novel in the normal nineteenth-century sense, where the characters are seen as engaged in various worldly pursuits and achievements. Instead, it is "a spiritual drama", a conflict in which the soul of each actor attempts to work out its adjustment to the cosmos. *Wuthering Heights*, he tells us, is not immoral, but "pre-moral"—a presentation of elemental energies displayed in their pure activity and not as subjected to moral evaluation.

As Lord David sees it, the theme of the novel is that of the conflict between two psychic groups, who by fate or chance[3] have become entangled. The cause of discord lies in the mating of the 'children of calm' (the Lintons) with the 'children of storm' (the Earnshaws).

"Together each group", writes Lord David, "following its own nature in its own sphere, combines to compose a cosmic harmony. It is the destruction and re-establishment of this harmony which is the theme of the story. It opens with the arrival at Wuthering Heights of an extraneous element—Heathcliff. He, too, is a child of the storm; and the affinity between him and Catherine Earnshaw makes them fall in love with each other. But since he is an extraneous element, he is a source of discord, inevitably disrupting the working of the natural order. He drives the father, Earnshaw, into conflict with the son, Hindley, and as a result Hindley into conflict with himself, Heathcliff. The order is still further dislocated by Catherine, who is seduced into uniting herself in an 'unnatural' marriage with Linton, the child of calm. The shock of her infidelity and Hindley's ill-treatment of him now, in its turn, disturbs the natural harmony of Heathcliff's nature, and turns him from an alien element in the established order, into a force active for its destruction. He is not therefore, as usually supposed, a wicked man voluntarily yielding to his wicked impulses. Like all Emily Brontë's characters, he is a manifestation of natural forces acting involuntarily under the pressure of his own nature. But he is a natural force which has been frustrated of its natural outlet, so that it inevitably becomes destructive; like a mountain torrent diverted from its channel, which flows out on the surrounding country, laying waste whatever may happen to lie in its way. Nor can it stop doing so, until the obstacles which kept it from its natural channel are removed."

This is a brilliant and persuasive defence; and it suggests that Emily's vision of the world was perhaps similar to that

3 It is possible that Emily favoured the idea of fate. We have traced the Stoic element in her writing, and predestination was one of the notions present in ancient Stoic philosophy. Marcus Aurelius for example writes: "Whatever happens to you was pre-ordained your lot from the first; and that chain of causes which constitutes fate tied your person and the event together from all eternity."

of the Stoic poet Cleanthes who, in his *Hymns to Zeus,* wrote:

> Yea, but Thou knowest even to find a place for superfluous things, and to order that which is disorderly, and things not dear to men are dear to Thee.
> Thus dost Thou harmonise into One all good and evil things, that there should be one everlasting Reason of them all.

Such a notion of God's economy has a spiritual breadth which Emily shares. But the moral implications of *Wuthering Heights* is something Lord David has in part misrepresented.

For if Heathcliff and the Earnshaws are children of the storm, and the conflict which the novel exhibits is not one between good and evil but between like and unlike, in what sense can the former's arrival be said to provide "an extraneous element", "a source of discord, inevitably disrupting the workings of the natural order"? Again, we are told by Lord David that it is the shock of "Catherine's infidelity and Hindley's ill-treatment of him" that "disturbs the natural harmony of Heathcliff's nature, and turns him from an alien element in the established order, into a force active for its destruction". But long before Catherine's marriage (there was no question of her being "seduced" into it, as Lord David suggests), Heathcliff had shown himself a "sullen child" and a "breeder of bad feeling in the house". And if it is true that Hindley persecuted him, it is also true that he played tricks on Hindley (we remember how he blackmailed Hindley into exchanging colts with him, because the handsomest—which Heathcliff had taken — proved itself after a while to be lame). And, once more, why should these two disagree if they are both of them children of storm?

The upshot of the matter is, that Lord David's elucidation of the hidden design in *Wuthering Heights* does not coincide at all points with the story in its details. This, I would say, is not because he has failed to discover Emily's buried intentions, but because he thinks she has realised these intentions in the novel completely.

In short, I would maintain that *Wuthering Heights* is a tale written according to a mystic's conception of the universe. This conception was the result of a revelation of cosmic forces —a dialectic that worked itself out in an end-stage of harmony and equilibrium. But the elements in this universal design were primal energies in their abstraction. What Emily, as I see it, failed to do was to show the play of these forces on the ethical and human level. "Beyond good and evil" is a mode of vision which we may suppose deity to enjoy. We may also believe that this form of apprehension is something the mystics occasionally share; but, then, most mystics possess a religion, and a religious morality, to which their vision can be safely referred. But Emily was without this interpretative framework. Her story may be true of how things are seen in heaven: it does not represent how things exist on earth.

Wuthering Heights is explained by Lord David as a kind of allegory; but allegory is a form of narrative which has to hold good on two levels: the symbolic or transcedental, and the physical or merely worldly. On the second of these, Emily failed.

Part of her failure, here, I think, was due to her limitation as a portrayer of character. Her range is too narrow; and even when within it, she is, by no means, sure. The children of storm—Heathcliff excepted—she is able to present convincingly. But her children of calm are largely unreal. She cannot comprehend types so different to herself. Her second weakness lies in her failure to envisage characters ethically. She has very little sense of good and evil as formative and determinative factors in the growth of personality. Her characters incline either, like Edgar, to encompass the nature of virtue in a formal and conventional fashion; or, like Linton Heathcliff, to bewail the fact that they are bad, but to see their badness as imposed upon them by a kind of predestination, or, thirdly, they show no concern with good and evil, and reflect their author's lack of concern.

It has sometimes been suggested that *Wuthering Heights*

is a book without a past or a future—a story which sprang from no literary precedents, and one without influence upon later fiction. Neither parts of this statement seem to me correct. The origins of *Wuthering Heights* lie quite clearly in English poetry, and the succession of this mode of story-telling can be traced through Swinburne's *Lesbia Brandon* to D. H. novels. Swinburne we know to have been tremendously impressed by *Wuthering Heights*.

"It may be true", he writes, "that not many will ever take it to their hearts; it is certain that those who do like it will like nothing very much better in the whole world of poetry or prose."

Lesbia Brandon, that strange novel, seems to show the influence of *Wuthering Heights*, both in spirit and in certain details. The death of Swinburne's heroine bears many points of resemblance to the scene in which Catherine lies ill and in fever.[4] What *Wuthering Heights* inaugurated was the novel of the pure drama of feeling. This was quite a different affair to the eighteenth-century novel of sentiment. Emily's principle characters — Catherine and Heathcliff — are figures hurled headlong on their way by the whirlwind force of their passions. They have no sense of wrong; and small sense of the personality of others. In this, they differ from the heroes and heroines of the eighteenth-century novel of sentiment; for here the characters submit to their passions, but know their acquiescense is a weakness.

Emily's novel has indeed paved the way for the modern novel of flux and sensation. The obsession of Catherine and Heathcliff with their own subjective feelings, their complete lack of any objective set of values, and their failure of interest in the outer world of opinion, leaves them a prey to the emotional solipsism which overtakes them both.

4 In his review of Miss Mary Robinson's biography of Emily Brontë Swinburne wrote that, "it is even somewhat less than exact to say that the scene of delirium 'is given with a masterly pathos that Webster need not have made more strong, nor Fletcher more lovely and appealing.' " This was the measure of his admiration for the scene.

D. H. Lawrence's characters are in a straight line of descent from the characters of *Wuthering Heights*. In them, the process of deliquescence in the social personality has gone one stage further.[5]

But *Wuthering Heights* exerted an influence on modern fiction in other ways, too. Idealised versions of the villanies of Heathcliff have been a feature in many later novels; until, after passing its height in the figure of the 'demon-lover', this fashion seems now to have reached its decline in the idea of the hero as cosh-boy and bandit. A third, more traditional, derivation is in the fiction of platonic passion, such as we find in Charles Morgan's novels.

[5] but this was something that Lawrence, unlike Emily, was equivocally aware of. "What ails me", he wrote to the psychologist Trigant Burrow, "is the absolute frustration of my primeval societal instinct. The hero illusion starts with the individualist illusion, and all resistances ensue. I think societal instinct much deeper than sex instinct." Lawrence was always trying to come to grips with the 'societal' need in his novels; and sometimes, in a rather grotesque fashion, succeeded. For Emily, the need hardly existed.

11

SUMMARY

A Postscript

When we look at Emily Brontë's achievement against the background of her life, we are apt to think of it as a unique but solitary thing — an extraordinary but lonely phenomenon. This has generally been the view which critics of the past have taken; and when we consider the discrepancy between her opportunities and her talents, such a perspective appears most natural.

It is possible, however, to regard her work in something of a less isolated manner; to see it in relation to other poets, other novelists, and other thinkers. This, I have endeavoured to do; and here it merely remains for me to summarise some of these comparisons.

We have seen how the notion of Emily as a nature-poet required enlargement; of how her achievement in this field was not that of a descriptive writer, of a rustic pastoralist concerned with country matters such as Robert Bloomfield or Tennyson Turner. Instead, we have observed her feeling her way, through a short-hand reference to the landscape she loved, towards a metaphysic of nature. But in the process of arriving at this, she was led to the creation of a regional type of poem which owed nothing to local idiom or place-names (such as Lord Tennyson employed in his Lincolnshire dialect pieces, or the Georgians in their 'itinerary' verses some half-a-century later). The local colour in these compositions was not achieved by small studied detail, but by one or two highly evocative images. It was the method of symbolism which Emily was using in these poems, and not the copyist's naturalism, which show her as an original nature-poet.

But Emily's concern with nature was not limited to a depiction of the physical background to human living. She wished to know what forces lay beyond that background, and this enquiry gave rise to the pantheism which is so potent a current in her writing. Here, the comparisons most ready are probably with Wordsworth and Hölderlin. But Emily possessed neither the first's sustained power for philosophic reflection (such as we find in *The Prelude*), nor the latter's instinct for synchronising the deities of Greece and the Christian Trinity. Unlike these two poets, then, her pantheism did not result in a system of religious belief, but found its consummation in a personal mysticism more closely allied to that of Novalis.

There was also the element of Stoicism in her, which came to its highest flowering in the poem *No coward soul is mine.* But in Emily's finest poetic achievement—in her six great poems, that is, it is hard to separate the stoical from the mystical elements. The metaphysical intensity of these pieces seems to fuse all the aspects of her mind into one single current of song.

As has been said, Emily renewed the metaphysical lyric in English after it had fallen into neglect with the passing of Shelley. More sustained than the shorter gnomic poems of Blake, her best metaphysical pieces must be said to lack both the psychological insight and drama of his *Prophetic Books* as well as the obscurity of style that goes with them.

Emily remains a subjective artist; and her six crowning poems mark the very peak in English of the subjective poetical philosophy of life. But when she tries to dramatise and *socialise* this private vision by the creation of characters, the narrowness of her perception is made clear. It is for this reason that the *Gondal* cycle, like the story of *Wuthering Heights,* reveals certain discrepancies of theme and certain unrealities of human behaviour. Like Nietzsche, whom she much resembled and whom in her fierceness of thought she anticipated, Emily was unable to realise the implications of her ideas within the context of a traditional society. It is always man alone that she sings and celebrates, or man in the single relationships of passion. But when she begins to imagine all those other contacts and responsibilities which the human person forms in passing through society, her writing is often immature and melodramatic. The shadow of the misanthropist Byron invalidates her thought even at that distance.

But what she achieved — what still remains positive — is something of no insubstantial order. Through her six great poems she must be considered as one of our major poets, while a larger number of other pieces reveal her as an interesting minor poet. As to *Wuthering Heights*—even though one may not assent to the judgment that pronounces it a flawless work of fiction—to have conceived the bare idea of it, the notion of a novel that should be poetic through its symbolic drama, rather than through any verbal graces—this itself is an innovation and an act of faith so unusual in the mundane art of novel-writing that its example wil intrigue and fascinate us always.

Stoic -
264,5

Gothic
p 261